DOMESDAY BOOK

Sussex

History from the Sources

DOMESDAY BOOK

A Survey of the Counties of England

LIBER DE WINTONIA

Compiled by direction of

KING WILLIAM I

Winchester
1086

DOMESDAY BOOK

text and translation edited by

JOHN MORRIS

2

Sussex

edited from a draft translation prepared by
Janet Mothersill

PHILLIMORE
Chichester
1976

1976

Published by

PHILLIMORE & CO. LTD.,
London and Chichester

Head Office: Shopwyke Hall,
Chichester, Sussex, England

© John Morris, 1976

ISBN 0 85033 145 5 (case)
ISBN 0 85033 146 3 (limp)

Printed in Great Britain by
Titus Wilson & Son Ltd.
Kendal

SUSSEX

Introduction

The Domesday Survey of Sussex

Notes
Appendix: the Hide
Index of Persons
Index of Places
Systems of Reference
Maps
Technical Terms

History from the Sources
General Editor: John Morris

The series aims to publish history
written directly from the sources
for all interested readers, both
specialists and others. The first
priority is to publish important
texts which should be widely
available, but are not.

DOMESDAY BOOK

The contents, with the folio on which each county begins, are:

Domesday Book is termed *Liber de Wintonia* (The Book of Winchester) in column 332c

INTRODUCTION

The Domesday Survey

In 1066 Duke William of Normandy conquered England. He was crowned King, and most of the lands of the English nobility were soon granted to his followers. Domesday Book was compiled 20 years later. The Saxon Chronicle records that in 1085

> at Gloucester at midwinter ... the King had deep speech with his counsellors ... and sent men all over England to each shire ... to find out ... what or how much each landholder held ... in land and livestock, and what it was worth ... The returns were brought to him.[1]

William was thorough. One of his Counsellors reports that he also sent a second set of Commissioners 'to shires they did not know, where they were themselves unknown, to check their predecessors' survey, and report culprits to the King.'[2]

The information was collected at Winchester, corrected, abridged, chiefly by omission of livestock and the 1066 population, and fair-copied by one writer into a single volume. Norfolk, Suffolk and Essex were copied, by several writers, into a second volume, unabridged, which states that 'the Survey was made in 1086'. The surveys of Durham and Northumberland, and of several towns, including London, were not transcribed, and most of Cumberland and Westmorland, not yet in England, was not surveyed. The whole undertaking was completed at speed, in less than 12 months, though the fair-copying of the main volume may have taken a little longer. Both volumes are now preserved at the Public Record Office. Some versions of regional returns also survive. One of them, from Ely Abbey,[3] copies out the Commissioners' brief. They were to ask

> The name of the place. Who held it, before 1066, and now?
> How many *hides*?[4] How many ploughs, both those in lordship and the men's?
> How many villagers, cottagers and slaves, how many free men and Freemen?[5]
> How much woodland, meadow and pasture? How many mills and fishponds?
> How much has been added or taken away? What the total value was and is?
> How much each free man or Freeman had or has? All threefold, before 1066,
> when King William gave it, and now; and if more can be had than at present?

The Ely volume also describes the procedure. The Commissioners took evidence on oath 'from the Sheriff; from all the barons and their Frenchmen; and from the whole Hundred, the priests, the reeves and six villagers from each village'. It also names four Frenchmen and four Englishmen from each Hundred, who were sworn to verify the detail.

The King wanted to know what he had, and who held it. The Commissioners therefore listed lands in dispute, for Domesday Book was not only a tax-assessment. To the King's grandson, Bishop Henry of Winchester, its purpose was that every 'man should know his right and not usurp another's'; and because it was the final authoritative register of rightful possession 'the natives called it Domesday Book, by analogy

---

[1] Before he left England for the last time, late in 1086. [2] Robert Losinga, Bishop of Hereford 1079-1095 (see *E.H.R.* 22, 1907, 74). [3] *Inquisitio Eliensis,* first paragraph. [4] A land unit, reckoned as 120 acres. [5] *Quot Sochemani.*

from the Day of Judgement'; that was why it was carefully arranged by Counties, and by landholders within Counties, 'numbered consecutively ... for easy reference'.[6]

Domesday Book describes Old English society under new management, in minute statistical detail. Foreign lords had taken over, but little else had yet changed. The chief landholders and those who held from them are named, and the rest of the population was counted. Most of them lived in villages, whose houses might be clustered together, or dispersed among their fields. Villages were grouped in administrative districts called Hundreds, which formed regions within Shires, or Counties, which survive today with minor boundary changes; the recent deformation of some ancient county identities is here disregarded, as are various short-lived modern changes. The local assemblies, though overshadowed by lords great and small, gave men a voice, which the Commissioners heeded. Very many holdings were described by the Norman term *manerium* (manor), greatly varied in size and structure, from tiny farmsteads to vast holdings; and many lords exercised their own jurisdiction and other rights, termed *soca*, whose meaning still eludes exact definition.

The Survey was unmatched in Europe for many centuries, the product of a sophisticated and experienced English administration, fully exploited by the Conqueror's commanding energy. But its unique assemblage of facts and figures has been hard to study, because the text has not been easily available, and abounds in technicalities. Investigation has therefore been chiefly confined to specialists; many questions cannot be tackled adequately without a cheap text and uniform translation available to a wider range of students, including local historians.

Previous Editions

The text has been printed once, in 1783, in an edition by Abraham Farley, probably of 1250 copies, at Government expense, said to have been £38,000; its preparation took 16 years. It was set in a specially designed type, here reproduced photographically, which was destroyed by fire in 1808. In 1811 and 1816 the Records Commissioners added an introduction, indices, and associated texts, edited by Sir Henry Ellis; and in 1861-1863 the Ordnance Survey issued zincograph facsimiles of the whole. Texts of individual counties have appeared since 1673, separate translations in the Victoria County Histories and elsewhere.

This Edition

Farley's text is used, because of its excellence, and because any worthy alternative would prove astronomically expensive. His text has been checked against the facsimile, and discrepancies observed have been verified against the manuscript, by the kindness of Miss Daphne Gifford of the Public Record Office. Farley's few errors are indicated in the notes.

[6] *Dialogus de Scaccario* 1,16.

The editor is responsible for the translation and lay-out. It aims at what the compiler would have written if his language had been modern English; though no translation can be exact, for even a simple word like 'free' nowadays means freedom from different restrictions. Bishop Henry emphasized that his grandfather preferred 'ordinary words'; the nearest ordinary modern English is therefore chosen whenever possible. Words that are now obsolete, or have changed their meaning, are avoided, but measurements have to be transliterated, since their extent is often unknown or arguable, and varied regionally. The terse inventory form of the original has been retained, as have the ambiguities of the Latin.

Modern English commands two main devices unknown to 11th century Latin, standardised punctuation and paragraphs; in the Latin, *ibi* ('there are') often does duty for a modern full stop, *et* ('and') for a comma or semi-colon. The entries normally answer the Commissioners' questions, arranged in five main groups, (i) the place and its holder, its hides, ploughs and lordship; (ii) people; (iii) resources; (iv) value; and (v) additional notes. The groups are usually given as separate paragraphs.

King William numbered chapters 'for easy reference', and sections within chapters are commonly marked, usually by initial capitals, often edged in red. They are here numbered. Maps, indices and an explanation of technical terms are also given. Later, it is hoped to publish analytical and explanatory volumes, and associated texts.

The Sussex Survey contains some informative statements about the hide which are parallelled in few other counties. An Appendix, listing the main evidence about the varied usages of THE HIDE , is therefore included in this volume.

The editor is deeply indebted to the advice of many scholars, too numerous to name, and especially to the Public Record Office, and to the publisher's patience. The draft translations are the work of a team; they have been co-ordinated and corrected by the editor, and each has been checked by several people. It is therefore hoped that mistakes may be fewer than in versions published by single fallible individuals. But it would be Utopian to hope that the translation is altogether free from error; the editor would like to be informed of mistakes observed.

The map outlines were drawn by Jim Hardy.

The preparation of this volume has been greatly assisted by a generous grant from the Leverhulme Trust Fund.

Conventions

* refers to a note to the Latin text.
[ ] enclose words omitted in the MS. ( ) enclose editorial explanations.

SVDSEXE

HIC ANNOTANT TENENTES TERRAS IN SVDSEXE.

.I. REX WILLELMVS

.II. Archiepˢ cantuariensͦ

.III. Epſ Ciceſtrenſis.

.IIII. Abb̄ Weſtmonaſter.

.V. Abb̄ Fiſcannenſis.

.VI. Oſbern epſ Execeſtr.

.VII. Abbatia Wintonienſͦ

.VII Abbatia de Labatailge.

.IX. Comes de Ow.

.X. Comes Moritonienſͦ

.XI. Comes Rogerius.

.XII. Wiłłs de Warenna.

.XIII. Wiłłs de Braioſe.

.XIIII. Odo de Winceſtre.

.XV. Eldred.

TERRA REGIS.

.I. REX WILLELMVS tenet in dn̄io *BOSEHAM*. Goduin comes tenuit. 7 t̄c̄ erant. LVI. 7 dimid. 7|XXXVIII. pro
hid geldauit. 7 m̄ ſimilit. Tra. ē

In dn̄io ſunt. VI. car. 7 XXXIX. uiłłi cū. L. bord hn̄t

XIX. car. Ibi æccła 7. XVII. ſerui. 7 VIII. molini de: IIII. lib

XXX. denar min. Ibi. II. piſcariæ de. VIII. ſot 7 X. denar.

Silua de. VI. porc.

Ad hoc m̄ p̄tin. XI. hagæ in Ciceſtre. T.R.E. quæ reddeb

VII. ſolid 7 IIII. den. Modo h̄t epſ decē de illis. a rege.

7 m̄ eſt una in m̄. Totū m̄ T.R.E. 7 poſt. ualuit. XL. lib.

Modo ſimilit. XL. lib. Tam̄ reddit. L. lib ad arſurā

7 penſū. quæ ualent. LXV. lib.   ⌐ 7 uñ bord.

ſ De iſto m̄ h̄t Engeler. II. hid de rege. 7 ibi h̄t. I. car

SUSSEX

LIST OF LANDHOLDERS IN SUSSEX

1	King William	[8a	St. Edward's Abbey]
2	The Archbishop of Canterbury	9	The Count of Eu
3	The Bishop of Chichester	10	The Count of Mortain
4	The Abbot of Westminster	11	Earl Roger
5	The Abbot of Fecamp	12	William of Warenne
6	Bishop Osbern of Exeter	13	William of Braose
7	Winchester Abbey	14	Odo of Winchester
8	Battle Abbey	[and]	Aldred

1

LAND OF THE KING

[In BOSHAM Hundred]

1 King William holds BOSHAM in lordship. Earl Godwin held it.
There were then 56½ hides; it paid tax for 38 hides; now the same.
Land for ...... In lordship 6 ploughs.
  39 villagers with 50 smallholders have 19 ploughs.
  A church; 17 slaves; 8 mills at £4 less 30d; 2 fisheries at 8s 10d;
    woodland at 6 pigs.
  11 sites in Chichester belong to this manor; they paid 7s 4d
    before 1066. Now the Bishop has 10 of them from the King,
    and 1 is now in the manor.
Value of the whole manor before 1066 and later £40; now the
same, £40. However, it pays £50 assayed and weighed, valued at £65.
  Engelhere has 2 hides of this manor from the King.
He has 1 plough and 1 smallholder.

Rex . W . ten in dñio *REREDFELLE* . de feudo epi Baioc.

Goduin tenuit . 7 tc 7 m̃ ſe deſd p . iii . hid . Tra . e

xxvi . car . In dñio ſunt . iiii . car . 7 xiiii . uilli cũ . vi .

bord hñt . xiiii . car . Ibi . iiii . ſerui . 7 ſilua de q̃t xx .

porc de paſnag . Parcus . e ibi .

T.R.E. ualeb . xvi . lib . 7 poſt: xiiii . lib . Modo: xii . lib .

7 tam̃ redd . xxx . lib .

TERRA ARCHIEPI.   *IN MELLINGES HVND.*

.II. Archieps Lanfranc ten M̃ *MELLINGES*.

7 eſt in Rap de Peneueſel . 7 T.R.E. deſd ſe p q̃t xx . hid .

Sed m̃ ñ ht archieps niſi . lxxv . hidas . quia comes

moritonij ht . v . hid ext hund . Tra toti M̃ . l . car .

In dñio ſunt . v . car . 7 cc . 7 xix . uilli cũ xxxv . bord

hñt . lxxiii . car . 7 xl.iii . croft .

Ibi . v . molini de . iiii . lib 7 x . ſolid . 7 ii . mil anguill .

Ibi . cc . ac pti . v . min . 7 ſilua . ccc . porc de paſnag .

De herbagio . xxxviii . ſol . 7 vi . den . 7 ccc.lv . porc herbag .

T.R.E. ualeb . xl . lib . Q̃do recep: xxx . lib . Modo:

lxx . lib . Hoc M̃ tenuit Godefrid ad firmã p . xc . lib .

⌐ De iſto M̃ ten Bainiard de archiepo . v . hid .

7 ibi ht in dñio . ii . car . 7 xiiii . uilli cũ . ii . bord hñt

ii . car . Ibi . xxxv . ac pti . 7 de herbagio . iii . porc .

Val . viii . lib .

⌐ De eod M̃ ten fili Boſelin de Archiepo . ii . hid . 7 ibi ht

in dñio . i . car . 7 xi . uilli cũ . ii . bord . hñt . iii . car . Ibi . ii .

molini de . x . ſolid . 7 de herbagio . ii . porc . 7 de ſilua . xx .

porc de paſnagio . Val . lx . ſol .

16 b

In ROTHERFIELD Hundred

2 King William holds ROTHERFIELD in lordship, from the Holding of the
Bishop of Bayeux. Earl Godwin held it. Then and now it answered
for 3 hides. Land for 26 ploughs. In lordship 4 ploughs.
   14 villagers with 6 smallholders have 14 ploughs,
    4 slaves; woodland at 80 pigs from pasturage; a park.
Value before 1066 £16; later £14; now £12; however, it pays £30.

2   LAND OF THE ARCHBISHOP

In MALLING Hundred

1a Archbishop Lanfranc holds the manor of (SOUTH) MALLING. It is in the
Rape of Pevensey. Before 1066 it answered for 80 hides, but now the
Archbishop has only 75 hides, because the Count of Mortain has 5 hides
outside the Hundred. In the whole manor, land for 50 ploughs.
In lordship 5 ploughs.
   219 villagers with 35 smallholders have 73 ploughs and 43 crofts.
   5 mills at £4 10s and 2,000 eels; meadow, 200 acres less 5;
    woodland, 300 pigs from pasturage; from grazing, 38s 6d;
    grazing, 355 pigs.
Value before 1066 £40; when acquired £30; now £70.
  Godfrey held this manor at a revenue for £90.

1b Baynard holds 5 hides of this manor from the Archbishop. He has
2 ploughs in lordship.
   14 villagers with 2 smallholders have 2 ploughs.
   Meadow, 35 acres; from grazing, 3 pigs.
Value £8.

1c Boselin's son holds 2 hides of this manor from the Archbishop.
He has 1 plough in lordship.
   11 villagers with 2 smallholders have 3 ploughs.
   2 mills at 10s; from grazing, 2 pigs; from the woodland, 20 pigs
    from pasturage.
Value 60s.

⨍ De ipso m̄ ten Godefrid . i . hid de archiepo . 7 ibi hŧ . ii . car
in dñio. 7 ii . uitti cū . iii . borđ . 7 uñ molin de . v . solid.
Silua . i . porc de pasnagio . Vat . l . sot.

⨍ De eođ m̄ ten Walter de archiepo . ii . part dimiđ hiđ
7 ibi hŧ . ii . car in dñio . 7 i . uitt 7 i . borđ cū . i . car . 7 iii . ac
p̄ti . 7 silua . iii . porc de pasnagio . 7 uñ porc de herbagio.

16 c   Vat . xl . sot.

⨍ De ipso adhuc m̄ ten canonici S̄ Michaeł . iiii . hiđ.
7 ibi . ē in dñio una car . 7 iiii . uitti cū . xvi . borđ hñt
ii . car . 7 uat . iii . lib.   ⨍ Alsihorne.

⨍ Witts de cahainges ten unā uirgā de isto m̄ . 7 est ad

IN ESTREV HVNĐ

I pse archieps ten ODINTVNE . de uestitu monachoʒ.
T.R.E. se defđ p̄ . vi . hiđ . 7 m̄ p̄ iiii . hiđ 7 dimidia.
q̄a aliud . ē in rapo comit de morit . Tra . ē . v . car.
In dñio sunt . ii . car . 7 x . uitti cū . iiii . borđ hñt . iii . car.
Ibi uñ molin de . xxxix . den . 7 xxii . ac p̄ti . 7 silua.
de . ii . porc.

T.R.E. ualeƀ . iiii . liƀ . 7 post . xl . sol . Modo . iiii . liƀ.   HĐ
Oli reddiđ . vi . liƀ . sed p̄durare n̄ potuit . IN FALEMERE

Canonici de Mellinges ten de archiepo STAMERE.
T.R.E. 7 m̄ p̄ . xx . hiđ se defđ . Tra . ē . xx . car . In dñio
sunt . iiii . 7 xlix . uitti cū . x . borđ hñt . xx . vi . car.
Silua de . vi . porc . T.R.E. 7 post . 7 m̄ . uat . xv . lib.
Huic m̄ adjacent . vii . hagæ in LEWES . redđtes
xxi . denar p̄ annū.

I pse archieps hŧ in LEWES . xxi . hag . reddentes
viii . sot . 7 viii . den p̄ annū . 7 p̄tiñ ad Mellinges . m̄.

1d Godfrey holds 1 hide of this manor from the Archbishop.
He has 2 ploughs in lordship.
2 villagers with 3 smallholders.
1 mill at 5s; woodland, 1 pig from pasturage.
Value 50s.

1e Walter holds 2 parts of ½ hide of this manor from the Archbishop.
He has 2 ploughs in lordship.
1 villager and 1 smallholder with 1 plough.
Meadow, 3 acres; woodland, 3 pigs from pasturage;
1 pig from grazing.
Value 40s.

1f Further, the Canons of St. Michael's hold 4 hides of this manor.   16 c
1 plough in lordship.
4 villagers with 16 smallholders have 2 ploughs.
Value £3.

1g William of Keynes holds 1 virgate of this manor.
It is at 'Alchin'.
[Value...]

In STREAT Hundred
2 The Archbishop holds WOOTTON himself for the monks' clothing.
Before 1066 it answered for 6 hides; now for 4½ hides,
because the other part is in the Count of Mortain's Rape.
Land for 5 ploughs. In lordship 2 ploughs.
10 villagers with 4 smallholders have 3 ploughs.
1 mill at 39d; meadow, 22 acres; woodland at 2 pigs.
Value before 1066 £4; later 40s; now £4; formerly it
paid £6, but it could not maintain it.

In FALMER Hundred
3 The Canons of Malling hold STANMER from the Archbishop.
Before 1066 and now it answered for 20 hides. Land for 20
ploughs. In lordship 4 ploughs.
49 villagers with 10 smallholders have 26 ploughs.
Woodland at 6 pigs.
Value before 1066, later, and now £15.
Attached to this manor are 7 sites in Lewes which pay 21d a year.

[In SWANBOROUGH Hundred]
4 The Archbishop has 21 sites himself in LEWES which pay 8s 8d a year.
They belong to the manor of Malling.

Ipse archieṗs ten *Pageham* in dñio . T.R.E. ſe defđ

ṗ . L . hiđ . 7 m̄ ṗ xxx.iiii . Tra . e̅ . xxx . car̄.

In dñio ſunt . vii . car̄ . 7 lxxiiii . uiłłi cū q̄t xx . borđ

iı . min hñt xxiii . car̄ . Ibi uñ moliñ de . x . ſoliđ.

7 q̄t xx . ac̄ pti . 7 parua ſilua ad clauſurā . De her

bagio . un porc̄ de unoqq̄ uiłło qui h̅t . vii . porcos.

T.R.E . 7 poſt. ualuit xl . liƀ . Modo: lx . liƀ . 7 tam̄ redđ

q̄t xx . liƀ . ſed nimis graue . e̅ . Ibi æccła . e̅ . 7 una æccła

in Ciceſtre . redđ . lxiiii . den̄　　　　　　　ſ bord̄.

De hoc m̄ ten Oiſmelin unā hiđ . de archiepo . Ibi h̅t . ii.

Ipſe archieṗs ten in dñio *Tangemere*.

Clerici tenuer̄ de archiepo T.R.E . defđ ſe ṗ . x . hiđ.

7 m̄ ṗ . vi . hiđ . Tra e̅ .　　　In dñio ſunt . ii . car̄ . 7 xv.

uiłłi cū . xv . borđ hñt . iiii . car̄ . Ibi æccła.

T.R.E . ualeƀ . vi . liƀ . 7 poſt: c . ſoliđ . Modo: vi . liƀ . 7 p̄po

ſit m̄ h̅t inde . xx . ſoł.

Ad hoc m̄ ptiñ . iiii . hagæ in Ciceſtre . redđ . xxii . den̄.

Ipſe archieṗs ten *Loventone . In Sillentone HĐ.*

in dñio . T.R.E . defđ ſe ṗ . xviii . hiđ . Modo ṗ . ix . hiđ

7 dimiđ . Tra . e̅　　　In dñio ſunt . iii . car̄ . 7 xiiii.

uiłłi cū . viii . borđ hñt . iiii . car̄ . Ibi uñ moliñ de . vi.

ſoliđ 7 xxvi . ac̄ pti.

T.R.E . 7 poſt . ualuit . xii . liƀ . Modo xv . liƀ.

De hoc m̄ ten Radulf̄ . iii . hiđ de archiepo . 7 ibi . i . uiłłs

cū . iii . borđ hñt . i . car̄ .　　　Val . iii . liƀ.

Ipſe Archieṗs ten *Petchinges In Rieberge Hvnđ.*

de ueſtitu monachoȝ fuit ſeṗ . T.R.E. ſe defđ ṗ . xii . hiđ.

7 m̄ ṗ . iii . hiđ 7 iii . uirg 7 dimiđ . Tra . e̅ . ix . car̄ . In dñio

In PAGHAM Hundred

5 The Archbishop holds PAGHAM himself, in lordship. Before 1066
it answered for 50 hides; now for 34. Land for 30 ploughs.
In lordship 7 ploughs.
  74 villagers with 80 smallholders, less 2, have 23 ploughs.
  A mill at 10s; meadow, 80 acres; a small wood for fencing;
    from grazing, 1 pig from each villager who has 7 pigs;
    the same throughout Sussex.
Value before 1066 and later £40; now £60; however, it pays £80,
but it is too heavy.
  A church; a church in Chichester which pays 64d.
  Osmelin holds 1 hide of this manor from the Archbishop.
He has 2 smallholders.

6 The Archbishop holds TANGMERE himself, in lordship. The clergy
held it from the Archbishop. Before 1066 it answered for
10 hides, now for 6 hides. Land for......In lordship 2 ploughs.
  15 villagers with 15 smallholders have 4 ploughs.
  A church.
Value before 1066 £6; later 100s; now £6.
  The reeve of the manor has 20s from it. 4 sites in
Chichester belong to this manor, which pay 22d.

In SINGLETON Hundred

7 The Archbishop holds LAVANT himself, in lordship. Before 1066
it answered for 18 hides; now for 9½ hides.
Land for .... In lordship 3 ploughs.
  14 villagers with 8 smallholders have 4 ploughs.
  A mill at 6s; meadow, 26 acres.
Value before 1066 and later £12; now £15.
  Ralph holds 3 hides of this manor from the Archbishop.
    1 villager with 3 smallholders have 1 plough.
Value £3.

In POLING Hundred

8 The Archbishop holds PATCHING himself; it was always for the monks'
clothing. Before 1066 it answered for 12 hides; now for 3 hides
and 3½ virgates. Land for 9 ploughs. In lordship 2 ploughs.

ſunt . ii . car . 7 xxii . uilli cū . xxi . borđ hñt . vi . car . Ibi æccła.

Silua . iiii . porc . T.R.E. ualeƀ . xii . liƀ . 7 poſt . x . liƀ . Modo . xv .
liƀ . Dudū fuit ad . xx . liƀ . ſed n̄ potuit pati . *In Bradfota hd.*

Iᵖſe archieps ten *Terringes* . qđ ſéᵖ fuit in monaſterio.

T.R.E. deſđ ſe ᵱ . xviii . hiđ . 7 m̄ ᵱ vii . hiđ 7 una uirg . Tra . ē
xiiii . car 7 dim . In dñio ſunt . iii . car . 7 xxvii . uilli cū . xiiii .
borđ hñt . x . car . Ibi . ii . æcclæ . 7 ſilua de . vi . porc.

T.R.E. ualeƀ . xiiii . liƀ 7 iiii . ſol . 7 poſt . x . liƀ . Modo . xv . liƀ.

⫰ De hoc m̄ ten Willts de braioſe . iiii . hiđ.

7 ibi hr̄ in dñio . i . car . 7 iiii . uilli cū . v . borđ hñt . i . car 7 dim .
Ibi . v . ac pti . De ſilua . x . deṇar . de paſnag . xx . ſoliđ . 7 ii . porc.
Val . lxx . ſoliđ.

Terra Eᵖi De Cicestre. *In Flexeberg hvnd.*

.II. Eᵖs de Cicestre ten in dñio *Biscopestone.*

T.R.E. ſe deſđ ᵱ . xx.v . hiđ . 7 m̄ ſimilit . Tra . ē
In dñio ſunt . iii . car . 7 xxx . uilli cū . ix . borđ hñt . xxx . car .
Ibi . xl . ac pti . Silua . iii . porc de paſnag . 7 de . iii . porcis .
uñ porc de herbag.

T.R.E. ualeƀ . xxvi . liƀ . 7 poſt . xi . liƀ . Modo . xx . liƀ.
De hoc m̄ ten Goisfriđ . iiii . hiđ . 7 Herold . ii . hiđ . 7 Ricarđ . iii . hiđ.
Ibi . vi . car in dñio . 7 xiii . borđ . Totū h⸳ Val . c . ſol 7 x . ſol.

In Hamfelde hvnd.

Iᵖſe eps ten in dñio *Hafelde* . T.R.E. ſe deſđ ᵱ xv . hiđ.
7 m̄ ᵱ . xi . hiđ 7 una uirgı . Tra . ē . xx . car . In dñio ſunt . ii . car .
7 xxiii . uilli cū . xv . borđ hñt . x . car . Ibi æccła . 7 xl . ac pti.
Molī 7 piſcaria deſuɴ ᵱ ſupfacto . W . de braioſe.

22 villagers with 21 smallholders have 6 ploughs. 16 d
    A church; woodland, 4 pigs.
Value before 1066 £12; later £10; now £15; previously it was at
£20, but it could not bear it.

In BRIGHTFORD Hundred

9 The Archbishop holds (WEST) TARRING himself; it was always in the
monastery('s lands). Before 1066 it answered for 18 hides;
now for 7 hides and 1 virgate. Land for 14½ ploughs.
In lordship 3 ploughs.
    27 villagers with 14 smallholders have 10 ploughs.
    2 churches; woodland at 6 pigs.
Value before 1066 £14 4s; later £10; now £15.

10 William of Braose holds 4 hides of this manor. He has 1 plough
in lordship.
    4 villagers with 5 smallholders have 1½ ploughs.
    Meadow, 5 acres; from the woodland 10d; from
      pasturage 20s; 2 pigs.
Value 70s.

[3]   LAND OF THE BISHOP OF CHICHESTER

In FLEXBOROUGH Hundred

1 The Bishop of Chichester holds BISHOPSTONE in lordship.
Before 1066 it answered for 25 hides; now the same.
Land for ...... In lordship 3 ploughs.
    30 villagers with 9 smallholders have 30 ploughs.
    Meadow, 40 acres; woodland, 3 pigs from pasturage;
      from grazing, 1 pig in 3.
Value before 1066 £26; later £11; now £20.
    Geoffrey holds 4 hides of this manor; Harold 2 hides;
Richard 3 hides. In lordship 6 ploughs.
    13 smallholders.
Value of all this 100s and 10[d?].

The Bishop himself holds
in HENFIELD Hundred

2 HENFIELD, in lordship. Before 1066 it answered for 15 hides;
now for 11 hides and 1 virgate. Land for 20 ploughs.
In lordship 2 ploughs.
    23 villagers with 15 smallholders have 10 ploughs.
    A church; meadow, 40 acres. A mill and a fishery are lacking,
      through encroachment by William of Braose.

De his hiđ ten Witłs . . . . de eᵱo . III . hiđ . 7 ibi hⁱ
in dñio . I . hiđ . 7 I . uiłłs cũ . x . borđ hñt dim̄ car . Silua
de . III . porc̄ . Totũ ⋒ T.R.E. ualeƀ . x . liƀ . 7 poſt; VII . liƀ.
Modo qđ eᵱs ten; x . liƀ . Qđ miles ten; XL . ſoł . 7 tam̄
fuit ad firmā . ᵱ XVIII . liƀ.

In *LEWES* ſunt . III . burges ad hoc ⋒ ᵱtintes . redđ . XXI . den.

IN BOCSE   HVNĐ.

Ipſe eᵱs ten in dñio *ALDINGEBORNE* . T.R.E. 7 m̄ ſe defđ
ᵱ . XXXVI . hiđ . Tra . e̅ . xx . car . In dñio ſunt . II . car . 7 XVI.
uiłłi cũ . XIII . borđ hñt . v . car . Ibi æccła 7 III . ſerui . 7 VI . ac
ᵱti . Silua . III . porc̄ de paſnag . 7 de herbag . I . porc̄ de . VI . porc̄.
Ad hoc ⋒ ᵱtin . XVI . hagæ . quæ redđ . VII . ſoł 7 VI . den.
⎠De hoc ⋒ ten ᵱbr . I . hiđ . Roƀt; v . hiđ . Hugo; III . hiđ.
Aluuard; I . hiđ . hi . III . clerici ſunt . 7 hi . IIII . milites . Herald.
III . hiđ . Murdac; III . hiđ . Anſfrid; I . hiđ . Louel; I . hidā.
Int om̄s hñt . VI . car in dñio . 7 XII . uiłłos 7 XXV . borđ.
Totũ ⋒ T.R.E. ualeƀ xv . lib . 7 poſt; x . lib . Modo qđ eᵱs ten;
x . liƀ . Qđ clerici; IIII . liƀ . Qđ milites; IIII . liƀ ſimiliter.

IN RISBERG HVNĐ.

Ipſe eᵱs ten *FERINGES* . In dñio . T.R.E. ſe defđ ᵱ XII . hiđ.
7 m̄ ᵱ . VIII . hiđ . Tra . e̅   In dñio ſunt . II . car . 7 xv uiłłi
cũ . XIIII . borđ hñt . v . car . Ibi . I . ſeru . 7 xx . ac ᵱti . 7 ſilua . IIII.
porc̄ . 7 ᵱ herbag; uñ porc̄ de . VII.

17 a

De iſto ⋒ ten Anſfrid . II . hiđ . 7 hⁱ in dñio dim̄ car cũ . IIII . borđ.
T.R.E. ualeƀ . VII . liƀ . 7 poſt; c . ſoł . M; VII . liƀ . Qđ Anſfrid
ten; uał .xx . ſoł.   *IN ESWENDE HVNĐ.*

Ipſe eᵱs ten *AMBRELIE* . T.R.E. 7 m̄ ſe defđ ᵱ XXIIII . hiđ.
Tra . e̅   In dñio ſunt . II . car . 7 xx . uiłłi cũ XIII ; borđ.
hñt . XII . car . 7 xxx . ac ᵱti . 7 ſilua . VII . porc̄ de paſnag.

William [a man-at-arms?] holds 3 of these hides from the Bishop.
He has 1 hide in lordship.
   1 villager with 10 smallholders have ½ plough.
   Woodland at 3 pigs.
Value of the whole manor before 1066 £10; later £7; now,
what the Bishop holds, £10; what the man-at-arms holds, 40s;
however, it was at a revenue for £18.
   In Lewes are 3 burgesses who belong to this manor; they pay 21d.

in BOX Hundred

3 ALDINGBOURNE, in lordship. Before 1066 and now it answered
   for 36 hides. Land for 20 ploughs. In lordship 2 ploughs.
     16 villagers with 13 smallholders have 5 ploughs.
     A church; 3 slaves; meadow, 6 acres; woodland, 3 pigs from pasturage;
       from grazing, 1 pig in 6 pigs.
     16 sites belong to this manor; they pay 7s 6d.
    A priest holds 1 hide of this manor; Robert, 5 hides;
    Hugh, 3 hides; Alfward, 1 hide; these 3 are clerics.
    Also, these 4 men-at-arms; Harold, 3 hides; Murdoch, 3 hides;
    Ansfrid, 1 hide; Lovell, 1 hide. Between them they have 6
    ploughs in lordship and
      12 villagers and 25 smallholders.
Value of the whole manor before 1066 £15; later £10;
now, what the Bishop holds £10; what the clerics hold £4;
what the men-at-arms hold likewise £4.

in POLING Hundred

4 FERRING, in lordship. Before 1066 it answered for 12 hides;
   now for 8 hides. Land for .... In lordship 2 ploughs.
     15 villagers with 14 smallholders have 5 ploughs.
     1 slave; meadow, 20 acres; woodland, 4 pigs;
     for grazing, 1 pig in 7.
    Ansfrid holds 2 hides of this manor. He has ½ plough   17 a
    in lordship, with 4 smallholders.
Value before 1066 £7; later 100s; now £7; value of what Ansfrid
holds, 20s.

in EASEWRITHE Hundred

5 AMBERLEY. Before 1066 and now it answered for 24 hides.
   Land for .... In lordship 2 ploughs.
     20 villagers with 13 smallholders have 12 ploughs.
     Meadow, 30 acres; woodland, 7 pigs from pasturage.

De isto ᷄M̃ tᷓ Wilłs cleric᷈ . ii . hiđ . 7 Ældred pᵇr . iii . hiđ .

Balduin᷈ . ii . hid 7 dimᷓ . Radulf᷈ . ii . hiđ | una virga minⁱ᷄ Teoderic . iii . hiđ . Huſcarleᵢ | ᵢᵢ·hiđ

Int omſ hn̄t . v . caᷓ . in dn̄io . 7 xvii . uiłłos 7 xxv ᵢ borđ hn̄tes

.v . caᷓ.'

Toᷓ ᷄M̃ T.R.E. ualeƀ xx . liƀ . 7 poſtᷓ xv ᵢ liƀ . Modoᷓ qđ eᵽs tᷓᷓ

xiiii . liƀ . Qđ alij de eᵽo tᷓ ᷓ uał vii . liƀ . ᷄ ℑN ᷄SV̄MERLEG HD̄.

Ipſe eᵽs tᷓ FILLEICHĀ in dn̄io . T.R.E. 7 m̂ ſe defđ ꝓ . xii .

hiđ . Tᷓa . ē . xii . caᷓ . In dn̄io ſunt . ii . caᷓ . 7 xvi . uiłłi cū . xiiii ᵢ

borđ hn̄t . vii . caᷓ . Ibi una āc p̂ti . 7 ſilua ad clauſurā .

De iſto ᷄M̃ tᷓ Giſleƀᷓ . iii . hiđ . Rozelin᷈ . i . hiđ . Vlf . i . hiđ .

7 in dn̄io hn̄t . iii . caᷓ . cū . xii . borđ .

Toᷓ ᷄M̃ T.R.E. ualeƀ x . liƀ . 7 poſtᷓ viii . liƀ . Modo . x . liƀ qđ

eᵽs tᷓ ᷓ . Qđ hōeſᷓ lxv . ſoł .

Ipſe eᵽs tᷓ SELEISIE . in dn̄io . T.R.E. 7 m̂ ſe defđ ꝓ . x . hiđᷓ

Tᷓa . ē . vii . caᷓ . In dn̄io ſunt . ii . caᷓ . 7 xvi . uiłłi cū xi . borđ ᵢ hn̄t

.v . caᷓ . Ibi . ii . ſerui . 7 vi . hagæ in Ciceſtre de . xxxviii . denaᷓᵢ

De iſto ᷄M̃ tᷓ Goisfrid . i . hiđ . 7 Wilłs dimiđ hiđ . 7 dim uirgᷓā .

7 hn̄t . i . caᷓ 7 dimiđ . cū uńo borđᵢ

Toᷓ ᷄M̃ T.R.E. ualeƀ xii . liƀ . 7 poſtᷓ x ᵢ liƀ . Modo dn̄iū epiᷓ xii . liƀ .

Hōum ejᷓ xl . ſoł .

Ipſe eᵽs tᷓ WESTRINGES . in dn̄io . T.R.E. 7 m̂ ſe defđ ꝓ . xiiii .

hiđ . Tᷓa . ē . viii . caᷓ . In dn̄io ſunt . ii . 7 xv . uiłłi cū . xii . borđ .

hn̄t . v . caᷓ . Ibi . i . moliñ de . xxx . denaᷓ . 7 xiii . hagæ de xxvi . den .

Herbagᷓ de . vii . porcis . unū .

De hoc ᷄M̃ tᷓ Radulf᷈ . i . hiđ . Herƀtᷓ᷈ iii . hiđ . 7 hn̄t in dn̄io . ii ᵢ

caᷓ 7 dimiđ . 7 ii . uiłłos cū xii . borđ . 7 dimiđ caᷓ̃ .

Toᷓ ᷄M̃ T.R.E. 7 poſt ualuit . viii . liƀ . Modo tn̄tđ uał qđ eᵽs hᷓ̄ .

Qđ hōeſᷓ l . ſoliđ .

William the cleric holds 2 hides of this manor; Aldred the priest 3
  hides; Baldwin 2½ hides; Ralph 2 hides less 1 virgate;
  Theodoric 3 hides; Guard 2 hides.
  Between them they have 5 ploughs in lordship and
    17 villagers and 25 smallholders who have 5 ploughs.
Value of the whole manor before 1066 £20; later £15;
now, what the Bishop holds £14; value of what the others hold
from the Bishop £7.

in SOMERLEY Hundred

6 SIDLESHAM, in lordship. Before 1066 and now it answered for
  for 12 hides. Land for 12 ploughs. In lordship 2 ploughs .
    16 villagers with 14 smallholders have 7 ploughs.
    Meadow, 1 acre; woodland for fencing.
    Gilbert holds 3 hides of this manor; Rozelin 1 hide;
      Ulf 1 hide. In lordship they have 3 ploughs, with
        12 smallholders.
Value of the whole manor before 1066 £10; later £8; now, what
the Bishop holds £10; what the men hold 65s.

7 SELSEY, in lordship. Before 1066 and now it answered
  for 10 hides. Land for 7 ploughs. In lordship 2 ploughs.
    16 villagers with 11 smallholders have 5 ploughs.
    2 slaves; 6 sites in Chichester at 38d .
    Geoffrey holds 1 hide of this manor; William ½ hide
      and ½ virgate. They have 1½ ploughs, with
        1 smallholder.
Value of the whole manor before 1066 £12; later £10; now,
the Bishop's lordship £12; his men's 40s.

8 (EAST?) WITTERING, in lordship. Before 1066 and now it
  answered for 14 hides. Land for 8 ploughs. In lordship 2.
    15 villagers with 12 smallholders have 5 ploughs.
    1 mill at 30d; 13 sites at 26d; grazing, 1 pig in 7.
    Ralph holds 1 hide of this manor; Herbert 3 hides.
      In lordship they have 2½ ploughs and
        2 villagers with 12 smallholders and ½ plough.
Value of the whole manor before 1066 and later £8; now, value
of what the Bishop has as much; what the men have 50s.

Ipſe eps ten̄ *PRESTETONE*. 7 ſēp fuit in monaſt . T.R.E . 7 m̄ ᵱ xx . ᵗⁱ

hid̄ ſe defd̄ . Tra .ē. xii . car̄ . In dn̄io .ē una 7 dimid̄ . 7 xxx . uiḹḹi

cū . xx . bord hn̄t . xii . car̄ . 7 in *LEWES* . iii . hagæ de . xviii . den̄.

Ibi æcc̄ḽa . 7 xv . ac̄ ᵽti . 7 ſilua de . ii . porc̄ de paſnag.

De hoc m̄ ten̄ Louel . ii . hid̄ . 7 ibi h̄t . ii . car̄ . 7 ix . uiḹḹos cū . iii.

bord̄ hn̄tibƷ . ii . car̄ . 7 un̄ molin̄ ibi.　　　Vaḽ . xl . ſoḽ

Totū m̄ T.R.E . ualeb xviii . lib̄ . 7 poſt ꞏ x . lib̄ . Modo . xviii . lib̄

　　　　　　　　　　　　　ᵛ
Oli fuit ad . xx . lib̄ . de firma.s; n̄ poterat reddere.

　　ᵈᵉ Cⁱᶜᵉſⁱʳᵉ
C anonici ten̄ cōmunit . xvi . hid̄ quæ nunq̄ geldaue r̄

ſicut dicunt . 7 ibi hn̄t . iiii . car̄ in dn̄io . Hoc uaḽ . viii . lib̄.

TERRA SC̄I PETRI WESTMONAST̄. *IN ISIWIRDE HVND̄.*

.ℍIII. A BBAS SC̄I PETRI de Weſtmonaſt ten̄ *PERHAM* . 7 de rege . E . tenuit

Tc̄ ſe defd̄ ᵱ . vii . hid̄ . m̄ ᵱ . iii ᵇʸ . Tra .ē. iiii . car̄ . In dn̄io .ē una.

7 viii . uiḹḹi cū . v . cot hn̄t . ii . car̄ . Ibi . ix . ac̄ ᵽti . Vaḽ 7 ualuit . iiii . lib̄.

¹⁷ᵇ TERRA ÆCC̄LÆ FISCANNENS̄. *IN GHESTELINGES HD̄.*

.V. A BBAS de Fiſcanno ten̄ de rege *RAMESLIE*.

　　7 de rege . E . tenuit . 7 tc̄ ſe defd̄ ᵱ xx . hid̄ . modo

ᵱ . xvii . hid̄ 7 dimid̄ . Tra .ē. xxxv . car̄.

In dn̄io ē una car̄ . 7 c . uiḹḹi un̄ min̄ ⁹ hn̄t . xl . iii . car̄.

Ibi . v . æcc̄læ reddt̄es . lxiiii . ſolid̄ . Ibi . c . ſaline dē . viii.

lib̄ 7 xv . ſolid̄ . 7 vii . ac̄ ᵽti . 7 ſilua . ii . porc̄ de paſnagio.

In ipſo m̄ .ē nouū burḡ . 7 ibi . lxiiii . burḡſes reddentes

viii . lib̄ . ii . ſolid̄ min̄ . In Haſtinges : iiii . burḡſes 7 xiiii ꞏ

bord̄ reddt̄ . lxiii . ſoḽ.

De iſto m̄ ten̄ Rob̄t ⁹ de haſtinges . ii . ḽiid̄ 7 dimid̄ dē abb̄e.

7 Herolf dimid̄ hid̄ . Ipſi hn̄t . iiii . uiḹḹos . 7 iiii . cot . 7 ii . car̄.

[in PRESTON Hundred]
9 PRESTON. It was always in the monastery('s lands).
    Before 1066 and now it answered for 20 hides.
    Land for 12 ploughs. In lordship 1½.
      30 villagers with 20 smallholders have 12 ploughs; in
        Lewes 3 sites at 18d.
      A church; meadow, 15 acres; woodland at 2 pigs from pasturage.
      Lovell holds 2 hides of this manor. He has 2 ploughs and
        9 villagers with 3 smallholders who have 2 ploughs.
      A mill.
      Value 40s.
    Value of the whole manor before 1066 £18; later £10; now £18;
      formerly it was at £25 revenue, but it could not pay it.

10 The Canons of Chichester hold 16 hides in common which have never
      paid tax, as they state. They have 4 ploughs in lordship.
      Value of this £8.

4   LAND OF ST. PETER'S OF WESTMINSTER

In EASEWRITHE Hundred
1 The Abbot of St. Peter's of Westminster holds PARHAM and held it
   from King Edward. Then it answered for 7 hides; now for 3.
   Land for 4 ploughs. In lordship 1.
     8 villagers with 5 cottagers have 2 ploughs.
     Meadow, 9 acres.
   The value is and was £4.

5   LAND OF FECAMP CHURCH   17 b

In GUESTLING Hundred
1 The Abbot of Fecamp holds RYE from the King, and held
   it from King Edward. Then it answered for 20 hides; now
   for 17½ hides. Land for 35 ploughs. In lordship 1 plough.
     100 villagers, less 1, have 43 ploughs.
     5 churches which pay 64s; 100 salt-houses at £8 15s;
       meadow, 7 acres; woodland, 2 pigs from pasturage.
     In this manor is a new Borough; 64 Burgesses pay £8 less 2s;
       in Hastings 4 burgesses and 14 smallholders pay 63s.
     Robert of Hastings holds 2½ hides of this manor from
   the Abbot; Herewulf ½ hide. They have
     4 villagers, 4 cottagers and 2 ploughs.

Totũ ⊙ T.R.E. ualeb . xxx . lib . Modo: L . lib dñiũ abbis.

Hominũ û . xl.iiii . fot.

Ipſe abb teñ STANINGES . Herald tenuit in fine regis . E.

7 tc ſe defd p qt . xx . hid 7 una . 7 inſup adhuc . xviii.

hidæ 7 vii . ac foris rap quæ nunq geldaueꝛ . Modo . lxvii.

hidæ . In rapo de Harundel ſunt xxxiii . hidæ 7 dimid.

7 aliæ in rapo Witti de braioſe . 7 tam abb teñ oms modo.

Terra toti ⊙: xl.i . car ; In dñio ſunt . vii . car.

7 c.lxxviii . uitti cũ . lxiii ; bord hñt . xl.viii . car.

Ibi . ii . æcclæ . ix . ſerui . 7 iiii . molini de . xlvii . ſolid

7 lxviii . porcis inſup . Ibi . c.xiii . ac pti . Silua . xlv.

porc de paſnag.

In burgo fueꝛ . c.xviii . maſuræ . 7 reddeb . iiii . lib 7 ii . fot.

Modo ſunt . c.xxiii . maſuræ . 7 reddt . c . ſolid 7 c . den.

7 hñt . i . car 7 dimid . Ad curia opabant ſic uillani . T.R.E.

T.R.E. ualeb qt xx 7 . vi . lib . 7 poſt: L . lib . M: c . lib.

7 tam eſt ad firma p . c.xxii . lib . . ii . ſot min.

Ipſe abb teñ de rege . BERIE . Goda comitiſſa tenuit

de rege . E . 7 tc ſe defd p ; xvi ; hid . Modo p . xii ; hid.

Tra . e xvi . car . In dñio ſunt ; ii . car . 7 xlviii . uitti

cũ . xxii . cot hñt . xviii . car . Ibi æccta ; 7 xxx ; ac pti.

7 ſilua ; xl . porc . 7 una piſcaria;

T.R.E ; 7 poſt: ualuit . xii . lib . Modo: xxiiii ; lib.

TERRA OSBERNI EPI.

.VI. Osbern eps teñ de rege æcctam de BOSEHAM.

7 de rege . E . tenuit . Huic æcctæ ptinebaꝫ . cxii . hidæ.

m̃ ſunt foris . xlvii . Hugo fili Rannulfi teñ ; xxx . hid.

7 Radulf de caiſned . xvii . hid.

Qdo Osbn recep: ſe defd æccta p . lxv . hid ; 7 m̃ ſimilit.

Value of the whole manor before 1066 £34; now, the Abbot's lordship
£50; the men's 44s.

In STEYNING Hundred

2 The Abbot holds STEYNING himself. Harold held it at the end of
King Edward('s life). Then it answered for 81 hides; in
addition a further 18 hides and 7 acres outside the Rape
which have never paid tax; now 67 hides. 33½ hides are in
the Rape of Arundel;the others are in the Rape of William of Braose.
but the Abbot holds them all now.
Land in the whole manor for 41 ploughs. In lordship 7 ploughs.
   178 villagers with 63 smallholders have 48 ploughs.
   2 churches; 9 slaves; 4 mills at 47s; in addition 68 pigs.
      Meadow, 113 acres; woodland, 45 pigs from pasturage.
   In the Borough there were 118 dwellings; they paid £4 2s.
      Now there are 123 dwellings; they pay 100s and 100d. [Their holders]
      have 1½ ploughs. Before 1066 they worked at the court like villagers.
Value before 1066 £86; later £50; now £100; however,
it is at a revenue for £122 less 2s.

In BURY Hundred

3 The Abbot holds BURY himself from the King. Countess Goda
held it from King Edward. Then it answered for 16 hides;
now for 12 hides. Land for 16 ploughs. In lordship 2 ploughs.
   48 villagers with 22 cottagers have 18 ploughs.
   A church; meadow, 30 acres; woodland, 40 pigs; a fishery.
Value before 1066 and later £12; now £24.

6 LAND OF BISHOP OSBERN (OF EXETER)

[In BOSHAM Hundred]

1 Bishop Osbern holds the church of BOSHAM from the King; he held it
from King Edward. 112 hides belonged to this church. Now 47 are
outside it; Hugh son of Ranulf holds 30 hides; Ralph of
Quesnay, 17 hides. When Osbern acquired it, the church answered

Tra̅.e̅   In dn̅io funt.ii.car̅.7 xxi.uitts

cu̅.xviii.borđ hn̅t.viii.car̅.Ibi.iii.molini de.xiiii.fot.

7 xii.ac̅ p̅ti.7 una falina de.ii.fot.7 una haga de.viii.đen.

Malger ten̅ de tra huj̅ æcctæ xii.hiđ p uno ꝏ Tornei. uocat'

7 geldat p.viii.hiđ.Ibi h̅t.xxxii.uittos cu̅.viii.car̅.

De eađ tra æcctæ.Radulf.i.hiđa Quiđa cleric.i.hiđ.7 iiii.clerici

17 c   ſ.i.hiđ comunit.

Ipfi hn̅t.iii.car in dn̅io.7 iii.uittos 7 x.borđ hn̅tes una̅

car̅ 7 dimiđ.7 æccta 7 p̅br ibi.7 ii.ferui.7 i.haga de.viii.

Totu̅ T.R.E.ualeƀ.ccc.liƀ.7 poft: l.liƀ.   ſ denar̅.

Modo.xvi.liƀ 7 x.fot qđ ep̅s ten̅.7 tam̅ h̅t de firma

xx.foliđ plus.Qđ Malger ten̅:vi.liƀ uat.7 tam̅ h̅t

.l.foliđ plus.Qđ alij tenent:iiii.liƀ 7 xv.foliđ uat.

Decima̅ æcctæ clerici tenent:7 uat.xl.foliđ.

T.R.E.ptinebat huic ꝏ.una hida in Icenore.Modo

ten̅ Warin ho̅ Rogerij comitis. IN HAMESFORD HĐ.

Ipfe ep̅s ten̅ HALESTEDE.7 de rege.E.tenuit.7 tc̅

p.xiii.hiđ fe defđ.m̅ p.v.hiđ 7 dimiđ.Tra̅.e̅

In dn̅io funt.ii.car̅.7 vii.uitti cu̅.xxiii.borđ hn̅t

ii.car̅.Ibi.ii.ferui.7 un̅ molin̅ de.iiii.fot.7 æccta ibi.

Silua.x.porc̅.Herbagiu̅:de.vii.porcis.i.

De hoc ꝏ ten̅ Ricard.i.hiđa.Osƀn cleric dim̅ hid.

Radulf p̅br.i.hiđa.quæ ptin̅ ad æcctam.

Totu̅ ꝏ T.R.E.7 poft.7 modo:uat xv.liƀ.

Durand ten de ep̅o PRESTETON IN SILLETONE HĐ.

T.R.E.7 m̅ fe defđ p.iii.hiđ.Tra̅.e̅   In dn̅io

una car̅ 7 dimiđ.7 iii.uitti cu̅.iiii.borđ hn̅t dimiđ

car̅.Ibi.vi.ac̅ p̅ti.7 parua filua ad claufura̅.

T.R.E.ualeƀ.iiii.liƀ.7 poft 7 modo:iii.liƀ.

for 65 hides, now the same. Land for ... In lordship 2 ploughs.
  21 villagers with 18 smallholders have 8 ploughs.
  3 mills at 14s; meadow, 12 acres; a salt-house at 2s;
     1 site at 8d.
   Mauger holds 12 hides of the land of this church as one
   manor, called THORNEY. He pays tax for 8 hides. He has
     32 villagers with 8 ploughs.
   Ralph has 1 hide of this church land; a cleric 1 hide, and
   4 clerics 1 hide in common.
   They have 3 ploughs in lordship;   17 c
     3 villagers and 10 smallholders who have 1½ ploughs.
     A church and a priest; 2 slaves; 1 site at 8d.
Total value before 1066 £300; later £50. Now, what the
Bishop holds, £16 10s; however, he has 20s more in revenue.
Value of what Mauger holds, £6; however, he has 50s more.
Value of what the others hold, £4 15s. The clerics hold the church
tithe, value 40s.
   Before 1066, 1 hide in Itchenor belonged to this manor;
now Warin, Earl Roger's man, holds it.

In DUMPFORD Hundred
2 The Bishop holds ELSTED himself. He held it from King Edward.
Then it answered for 13 hides; now for 5½ hides. Land for ....
In lordship 2 ploughs.
  7 villagers with 23 smallholders have 2 ploughs.
  2 slaves; a mill at 4s; a church; woodland, 10 pigs;
   grazing, 1 pig in 7.
  Richard holds 1 hide of this manor; Osbern the cleric, ½ hide;
   Ralph the priest 1 hide, which belongs to the church.
Value of the whole manor before 1066, later and now £15.

In SINGLETON Hundred
3 Durand holds PRESTON from the Bishop. Before 1066 and now it
answered for 3 hides. Land for .... In lordship 1½ ploughs.
  3 villagers with 4 smallholders have ½ plough.
  Meadow, 6 acres; a small woodland for fencing.
Value before 1066 £4; later and now £3.

Ricard ten de epo *LEVITONE*. *In Redrebrige Hd*.

Goduin tenuit de rege . E . in elemosina . 7 tc 7 m̃

se defd ꝑ . vi . hid . Tra . ē   In dñio sunt . ii . car.

7 xi . uilli cũ . vii . bord hñt . iiii . car.

Ibi æccła . 7 in cicestre una haga de . iii . den . 7 xii . ãc

p̃ti . Silua . x . porc . 7 de . vii . porcis unũ.

T.R.E . ualeb . x . lib . 7 post. vi . lib . Modo. x . lib.

Oĩs hæ træ ꝑtinueꝛ 7 ꝑtin æcclæ de Bosehã in elem.

TERRA SCI PETRI DE WINTONIA.

.VII. **A**BBAS SCI PETRI Wintoniæ . ten *SVESSE* . Sep

fuit in monasterio . T.R.E . se defd ꝑ xxviii . hid.

7 m̃ ꝑ xxvii . hid . Tra . ē . xxviii . car.

In dñio est una car . 7 xlvi . uilli cũ . iiii . bord hñt

xxi . car . Ibi æccła . 7 cxxx . ãc p̃ti.

In *LEWES* . x . burgſes de . lii . denar . 7 de uillanis

xxxviii . mil alleciũ 7 q̃ngent . ꝑ marsuins . iiii . lib.

ꝑ forisfactura uillanoꝗ . ix . lib . 7 iii . sũmas de pisis.

In totis ualentijs T.R.E . 7 post. ualuit . xx . lib.

Modo. tñtd app̃ciat. sed taĩ redd . xxviii . lib.

In Estocbrige Hd.

Ipse abb ten *CLONINCTVNE* . T.R.E . tenuit abbatia.

7 tc 7 m̃ ꝑ . v . hid se defd . Tra . ē   In dñio

est una car . 7 xv . uilli cũ . iiii . bord hñt . vi . car 7 dim.

Ibi . ii . serui . 7 xxv . ãc p̃ti . 7 silua ad clausuram.

In Cicestre . una haga de . iiii . den . De pasnagio.

uñ porc 7 dimid.

T.R.E. ualeb iiii . lib 7 x . sol 7 vii . den . Modo. vi . lib.

In ROTHERBRIDGE Hundred

4 Richard holds (EAST) LAVINGTON from the Bishop. Godwin the priest
held it from King Edward in alms. Then and now it answered
for 6 hides. Land for ... In lordship 2 ploughs.
    11 villagers with 7 smallholders have 4 ploughs.
    A church; one site in Chichester at 3d; meadow, 12 acres;
      woodland, 10 pigs; 1 pig in 7.
Value before 1066 £10; later £6; now £10.

5 All these lands belonged and belong to the church at Bosham, in alms.

7   LAND OF ST. PETER'S OF WINCHESTER

[In HOLMESTROW Hundred]

1 The Abbot of St. Peter's of Winchester holds SOUTHEASE.
It was always in the monastery('s lands). Before 1066 it
answered for 28 hides; now for 27 hides. Land for 28
ploughs. In lordship 1 plough.
    46 villagers with 4 smallholders have 21 ploughs.
    A church; meadow, 130 acres.
    In Lewes 10 burgesses at 52d. From the villagers 38,500 herrings;
      for porpoises £4; for the villagers' fines £9; 3 packloads of peas.
Total value before 1066 and later £20, now assessed at
as much; however, it pays £28.

In STOCKBRIDGE Hundred

2 The Abbot holds DONNINGTON himself. The Abbey held it before 1066.
Then and now it answered for 5 hides.
Land for .... In lordship 1 plough.
    15 villagers with 4 smallholders have 6½ ploughs.
    2 slaves; meadow, 25 acres; woodland for fencing;
      one site in Chichester at 4d; from pasturage, 1½ pigs.
Value before 1066 £4 10s 7d; now £6.

TERRA ÆCCLÆ DE LABATAILGE. *In WANDELMESTREI HD.*

VI. ABBAS SCI MARTINI de Labatailge ten *ALSISTONE.* de rege. Alnod tenuit de rege. E. 7 tc defd se ꝑ . L . hid.

7 m̃ ꝑ . XLIIII . hid 7 dim̃ . Tra . ẽ . XXVIII . car.

De his hid jaceꝏ . III . hid 7 dimid in Rap de Haſtinges.

7 II . hidæ in Rap de Lewes . 7 VII . burgenſes.

In dñio hñ abb . IIII . car . 7 LXV . uilti cũ . VII . bord . hñt

XXI . car . 7 dimid . Ibi . XII . ſerui . 7 L . ac pti . Silua. IIII . porc.

de paſnag . 7 VI . porc de herbagio.

De . V . hid ſupdictis . ten Rob̃t . I . hid 7 III . uirg de abbe.

Reinbert . V . uirg . Goiſfrid dimid hid . Alured . III . uirg.

Ipſi hñt in dñio . IIII . car . 7 V . uillos 7 uñ bord cũ . I . car

7 dimid.

Totũ m̃ T.R.E. ualeb . XLVIII . lib . 7 poſt. XXX . lib . Modo.

XXXVI . lib qd abb ten . Qd hoes ej . IIII . lib 7 V . ſolid.

Ipſe abb ten de rege . IIII . hid *IN TOTENORE HVND.*

Alnod tenuit de rege. E. 7 tc 7 m̃ se defd ꝑ IIII . hidis.

Ibi hñ abb . VI . uillos cũ . III . car . Apⷦciatũ eſt in alio m̃.

Ipſe abb hñ in ſuo rapo . VI . hid 7 dimid . H̃ tra ꝑ . VI . hid ſe

defd . 7 dimid fuit qeta . quia foris rap.

In his hid ten iſdẽ abb in dñio *BOCHEHA*. Olbolt tenuit de Go

duino com . Tc 7 m̃ se defd ꝑ dim hida . modo . ẽ una v in rapo

comitis de Ow . In dñio hñ abb . I . car . 7 IIII . bord cũ una car.

Ibi . III . ac pti . 7 ſilua . II . porc . T.R.E. 7 m̃. ual . XX . ſol.

In *BECE* q ten Oſbn de com de Ow . hñ abb . III . v træ . 7 ibi ſunt

III . uilti cũ . I . car . Val . VI . ſol.

In *WASINGATE* q ten Reinbt. hñ abb una v træ . cũ uno uillo

7 dimid car . Ibi ſilua . II . porc . Val . IIII . ſol.

In ALCISTON Hundred

1 The Abbot of St. Martin's of Battle holds ALCISTON from the King.
   Young Alnoth held it from King Edward. Then it answered for 50
   hides; now for 44½ hides. Land for 28 ploughs. 3½ of these
   hides lie in the Rape of Hastings; and 2 hides in the Rape of
   Lewes; 7 burgesses. The Abbot has 4 ploughs in lordship.
      65 villagers with 7 smallholders have 21 ½ ploughs.
      12 slaves; meadow, 50 acres; woodland, 4 pigs from
        pasturage; 6 pigs from grazing.
      Of the said 5 hides, Robert holds 1 hide and 3 virgates
      from the Abbot; Reinbert 5 virgates; Geoffrey ½ hide;
      Alfred 3 virgates. In lordship they have 4 ploughs.
      5 villagers and 1 smallholder with 1½ ploughs.
   Value of the whole manor before 1066 £48; later £30;
   now, what the Abbot holds £36; what his men hold £4 5s.

In TOTNORE Hundred

2 The Abbot holds 4 hides himself from the King. Young Alnoth
   held them from King Edward. Then and now it answered
   for 4 hides. The Abbot has
      6 villagers with 3 ploughs.
   It is assessed in another manor.

In his Rape

3 the Abbot has 6½ hides himself. This land answered for 6
   hides. ½ (hide) was exempt because it was outside the Rape.
   In these hides the Abbot also holds UCKHAM in lordship.
   Wulfbald held it from Earl Godwin. Then and now it answered
   for ½ hide. Now 1 virgate is in the Count of Eu's Rape.
   The Abbot has in lordship 1 plough;
      4 smallholders with 1 plough.
   Meadow, 3 acres; woodland, 2 pigs.
   Value before 1066 and now 20s.

The Abbot has

4 in BEECH, which Osbern holds from the Count of Eu, 3 virgates
   of land.
      3 villagers with 1 plough.
   Value 6s.

5 in BATHURST, which Reinbert holds, 1 virgate of land, with
      1 villager and ½ plough.
      Woodland, 2 pigs.
   Value 4s.

In *WILMINTE* q̃ teñ com̃ moritoñ . h̃t abb̃ . vi . uirg̃ træ . 7 ibi
ſunt . vi . uiłłi cũ . iiii . car̃ . 7 ſilua . ii . porc̃ . Vał . xv . ſoł.

In *NIREFELD* q̃ teñ com̃ de Ow . h̃t abb̃ . vi . uirg̃ tre . 7 ibi ſuɴ
.v . uiłłi 7 uñ borđ cũ . iii . car̃ .   Vał . x . ſoliđ.

In *PENEHEST* q̃ teñ Oſbñ de com̃ de Ow . h̃t abb̃ dim̃ hiđ . 7 ibi
ii . uiłłi ſunt cũ . ii . car̃ . 7 una ãc p̃ti . 7 ſilua . ii . porc̃ . Vał . xv . ſoł.

In Manerio *Hov* q̃đ teñ com̃ de Ow . h̃t abb̃ dim̃ hiđ . 7 ibi ſunt
ii . uiłłi cũ una car̃ . Vał . v . ſoł ⌐ car̃ . 7 una ãc p̃ti . Vał . iiii . ſoł.

In *PILESHĀ* q̃ teñ com̃ de Ow . h̃t abb̃ unã v̄ . 7 uñ uiłłm̃ cũ una

In *CEDESFELD* q̃ teñ Werenc de com̃ de Ow . h̃t abb̃ . iii . v̄ in dñio.

In *BOLLINTVN* q̃ teñ com̃ de Ow . h̃t abb̃ . ii . hiđ unã v̄ min.
7 ibi ſunt . vii . uiłłi cũ . v . car̃ . Vał xx . ſoł ⌐ cũ . i . uiłło . Vał . xii . deñ.

In *CROHERST* q̃ teñ Walter de com̃ de Ow . h̃t abb̃ unã v̄ træ.

In *WITINGES* q̃ teñ Ingelrann de com̃ . h̃t abb̃ . i . uirg̃ træ waſtã.

In *HOLINTVN* q̃ teñ com̃ de Ow . h̃t abb̃ unã v̄ træ waſtã.

Adhuc . ē una ſilua foris rap̃ de . v . porc̃.

De om̃i hac t̃ra h̃t abb̃ in dñio . ii . hiđ 7 dim̃ . 7 ibi . i . car̃
cũ . xxi . borđ . 7 ii . molinos ſine cenſu . Vał . xl . ſoł.

Hæ hidæ ñ geldaueř in rapo.

6   in WILMINGTON, which the Count of Mortain holds, 6 virgates of land.
    6 villagers with 4 ploughs.
    Woodland, 2 pigs.
    Value 15s.

7   in NETHERFIELD, which the Count of Eu holds, 6 virgates of land.
    5 villagers and 1 smallholder with 3 ploughs.
    Value 10s.

8   in PENHURST, which Osbern holds from the Count of Eu, ½ hide.
    2 villagers with 2 ploughs.
    Meadow, 1 acre; woodland, 2 pigs.
    Value 15s

9   in the manor of HOOE, which the Count of Eu holds, ½ hide.
    2 villagers with 1 plough.
    Value 5s.

10 in FILSHAM, which the Count of Eu holds, 1 virgate, and
    1 villager with 1 plough.
    Meadow, 1 acre.
    Value 4s.

11 in CATSFIELD, which Waring holds from the Count of Eu,
    3 virgates, in lordship.

12 in BULLINGTON, which the Count of Eu holds,
    2 hides less 1 virgate.
    7 villagers with 5 ploughs.
    Value 20s.

13 in CROWHURST, which Walter holds from the Count of Eu, 1 virgate of land,
    with 1 villager.
    Value 12d

14 in WILTING, which Ingelrann holds from the Count, 1 virgate of land, waste.

15 in HOLLINGTON, which the Count of Eu holds, 1 virgate of land, waste.
    Further, a woodland outside the Rape, at 5 pigs.

16 Of all this land the Abbot has 2½ hides in lordship. 1 plough, with
    21 smallholders.
    2 mills without dues.
    Value 40s.
    These hides did not pay tax in the Rape.

TERRA SCI EDWARDI.

IN BENESTEDE HVND Abbatia de S̄ EDWARDO ten 7 tenuit T.R.E.

FALCHEHÁ. Tc se defd p̄.xxi.hida. Modo p̄.xv.hid 7 dimid.

Tra.ē.xii.car. In dn̄io est una car. 7 xlviii.uilli 7 xix.cot

cū.xv.car. Ibi æccla. 7 piscaria de.v.solid. 7 In cicestre.vi.burgenses

de.vii.solid. Ibi.viii.āc p̄ti. Silua de.xxx.porc.

T.R.E.uale b̄.x.lib. Modo: xx.lib.

18 a

TERRA COMITIS DE OW.

C.IX. COMES DE OW.ten in dn̄io m̄.qd uocat Hor.

Goduin com tenuit. 7 T.R.E. 7 m̄ se defd p̄.xii.

hid.Tra.ē.xliiii.car. In dn̄io sunt.ii.car. 7 xliiii.uilli

cū xii.bord hn̄t.xxviii.car. Ibi æcclesiola. 7 i.molin de

vii.solid. 7 lxx 7 una āc p̄ti. 7 xxx.salinæ de xxxiii.sol.silua

x.porc de pasnag. De herbag.vii.porc.

De tra uillo₂ huj m̄ ten Reinbt dim hid.Robt.ii.

uirg 7 dimid. Osbn.ii.uirg. Alured.ii.uirg. Girald.ii.uirg.

Ingelrann.ii.uirg.Witbt.iiii.uirg 7 dim.Werelc.ii.uirg.

Robt alt.ii.uirg.

Int om̄s hn̄t in dn̄io.iii.car 7 dim. 7 xii.uillos 7 iii.bord

cū.vii.car.

Tot m̄ T.R.E.uale b̄.xxv.lib. 7 post: vi.lib. Modo dn̄ium

comitis: xiiii.lib. Militū ej: vii.lib 7 vii.sol.

Werenc ten de com CEDESFELLE. Elfelm tenuit de rege.E.

7 potuit ire cū tra quo uoluit. Tc se defd p̄ una hida 7 dim.

m̄ p̄ una hida 7 i.uirg. Tra.ē.vii.car. In dn̄io.ē una car.

7 xi.uilli cū.ii.bord hn̄t.viii.car. Ibi æcclesiola. 7 i.molin ad

hallā seruie₅. Ibi.iiii.āc p̄ti. 7 silua.iii.porc.7 herbag.v.porc.

T.R.E.uale b̄.l.sol. 7 post: xx.sol. Modo.lx.sol.

[8a] LAND OF ST. EDWARD'S [ABBEY, SHAFTESBURY]

In BINSTED Hundred

1 St. Edward's Abbey holds and held FELPHAM before 1066.
  Then it answered for 21 hides; now for 15½ hides.
  Land for 12 ploughs. In lordship 1 plough.
    48 villagers and 19 cottagers with 15 ploughs.
    A church; a fishery at 5s; 6 burgesses in Chichester
      at 7s. Meadow, 8 acres; woodland at 30 pigs.
  Value before 1066 £10; now £20.

9 LAND OF THE COUNT OF EU
(Hastings Rape)

18 a

[In NINFIELD Hundred]

1 The Count of Eu holds the manor called HOOE in lordship.
  Earl Godwin held it. Before 1066 and now it answered for
  12 hides. Land for 44 ploughs. In lordship 2 ploughs.
    44 villagers with 12 smallholders have 28 ploughs.
    A small church; 1 mill at 7s; meadow, 71 acres;
      30 salt-houses at 33s; woodland, 10 pigs from
      pasturage; from grazing, 7 pigs.
  Reinbert holds ½ hide of the villagers' land of this manor;
  Robert 2½ virgates; Osbern 2 virgates; Alfred 2 virgates;
  Gerald 2 virgates; Ingelrann 2 virgates; Withbert 4½
  virgates; Waring (?) 2 virgates; another Robert 2 virgates.
  Between them they have 3½ ploughs in lordship; and
    12 villagers and 3 smallholders with 7 ploughs.
  Value of the whole manor before 1066 £25; later £6;
  now the Count's lordship £14; his men-at-arms' £7 7s.

2 Waring holds CATSFIELD from the Count. Alfhelm held it from
  King Edward. He could go where he would with the land.
  Then it answered for 1½ hides; now for 1 hide and 1 virgate.
  Land for 7 ploughs. In lordship 1 plough.
    11 villagers with 2 smallholders have 8 ploughs.
    A small church; 1 mill which serves the Hall; meadow,
      4 acres; woodland, 3 pigs; grazing, 5 pigs.
  Value before 1066 50s; later 20s; now 60s.

Wibtus ten̄ de comite _MEDEHEI_ . Ofuuard tenuit de Rege . E.

7 quo uoluit cū tra ire potuit . 7 tc̄ 7 m̄ fe defđ ꝑ . iii . uirḡ.

Tra . ē . iiii . car̄ . In dn̄io . ē una car̄ . 7 iiii . uilli cū . iiii . car̄.

7 v . falinæ de . lxiiii . den̄ . 7 ii . ac̄ p̄ti 7 dim̄ . 7 filua . iii . porc̄

de pafnaḡ.

Ŧ.R.E . ualeƀ . iiii . liƀ . 7 poft.̷ xx . fol . Modo . c 7 x . folid̄.

Robt̄ ten̄ de com̄ _NEREWELLE_ . Blac tenuit de . R . E . 7 cū tra

quo uoluit ire uoluit . Tc̄ fe defđ ꝑ . iii . hiđ . m̄ ꝑ . ii . hiđ 7 dim̄.

Tra . ē . xii . car̄ . In dn̄io h̄t̄ Robt̄ . i . car̄ . 7 æcclam 7 i . bord̄.

⌐ De tra huj ꝳ ten̄ ipfe comes de Ow . v . uirḡ . in dn̄io.

Osƀn̄ . iii . uirḡ . Werenc . ii . uirḡ . Reinƀt̄ . vii . uirḡ.

In dn̄io h̄n̄t̄ . ii . car̄ . 7 viii . uilli 7 ii . borđ h̄n̄t̄ . vi . car̄.

Prædict Robt̄ coquus ten̄ cap̄ ꝳ . 7 ii . uirḡ tan̄tm̄ tenet.

7 q̄đa uillan̄ ten̄ alias.

Toŧ ꝳ T.R.E . ualeƀ . vi . liƀ . 7 poft . xx . fol . Modo totū.̷ c.v . fol.

IN FOLSALRE HVND̄.

Wibt̄ ten̄ de com̄ _HERSTE_ . Edmer p̄ƀr tenuit T.R.E . 7 cū

tra potuit ire quo uoluit . 7 tc̄ 7 m̄ fe defđ ꝑ . v . hiđ . Tra . ē . xii.

car̄ . In dn̄io funt . iii . car̄ . 7 xxx . uilli cū . xii . cot h̄n̄t̄ . xvi . car̄.

Ibi æccla . 7 vii . ac̄ p̄ti . 7 filua.̷ ii . porc̄.

T.R.E . ualeƀ . vi . liƀ . 7 poft.̷ xx . fol . Modo.̷ x . liƀ.

Wilts ten̄ de com̄ _WERLINGES_ . Alnod tenuit de rege . E.

7 quo uoluit cū tra ire potuit . 7 tc̄ 7 m̄ fe defđ ꝑ . v . hiđ . Tra . ē

xvi . car̄ . In dn̄io funt . ii . car̄ . 7 xxx . uilli cū . x . cot h̄n̄t̄ xviii.

car̄ . Ibi iii . falinæ de . vii . fol . Silua.̷ xxx . porc̄ . 7 xxx . ac̄ p̄ti.

⌐ De tra huj ꝳ ten̄ Girard . i . hiđ . Radulf . i . hiđ . Wennenc

.ii . uirḡ . Ibi xii . uilli cū . iiii . cot cū ix . car̄ . 7 viii . ac̄ p̄ti.

Toŧ ꝳ T.R.E | ualeƀ . x . liƀ . Modo qđ Wilts ten̄.̷ x . liƀ . Qđ milites.̷

⌐ iiii . liƀ.

3 Wibert holds *MEDEHEI* from the Count. Osward held it from
King Edward; he could go where he would with the land.
Then and now it answered for 3 virgates. Land for 4 ploughs.
In lordship 1 plough.
  4 villagers with 4 ploughs.
  5 salt-houses at 64d; meadow, 2½ acres; woodland,
    3 pigs from pasturage.
Value before 1066 £4; later 20s; now 110s.

4 Robert holds NINFIELD from the Count. Black held it from
King Edward; he [could] go where he would with the land.
Then it answered for 3 hides; now for 2½ hides. Land for 12 ploughs.
Robert has 1 plough in lordship; and
  a church and 1 smallholder.
The Count of Eu holds 5 virgates of the land of this manor
himself in lordship; Osbern 3 virgates; Waring 2 virgates;
Reinbert 7 virgates. They have 2 ploughs in lordship.
  8 villagers and 2 smallholders have 6 ploughs.
The said Robert Cook holds the head of the manor. He holds
  only 2 virgates; a villager holds the others.
Value of the whole manor before 1066 £6; later 20s; now 105s.

In FOXEARLE Hundred

5 Wibert holds HERSTMONCEUX from the Count. Edmer the priest
held it before 1066; he could go where he would with the land.
Then and now it answered for 5 hides. Land for 12 ploughs.
In lordship 3 ploughs.
  30 villagers with 12 cottagers have 16 ploughs.
  A church; meadow, 7 acres; woodland, 2 pigs.
Value before 1066 £6; later 20s; now £10.

6 William holds WARTLING from the Count. Alnoth held it from
King Edward; he could go where he would with the land.
Then and now it answered for 5 hides. Land for 16 ploughs.
In lordship 2 ploughs.
  30 villagers with 10 cottagers have 18 ploughs.
  3 salt-houses at 7s; woodland, 30 pigs; meadow, 30 acres.
Gerard holds 1 hide of this manor's land; Ralph 1 hide;
Venning the priest 2 virgates.
  12 villagers with 4 cottagers with 9 ploughs.
  Meadow, 8 acres.
Value of the whole manor before 1066 and later £10; now,
what William holds £10; what the men-at-arms hold £4.

Rotbt de Cruel ten de com *ESSEBORNE*. Seuuard
tenuit de rege. E. 7 tc 7 m̃ se defd p̄. ii. hid. 7 dim. Tra ē. xii. car. In dñio. ē una.
7 xxi. uitts cū. iii. cot hñt. xiiii. car. Ibi æccta. 7 iii. salinæ
de. lviii. deñ.

T.R.E. ualeb. vi. lib. 7 post. xx. sot. Modo. ix. lib.

FRANCWELLE ten com de Ow. 7 vi. milites de eo.
Vn eoȝ Norman tenuit T.R.E. 7 tc 7 m̃ se defd p una hid
7 dimid. Tra. ē. ii. car.

De hac tra ht isd Norman dim hid. Radulf. ii. uirg.
Hugo. ii. uirg. Osbn. ii. uirg. Wenenc. i. uirg. Girard. i. v.
In dñio. i. car. 7 viii. uitti 7 i. cot cū. iiii. car.
In ⊙. xii. ac p̃ti 7 silua. ii. porc.

Tot ⊙ T.R.E. ualeb. xl. sot. 7 post. x. sot. Modo. xl. vi. sot.

Ingelrahn ten de com unã hid in eod hund. Duo libi
hões tenuer T.R.E. 7 quo uoluer cū tra ire potuer. Tc 7 m̃
p una hid se defd. Tra. ē. iiii. car. In dñio. ē una. 7 vi.
uitti cū. iiii. cot hñt. iiii. car.

T.R.E. ualeb. xxx. sot. 7 post. xx. solid. Modo. xxx. solid.

Olaf ten de com unã uirg in ipso hund. Hernetoc
tenuit T.R.E. 7 q̃ libuit ire potuit. 7 p. i. uirg tc 7 m̃ se defd.
Tra. ē. i. car. 7 ibi. ē in dñio. cū uno uitto 7 ii. cot. Vat x. sot. 7 ualuit.

IN BEXELEI HVND.

BEXELEI ten Osbn de comite. T.R.E. tenuit eps
Alricus q̃a. ē de episcopatu. 7 post tenuit. donec rex. W.
dedit comiti castellariã de Hastinges. T.R.E. 7 m̃ se
defd p. xx. hid. Tra. ē xxvi. car.

De tra huj ⊙ ten ipse comes in dñio. iii. hid.
7 ibi ht. i. car. 7 vii. uitt cū. iiii. car.

9

7 Robert of Criel holds ASHBURNHAM from the Count. Siward held   18 b
it from King Edward. Then and now it answered for 2½ hides.
Land for 12 ploughs. In lordship 1.
  21 villagers with 3 cottagers have 14 ploughs.
  A church; 3 salt-houses at 58d.
Value before 1066 £6; later 20s; now £9.

8 The Count of Eu holds FRANKWELL, and 6 men-at-arms from him.
One of them, Norman, held it before 1066. Then and now it
answered for 1½ hides. Land for 2 ploughs.
  Norman also has ½ hide of this land; Ralph 2 virgates; Hugh 2 virgates;
Osbern 2 virgates; Venning 1 virgate; Gerard 1 virgate.
In lordship 1 plough;
  8 villagers and 1 cottager with 4 ploughs.
  In the manor, meadow, 12 acres; woodland, 2 pigs.
Value of the whole manor before 1066 40s; later 10s; now 46s.

9 Ingelrann holds 1 hide from the Count in the same Hundred.
Before 1066 2 free men held it; they could go where they would
with the land. Then and now it answered for 1 hide.
Land for 4 ploughs. In lordship 1.
  6 villagers with 4 cottagers have 4 ploughs.
Value before 1066, 30s; later 20s; now 30s.

10 Olaf holds 1 virgate from the Count in this Hundred. Hernetoc
held it before 1066; he could go wherever he would. Then and now
it answered for 1 virgate. Land for 1 plough.
It is there, in lordship, with
  1 villager and 2 cottagers.
The value is and was 10s.

  In BEXHILL Hundred
11 Osbern holds BEXHILL from the Count. Before 1066 Bishop Alric
held it because it is the Bishopric's; he held it later until King William
gave the castelry of Hastings to the Count. Before 1066 and
now it answered for 20 hides. Land for 26 ploughs.
The Count holds 3 hides of the land of this manor himself in
lordship. He has 1 plough;
  7 villagers with 4 ploughs.

De ead̃ t̃ra h̃t Osb̃n . x . hid̃ . Weñenc . i . hid̃ . Wilłs de

sept mueles . ii . hid̃ 7 dim . dim v̊ min . Rob̃t . i . hid̃ 7 dim v̊ .

Reinb̃t dim h̃d̃ . Anſchitil dim h̃d̃ . Rob̃t dim hidā .

Goisfrid 7 Roger clerici . i . hidā in p̃benda . Ibi . ii . ecclæ .

In dñio . iiii . car̃ . 7 xlvi . uilł 7 xxvii . cot cū . xxviiii . car̃ .

In toto m̃ꝰ vi . ắc p̃ti .

Tot̃ m̃ T . R . E . ualeb̃ . xx . lib̃ . 7 poſtꝰ waſta fuit . Modoꝰ

xviii . lib̃ 7 x . fol̃ . De hisꝰ pars comitis . xl . fol̃ capit .

Osb̃n ten de com . ii . uirg̃ t̃ræ in eod̃ hund . 7 ꝑ . ii . uirg̃

ſe defd̃ ſẽp . Ibi h̃t . v . bou in car̃ . Valuit viii . fol̃ . m̃ . xvi . fol̃ .

Bolintvn tenuit Leuenot de rege . E . 7 ꝑ . v . hid̃ ſe defd̃

7 tc̃ 7 m̃ . Tra . ẽ . v . car̃

De hac t̃ra ten com in dñio . iii . uirg̃ . 7 ibi h̃t xx . burgſes .

7 v . cot cū . ii . car̃ .

Abbatia de Vltreſport ten . iii . hid̃ . ii . v̊ min . 7 ꝑ tanto

ſe defd̃ . In dñio . i . car̃ . 7 xiii . uilłi cū xiii . cot h̃nt . v . car̃ .

car̃ . xx . ắc p̃ti .

T . R . E . ualeb̃ tot̃ m̃ . vi . lib̃ . 7 poſtꝰ l . fol̃ . Modo h̃t comꝰ

xliii . fol̃ . 7 monachi . iiii . lib̃ .   In Baldeslei hvnd̃ .

Wileshā tenuit rex . E . in dñio . Ibi . xv . hidæ ſunt .

quẽ∣geldañ neqₖ geldauer̃ . Tra . ẽ . xxx . car̃ .

De hac t̃ra ten ipſe comes . viii . hid̃ . 7 i . v̊ . 7 ibi h̃t . ii . car̃ .

7 xlviii . uilłi cū . vii . cot h̃nt xxx.iiii . car̃ .

De t̃ra ejd̃ m̃ ten Goisfrid . ii . hid̃ . Rob̃t . i . hid̃ 7 uñā v̊ .

Wilłs dim hid̃ . Hugo Arbaliſt . v . uirg̃ . Ingelrañ . ii . v̊ .

Rob̃tus dimid̃ hid̃ . Walteri . v . uirg̃ . Safuuard una . v̊ .

Weñenc . unā v̊ . Ofuuard . ii . v̊ . Roger daniel dim hid̃ .

In dñio . vi . car̃ 7 dimid̃ . 7 xiii . uilłi 7 xvii . cot . 7 iii .

ſerui cū . vii . car̃ 7 dimid̃ .   In m̃ . xxx . ắc p̃ti .

7 Silua . viii . porc .

Osbern has 10 hides of this land; Venning 1 hide;
William of Sept-Meules 2½ hides less ½ virgate; Robert St Leger
1 hide and ½ virgate; Reinbert ½ hide; Ansketel ½ hide;
Robert of Criel ½ hide; the clerics Geoffrey and Roger
1 hide in prebend; 2 churches. In lordship 4 ploughs;
46 villagers and 27 cottagers with 29 ploughs.
In the whole manor, meadow, 6 acres.
Value of the whole manor before 1066 £20; later it was
waste; now £18 10s; the Count's part takes 40s thereof.

12 Osbern holds 2 virgates of land from the Count in this Hundred.
It always answered for 2 virgates. He has 5 oxen in a plough.
The value was 8s; now 16s.

13 Leofnoth held BULLINGTON from King Edward. Then and now
it answered for 5 hides. Land for 5 ploughs.
The Count holds 3 virgates of this land in lordship. He has
20 burgesses; 5 cottagers with 2 ploughs.
Treport Abbey holds 3 hides less 2 virgates. It answers
for as much. In lordship 1 plough.
13 villagers with 13 cottagers have 5 ploughs.
Meadow, 20 acres.
Value of the whole manor before 1066 £6; later 50s;
now the Count has 43s; the monks £4.

In BALDSLOW Hundred
14 King Edward held FILSHAM in lordship. There are 15 hides there,
which do not and did not pay tax. Land for 30 ploughs.
The Count holds 8 hides and 1 virgate of this land himself.
He has 2 ploughs.
48 villagers with 7 cottagers have 34 ploughs.   18 c
Geoffrey holds 2 hides of this manor's land; Robert 1 hide
and 1 virgate; William ½ hide; Hugh Bowman 5 virgates;
Ingelrann 2 virgates; Robert Cook ½ hide; Walter 5 virgates;
Sasward 1 virgate; Venning the priest 1 virgate;
Osward 2 virgates; Roger Daniel ½ hide.
In lordship 6½ ploughs;
13 villagers, 17 cottagers and 3 slaves with 7½ ploughs.
In the manor, meadow, 30 acres; woodland, 8 pigs.

Tot m̃ T.R.E. ualeb xiiii . lib . Poſtea uaſtatũ fuit

Modo . xxii . lib . De his cõputat in parte cõm xiiii . lib.

ᚠ Vluuard p̃r huj m̃ ten æcclam cũ una v̄ . ſed non

ptiñ ad . xv . hid . Vlmer tenuit de rege .E. nec tc

geldauit nec m̃ facit . Val . v . ſolid.

HORINTONE tenuer̃ Goduin 7 Aleſtan T.R.E. 7 q̃ uole

bant cũ tra ire poteraņ . Tc ſe defd̃ p . iiii . hid 7 dimid.

Modo p . iii . hid 7 . ii . v̄ . Tra . ē . viii . car.

De hac tra ten comes in dñio unã hid 7 dim . 7 ii . v̄.

7 ibi h̃t . i . car . 7 xii . uiłłos cũ . iiii . car.

De ipſa tra h̃t Reinb̃ dimid hid . Wiłłs unã hid.

Hugo dimid hd̃ . Vluuard . ii . v̄.

In dñio una car̃ . 7 iii . uiłł 7 iii . cot cũ . iii . car.

In m̃ . ii . ac p̃ti . 7 ſilua . ii . porc.

Tot m̃ T.R.E. ualeb xxx . ſoł . 7 poſt . xx . ſoł . M̃. lviii . ſoł.

CROTESLEI tenuit Golduin T.R.E. 7 potuit ire quo

uoluit . 7 tc 7 m̃ p . vi . hid ſe defd̃ . Tra . ē . viii . car̃.

De hac tra ten dimid hid . 7 ibi un uiłłs . ē cũ . i . car.

De ead tra ten Wiłłs 7 Goduin de eo . iiii . hid 7 dim̃.

Reinb̃ dim hid . Hugo dim hid.

Ibi hñt xxiiii . uiłłos 7 ii . cot cũ viii . car.

In m̃ . xxvii . ac p̃ti.

Tot m̃ T.R.E | ualeb . c . ſolid . Modo . vi . lib 7 vii . ſolid

WESTEWELLE tenuit Weneſtan T.R.E. 7 potuit ire

quo uoluit . Tc 7 m̃ ſe defd̃ p una hd̃ 7 ii . v̄ . Tra . ē

iii . car̃ . Wib̃t tenet de com̃ . 7 h̃t in dñio . i . car̃ 7 dim.

7 vii . uiłł 7 i . cot cũ . iii . car.

T.R.E. ualeb . xx . ſoł . 7 poſt. lxx . ſoł . M̃. lxxii . ſoł.

CROHEST tenuit Herald comes . Tc p . vi . hid ſe defd̃.

Modo p . iii . hid . Tra . ē . xx.ii . car̃ . Walter fili Lãb̃ti

Value of the whole manor before 1066 £14; later, it was wasted; now £22; £14 of this is accounted in the Count's part.

Wulfward the priest holds the church of this manor with 1 virgate, but it does not belong to the 15 hides. Wulfmer held it from King Edward; it did not pay tax then nor does it now. Value 5s.

15 Godwin and Alstan held HOLLINGTON before 1066; they could go where they would with the land. Then it answered for 4½ hides; now for 3 hides and 2 virgates. Land for 8 ploughs. The Count holds 1½ hides and 2 virgates of this land in lordship. He has 1 plough and
  12 villagers with 4 ploughs.
Reinbert has ½ hide of this land; William 1 hide; Hugh ½ hide; Wulfward 2 virgates. In lordship 1 plough;
  3 villagers and 3 cottagers with 3 ploughs.
  In the manor, meadow, 2 acres; woodland, 2 pigs.
Value of the whole manor before 1066, 30s; later 20s; now 58s.

16 Goldwin held 'CORTESLEY' before 1066; he could go where he would. Then and now it answered for 6 hides. Land for 8 ploughs.....holds ½ hide of this land.
  1 villager with 1 plough there.
William holds 4½ hides of this land and Godwin from him;
  Reinbert ½ hide; Hugh ½ hide. They have
  24 villagers and 2 cottagers with 8 ploughs.
  In the manor, meadow, 27 acres.
Value of the whole manor before 1066 and later 100s; now £6 7s.

17 Winstan held WESTFIELD before 1066; he could go where he would. Then and now it answered for 1 hide and 2 virgates. Land for 3 ploughs. Wibert holds from the Count. He has in lordship 1½ ploughs;
  7 villagers and 1 cottager with 3 ploughs.
Value before 1066, 20s; later 70s; now 72s.

18 Earl Harold held CROWHURST. Then it answered for 6 hides; now for 3 hides. Land for 22 ploughs. Walter son of Lambert

ten de comite . 7 ht . II . car̃ in dñio . 7 XII . uilt 7 VI . cot

hñt XII . car̃ . Ibi . XV . ãc p̃ti . 7 ſilua.' IIII . porc̃.

Quidã Walo ten dimid hid . 7 II . v̄ . Ibi . III . uilti . cũ . I . c̃.

T . R . E . ualeb . VIII . lib . Modo.' c . ſot . Vaſtat̃ fuit.

WILTINGHA tenuer̃ . II . libi hões T . R . E . Tc̃ 7 modo

ſe defd p . IIII . hid . Tra . e̅ . IX . car̃.

De hac tra ten Ingelrann de comite . II . hid . 7 . II . v̄.

Reinbt dimid hid 7 II . v̄ . Radulf dim hid . Robt . II . v̄.

Ibi ſuɴ in dñio . III . car̃ . 7 IX . uilt 7 v . cot cũ . VI . car̃.

Ibi . XVI . ãc p̃ti . Tot c̃ T . R . E . ualeb c . ſot . M̃.' IIII . lib.

Vaſtat̃ fuit . Comes ht̄ in parco ſuo . I . uirg de hoc c̃.

In eod hund ten Ingelrañ de com̃ . III . v̄ . q̃s tenuer̃ . II . libi

hões T . R . E . ſed geld nunq | dider̃ . Ibi . III . uilti cũ . II . car̃ . Val . X . ſot.

IN HAILESALTEDE HVND.

WATLINGETONE tenuit Herald . Tc̃ 7 m̃ p dim hid ſe defd.

Tra . e̅ . VI . car̃ . Reinbt ten de com̃ . 7 ibi ht̄ . II . car̃ 7 VI . uilt

7 III . cot cũ . III . car̃ . Ibi . X . ãc p̃ti . 7 ſilua . VI . porc̃.

T . R . E . 7 m̃ ual . L . ſot . Vaſtat̃ fuit.

Iſdẽ Reinbt ten de comite *MONTIFELLE* . God tenuit T . R . E.

7 quo uoluit ire potuit . Tc̃ 7 m̃ p una hida ſe defd . Tra . e̅ . VIII . car̃.

In dñio ſunt . II . 7 IX . uilti cũ . II . cot hñt . VI . car̃ . Ibi . VIII . ãc p̃ti.

7 ſilua . X . porc̃ . T . R . E . ualeb . III . lib 7 poſt.' XX . ſot . Modo.' IIII . lib.

Herolf ten de com̃ *NEDREFELLE* . Goda tenuit de rege . E . Tc̃ ſe

defd p una hid 7 dim . Modo p una tñt . Tra . e̅ . IIII . car̃ . In dñio

eſt una . 7 VII . uilti hñt . III . car̃ . Ibi . VIII . ſalinæ de . VIII . ſolid.

7 ſilua . X . porc̃ . T . R . E . ualeb . c . ſot . M̃ . L . ſot . Vaſtata fuit.

holds it from the Count. He has 2 ploughs in lordship.
12 villagers and 6 cottagers have 12 ploughs.
Meadow, 15 acres; woodland, 4 pigs.
One Walo holds ½ hide and 2 virgates.
3 villagers with 1 plough there.
Value before 1066 £8; now 100s; it was wasted.

19 Before 1066, 2 free men held WILTING. Then and now it
answered for 4 hides. Land for 9 ploughs.
Ingelrann holds 2 hides and 2 virgates of this land from
the Count; Reinbert ½ hide and 2 virgates; Ralph ½ hide;
Robert 2 virgates. In lordship 3 ploughs;
9 villagers and 5 cottagers with 6 ploughs.
Meadow, 16 acres.
Value of the whole manor before 1066, 100s; now £4;
it was wasted.
The Count has 1 virgate of this manor in his park.

20 In the same Hundred Ingelrann holds 3 virgates from the Count   18 d
which 2 free men held before 1066; but they never paid tax.
3 villagers with 2 ploughs.
Value 10s.

In NETHERFIELD Hundred

21 Earl Harold held WHATLINGTON. Then and now it answered
for ½ hide. Land for 6 ploughs. Reinbert holds from the
Count. He has 2 ploughs.
6 villagers and 3 cottagers with 3 ploughs.
Meadow, 10 acres; woodland, 6 pigs.
Value before 1066 and now 50s. It was wasted.

22 Reinbert also holds MOUNTFIELD from the Count. Goda held it
before 1066; he could go where he would. Then and now it
answered for 1 hide. Land for 8 ploughs. In lordship 2.
9 villagers with 2 cottagers have 6 ploughs.
Meadow, 8 acres; woodland, 10 pigs.
Value before 1066 £3; later 20s; now £4.

23 Herewulf holds NETHERFIELD from the Count. Goda held it from
King Edward. Then it answered for 1½ hides; now for 1 only.
Land for 4 ploughs. In lordship 1.
7 villagers have 3 ploughs.
8 salt-houses at 8s; woodland, 10 pigs.
Value before 1066, 100s; now 50s; it was wasted.

In hoc *HVND* ten Hugo.uñ ⊗ de comite.q̃d Alnod tenuit

T.R.E.⁊ q̃libet cũ eo ire potuit.⁊ tc̃ ꝓ una h̃d ⁊ dim̃ ſe defd̃.Modo

ꝓ una tñt.Tra.ē.iiii.caꝛ.In dñio.ē una caꝛ.⁊ xii.uiłł cũ.v.caꝛ.

Ibi.v.ãc p̃ti.⁊ ſilua.iiii.porc̃.T.R.E.uałb̃ c.ſoł.⁊ poſt:́ xx.M.́ꟙ.ꟙ.ſoł.

Iſd̃e Osbñ ten.i.v de com̃ in *BECHE*.Vlbald tenuit.T.R.E.

Tc̃ ꝓ una uirg̃.m̃ ꝓ nichilo.Tc̃ uałb̃.ii.ſoł.́ m̃ nichil.

Wenenc ten de com̃ *BRVNHĀ*.Eddid tenuit T.R.E.⁊ q̃libet

ire potuit.⁊ ꝓ dim̃ h̃d ſe defd̃.tc̃ ⁊ m̃.Tra.ē.iii.caꝛ.In dñio.ē una.

⁊ iiii.uiłłi ⁊ ii.cot cũ.ii.caꝛ.Vna ãc p̃ti.Silua.ii.porc̃.

T.R.E.⁊ m̃:́ xx.ſoł.Vaſtata fuit.

Hugo ten de com̃ una v In *ESLEDE*.Leuuiñ tenuit de Leuuino

Nunꝗ geldauit.Ibi.i.caꝛ.⁊ ſilua.iii.porc̃.Valuit.v.ſoł.M̃.xii.ſt

Iſd̃e Hugo ten.ii.v ꝑtinent in *ELLEDE*. *IN STAPLEHĀ HVND*.

Leuuiñ tenuit.⁊ ꝓ.ii.v ſe defd̃ tc̃ ⁊ m̃.Ibi uñ uiłłs cũ.i.caꝛ.

Ipſe com̃ ten unã v ꝑtiñ In *ESLEDE*.Leuuiñ tenuit.

Nunꝗ geld dedit.Tra.ē.i.caꝛ.⁊ ibi.ē cũ.i.uiłło.Tc̃.iiii.ſoł.m̃.v.ſoł.

In eod̃ hund ten Hugo de com̃ una v.Can tenuit T.R.E.Tc̃

⁊ m̃ ꝓ una v ſe defd̃.Tra.ē una caꝛ.Ibi.ē cũ.i.uiłło.Vał.iiii.ſoł.⁊ uał.

BRISLINGA ten comes de Ow.T.R.E.tenueꝛ.ii.frs de rege.

ꝓ una hida ſe defd̃ tc̃ ⁊ m̃.In dñio.ē una caꝛ.⁊ æccła.⁊ ſilua:́

De iſta h̃d ten Robt.iiii.v de com̃.⁊ ibi h̃t   Ɫ de.v.ſoł.

x.uiłł cũ.ii.cot.h̃ntes.vii.caꝛ.

T.R.E.uałb̃.c.ſoł.⁊ poſt:́ x.ſoł.Modo:́ xlii.ſoł.

24 In this Hundred Hugh holds a manor from the Count, which
Alnoth held before 1066; he could go wherever he would with it.
Then it answered for 1½ hides; now for 1 only. Land for 4 ploughs.
In lordship 1 plough;
  12 villagers with 5 ploughs.
  Meadow, 5 acres; woodland, 4 pigs.
Value before 1066, 100s; later 20[s]; now 50s.

25 Osbern also holds 1 virgate in BEECH from the Count. Before 1066
Wulfbald held it. Then it answered for 1 virgate; now for nothing.
Value then 2s; now nothing.

26 Venning the priest holds BROOMHAM from the Count. Edith held it
before 1066; she could go wherever she would. Then and now it
answered for ½ hide. Land for 3 ploughs. In lordship 1;
  4 villagers and 2 cottagers with 2 ploughs.
  Meadow, 1 acre; woodland, 2 pigs.
Value before 1066 and now 20s; it was wasted.

27 Hugh holds 1 virgate from the Count in EYELID. Leofwin held
it from Earl Leofwin. It never paid tax.
  1 plough; woodland, 3 pigs.
The value was 5s; now 12s.

In STAPLE Hundred
28 Hugh also holds 2 virgates which belong to EYELID. Earl Leofwin
held it. Then and now it answered for 2 virgates.
  1 villager with 1 plough.

29 The Count holds 1 virgate himself which belongs to EYELID.
Earl Leofwin held it. It never paid tax. Land for 1 plough.
It is there, with
  1 villager.
[Value] then 4s; now 5s.

30 In the same Hundred Hugh holds 1 virgate from the Count. Cana
held it before 1066. Then and now it answered for 1 virgate.
Land for 1 plough. It is there, with
  1 villager.
The value is and was 4s.

[In NETHERFIELD Hundred]
31 The Count of Eu holds BRIGHTLING. Before 1066 two brothers
held it from the King. Then and now it answered for 1 hide.
In lordship 1 plough.
  A church; woodland at 5s.
Robert holds 4 virgates of this hide from the Count. He has
  10 villagers with 2 cottagers who have 7 ploughs.
Value before 1066, 100s; later 10s; now 42s.

DALINTONE ten cõm de ow . Norman tenuit T ⸝R . E . 7 ɋlibet.
ire potuit . 7 ꝑ una hiđ ſe defđ . M̃ ꝑ nichilo . T̃ra . ē
De iſta hida h̃t cõm medietatē in foreſta . 7 ual . v . ſol.
Wilts h̃t aliã medietatē . 7 ibi h̃t . i . car in dñio . cũ . ii . cot.
Iſdē Wilts h̃t unã v̄ 7 dim in *FOXER HVND* . Rex . E . tenuit.
7 nunꝗ geldauit . Ibi . i . uill 7 ii . cot h̃nt . i . car.
Totũ T . R . E . ualb̃ xL . ſol . Modo: xxxv . ſol.
Wilbᵗ ten de cõm *WARBORGETONE* . I̅N H̅A̅V̅O̅C̅H̅E̅S̅B̅E̅R̅I̅E̅ H̃D.
Goda comitiſſa tenuit . T̃c 7 m̃ ꝑ una hiđ ſe defđ . T̃ra . ē . ii . car.
In dñio . ē una . 7 ii . uilti cũ . vi . cot h̃nt . i . car . Valuit xL . ſol . M̃ . xx . ſol.
In *BELINGEHÁ* h̃t comes . i . hiđ in dñio . Eddiđ regina tenuit.
Nunꝗ geldauit . T̃ra . ē . iii . car . In dñio . ē una . 7 iii . uill h̃nt . ii . car

19 a

T . R . E . ualb̃ xx . ſol . 7 poſt: x . ſol . Modo: xx . ſoliđ.
Ipſe cõm h̃t dim̃ h̃d in *BELINGHÁ* . Rex . E . tenuit . 7 nunꝗ
geldauit . Ibi ſunt . ii . uilti cũ . iii . car . Valuit 7 ual . x . ſoliđ.
Itē in *BELINGHÁ* ten comes . iiii . hiđ dimiđ v̄ min . Goda
comitiſſa tenuit . 7 nunꝗ geldauit . T̃ra . ē . x . car . Ibi . xviii.
uilti h̃nt . xiii . car . T . R . E . ualb̃ . iiii . lib̃ . 7 poſt: xL . ſol . M̃: Lxx . ſol.
Ipſe comes ten in dñio . i . h̃d 7 dim̃ | de ꝏ *FERLA* . T . R . E.
tenuit abbatia Wiltun . Nõꝗ geldauit . T̃ra . ē . vi . car.
Ibi . ix . uilti h̃nt . viii . car . T . R . E . 7 m̃ ual xxx . ſol.
Iſdē cõm ten uirg 7 dim̃ de *HERLINTONE* . Abbatia
de Wiltun tenuit T . R . E . Nunꝗ geldauit . T̃ra . ē . i . car.
Ibi . v . uilti h̃nt . iii . car . T . R . E . 7 m̃: ual . vii . ſol.
Iſdē cõm h̃t unã v̄ 7 dimiđ de ꝏ *LESTONE* . Goda
comitiſſa tenuit . Nunꝗ geldauit . Ibi . iii . uilti h̃nt . ii . car.
T . R . E . 7 m̃ ual viii . ſoliđ.

32 The Count of Eu holds DALLINGTON. Norman held it before 1066;
   he could go wherever he would. It answered for 1 hide;
   now for nothing. Land for ....
   The Count has the half of this hide in the Forest.
   Value 5s.
   William has the other half. He has 1 plough in lordship, with
   2 cottagers.
   In FOXEARLE Hundred
33 William also has 1½ virgates. King Edward held it. It never paid tax.
   1 villager and 2 cottagers have 1 plough.
   Value of the whole before 1066, 45s; now 35s.
   In HAWKSBOROUGH Hundred
34 Wibert holds WARBLETON from the Count. Countess Goda
   held it. Then and now it answered for 1 hide. Land for 2 ploughs.
   In lordship 1.
   2 villagers with 6 cottagers have 1 plough.
   The value was 40s; now 20s.
   [In the Rape of PEVENSEY]
35 The Count has 1 hide in BEDDINGHAM, in lordship. Queen Edith
   held it. It never paid tax. Land for 3 ploughs. In lordship 1.
   3 villagers have 2 ploughs.
   Value before 1066, 20s; later 10s; now 20s.   19 a
36 The Count has ½ hide in BEDDINGHAM himself. King Edward
   held it. It never paid tax.
   2 villagers with 3 ploughs.
   The value was and is 10s.
37 Also in BEDDINGHAM the Count holds 4 hides less ½ virgate.
   Countess Goda held it. It never paid tax. Land for 10 ploughs.
   18 villagers have 13 ploughs.
   Value before 1066 £4; later 40s; now 70s.
38 The Count holds 1½ hides and 1 virgate of the manor of
   (WEST) FIRLE himself, in lordship. Wilton Abbey held it
   before 1066. It did not pay tax. Land for 6 ploughs.
   9 villagers have 8 ploughs.
   Value before 1066 and now 30s.
39 The Count also holds 1½ virgates of ARLINGTON. Wilton Abbey
   held it before 1066. It never paid tax. Land for 1 plough.
   5 villagers have 3 ploughs.
   Value before 1066 and now 7s.
40 The Count also has 1½ virgates of the manor of LAUGHTON.
   Countess Goda held it. It never paid tax.
   3 villagers have 2 ploughs.
   Value before 1066 and now 8s.

Isdē cōm teñ unā v̄ træ ptinent ad *HECHESTONE*.

Agemund tenuit T.R.E. 7 q̄libet ire potuit. Neq̄ geldau.

Ibi . ii . uitti hñt . ii . car̄ . T.R.E. 7 m̄ . uat . iiii . fot.

Isdē cōm teñ dimid h̄d 7 dim v̄ de M̄ *RIPE*. Herald cōm

tenuit 7 nunq̄ geldauit. Ibi . ii . uitti hñt . i . car̄.

Vat 7 ualuit . v . fot.

Isdē cōm teñ unā v̄ in M̄ *TELITONE* . Herald cōm tenuit.

7 nunq̄ geldauit. Ibi . ii . uitti hñt . i . car̄ . Vat 7 ualuit . v . fot.

In M̄ *ESDENE* . unā v̄ 7 dim . Goda comit tenuit . nūq̄ geld.

Ibi . ii . uitti hñt . i . car̄ . Vat 7 ualuit . iii . fot.

In M̄ *WILLENDONE* Goda comitiffa . i . v̄ 7 dimid tenuit.

7 ñq̄ geldauit. Ibi cōm . ii . uitt cū . ii . car̄ ht. Vat . v . fot 7 ualuit.

Ibid Vlmer pbr unā v̄ tenuit. 7 q̄libet ire potuit 7 nunq̄ geldau.

Ibi cōm ht uñ uitt cū . i . car̄ . Vat 7 ualuit . iii . fot.

Ibid Aluuin tenuit |unā v̄ 7| qrt uit a de M̄ *SASINGHA* . 7 q̄libet ire pot.

7 ñq̄ geldau. Ibi cōm ht . ii . uitt cū . ii . car̄ . Vat 7 ualuit . x . fot.

Wibt de cōm teñ dimid hid *In RADINTONE* . Cana q̄dā

tib h̄o tenuit . 7 ñq̄ geldauit. Ibi . iii . uitti hñt . ii . car̄.

Vat 7 ualuit . viii . folid.

In *DENE* Goda comitiffa . i . hid tenuit. ñq̄ gtdt. Ibi Wibt

ht . ii . uittos cū . ii . car̄ . Vat 7 ualuit . xiiii . fot.

In *LESTONE* Goda comit unā h̄d tenuit . 7 ñq̄ gtdt . Ibi Wibt

ht . iiii . uitt cū . iii . car̄ . Vat 7 ualuit xiii . fot.

In *BORTONE* Vlmer q̄dā tib h̄o tenuit . 7 ñq̄ gtdt . dim hidā.

Ibi Wibt . i . uitt 7 i . cot cū . i . car̄ ht . Tc 7 m̄ . viii . fot.

41 The Count also holds 1 virgate of land which belongs to ECKINGTON.
Agemund held it before 1066; he could go wherever he would.
It did not pay tax.
  2 villagers have 2 ploughs.
Value before 1066 and now 4s.

42 The Count also holds ½ hide and ½ virgate of the manor of RIPE.
Earl Harold held it. It never paid tax.
  2 villagers have 1 plough.
The value is and was 5s.

43 The Count also holds 1 virgate in the manor of TILTON.
Earl Harold held it. It never paid tax.
  2 villagers have 1 plough.
The value is and was 5s.

44 In the manor of EAST DEAN Countess Goda held 1½ virgates.
It never paid tax.
  2 villagers have 1 plough.
The value is and was 3s.

45 In the manor of WILLINGDON Countess Goda held 1½ virgates.
It never paid tax. The Count has
  2 villagers with 2 ploughs.
The value is and was 5s.

46 Wulfmer the priest also held 1 virgate there. He could go
wherever he would. It never paid tax. The Count has
  1 villager with 1 plough.
The value is and was 3s.

47 There Alwin also held 1 virgate and 1 furlong of the manor of
SESSINGHAM; he could go wherever he would. It never paid tax.
The Count has
  2 villagers with 2 ploughs.
The value is and was 10s.

48 Wibert holds ½ hide in RATTON from the Count. Cana, a free man,
held it. It never paid tax.
  3 villagers have 2 ploughs.
The value is and was 8s.

49 In (EAST) DEAN Countess Goda held 1 hide. It never paid tax. Wibert has
  2 villagers with 2 ploughs.
The value is and was 14s.

50 In LAUGHTON Countess Goda held 1 hide. It never paid tax. Wibert has
  4 villagers with 3 ploughs.
The value is and was 13s.

51 In BROUGHTON Wulfmer, a free man, held ½ hide. It never paid tax.
Wibert has
  1 villager and 1 cottager with 1 plough.
[Value] then and now 8s.

Osbn fili Goisfridi de com ten . v . hid In *LESTONE* . Goda ^{comit'}

tenuit . 7 ñq gldt . Tra . ē . x . car . Ibi . xv . uilli hñt . xv . car .

T.R.E. iiii . lib ualeb . 7 post. xl . sol . Modo . iiii . lib.

In *STOCHINGHA* . Leuenot dim hd tenuit . 7 ñq gldt .

Ibi ht Osbn . i . cot . redd xii . den . Tc . iii . sol . m . ii . solid .

In *ACHINGEWORDE* Brictuin lib ho dim hd tenuit . 7 ñq

gldt . Ibi ht Osbn in dnio . i . car . 7 i . uilt cu . i . car . 7 ii . acs pti .

Tc 7 post 7 m . ual . x . sol .

In *ECHENTONE* Agemund . i . hd de rege . E . tenuit . 7 ñq gldt .

Tra . ii . car . Ibi Osbn ht . iii . uilt cu . iii . cai . Tc 7 post 7 m . xiiii . sol .

19 b

In *FERLE* tenuit . una v de rege .E. Abbatia de Wiltun .

7 nunq geldauit . Ibi ht Osbn un uilt cu . i . car .

Tc 7 m . ual . xxx . den.

In *PRESTITONE* Botiz lib ho tenuit dim hid . 7 ñq

gldt . Ibi ht Osbn . v . uilt cu . iii . car . Tc 7 m ; v . solid .

In *WALDERE* . Ælueua liba femina dim v tenuit .

7 nunq gldt . Ibi ht Osbn . i . uilt cu . v . bob . Val . ii . sol .

In *RIPE* Herald ^{com} tenuit una v . Nunq gldt . Ibi Aluuin

ho comitis de Ow ht . i . car in dnio . 7 i . uilt . 7 i . cot

cu . i . car . Ibi . iii . ac pti . 7 silua . iii . porc . Tc 7 post. iiii . sol .

m . x . sol . *IN ESSESWELLE HVND . HOC HVND*

NVNQ GELDAVIT .

Walteri fili Lanbti ten de comite *HASLESSE .*

Alric eps tenuit in feudo de rege . E . Tc 7 m

iiii . hidæ 7 dim . Tra . ē . ix . car . Ibi in dnio . ii . car .

7 vi . uilti 7 un cot cu . vii . car . Ibi æccla . 7 silua .

x . porc . De hac tra ten Walo . i . hd . 7 ibi ht . iiii . uilt

cu . ii . car 7 i . cot . Tot M T.R.E ualeb . cxiiii . sol .

Modo . vii . lib . Vastatu fuit .

52 Osbern son of Geoffrey holds 5 hides from the Count in LAUGHTON.
Countess Goda held it. It never paid tax.
Land for 10 ploughs.
  15 villagers have 15 ploughs.
Value before 1066 £4; later 40s; now £4.

53 In 'STOCKINGHAM' Leofnoth held ½ hide. It never paid tax. Osbern has
  1 cottager who pays 12d.
[Value] then 3s; now 2s.

54 In ETCHINGWOOD Brictwin, a free man, held ½ hide. It never
paid tax. Osbern has 1 plough in lordship.
  1 villager with 1 plough.
  Meadow, 2 acres.
Value then, later and now 10s.

55 In ECKINGTON Agemund held 1 hide from King Edward. It never
paid tax. Land for 2 ploughs. Osbern has
  3 villagers with 3 ploughs.
[Value] then, later and now 14s.

56 In (WEST) FIRLE Wilton Abbey held 1 virgate from King Edward.   19 b
It never paid tax. Osbern has
  1 villager with 1 plough.
Value then and now 30d.

57 In PRESTON Botic, a free man, held ½ hide. It never paid tax. Osbern has
  5 villagers with 3 ploughs.
[Value] then and now 5s.

58 In WALDRON Aelfeva, a free woman, held ½ virgate. It never paid tax.
Osbern has
  1 villager with 5 oxen.
Value 2s.

59 In RIPE Earl Harold held 1 virgate. It never paid tax.
Alwin, the Count of Eu's man, has 1 plough in lordship.
  1 villager and 1 cottager with 1 plough.
  Meadow, 3 acres; woodland, 3 pigs.
[Value] then and later 4s; now 10s.

In SHOYSWELL Hundred. THIS HUNDRED NEVER PAID TAX.
60 Walter son of Lambert holds HAZELHURST from the Count.
Bishop Alric held it as a Holding from King Edward. Then and
now 4½ hides. Land for 9 ploughs. In lordship 2 ploughs;
  6 villagers and 1 cottager with 7 ploughs.
  A church; woodland, 10 pigs.
Walo holds 1 hide of this land. He has
  4 villagers with 2 ploughs and 1 cottager.
Value of the whole manor before 1066, 114s; now £7; it was wasted.

In *CAVELTONE* tenuer̃ unā v̆ duo libi hões Leuuin 7 Eduard

Ibi hr̃ com . ii . uill cũ . i . car̃ . Tc̃ 7 post . 7 m̃ . xl . den̆.

In *ESSERINTONE* tenuit Leuuin un lib hõ unā v̆ . Ibi hr̃

com . ĭi . uill cũ . i . car̃ . Tc̃ 7 post . 7 m̃ . vi . sol.

In *ALSITONE* tenuit abbatia de Wiltun unā v̆ . Ibi hr̃ com

un uill cũ . i . car̃ . Tc̃ 7 post 7 m̃ . v . sol.

Reinbr̃ ten de comite una v̆ In *RADETONE* . Vlf un

lib hõ tenuit . Ibi una car̃ in dñio 7 xv . ac pti . 7 iii . cot.

redd̃ . ii . sol . Tc̃ 7 post 7 m̃ . v . sol.

In *ALSITONE* tenuit Abbatia de Wiltun . unā v̆ . Ibi hr̃

Reinbr̃ . ii . car̃ 7 iii . cot . 7 siluā . ii . porc̃ . Tc̃ 7 post . 7 m̃ . v . sol.

In *WIGENTONE* tenuit Goda unā v̆ . Ibi hr̃ Reinbr̃

in dñio . i . car̃ cũ . i . cot . Tc̃ . v . sol . M̊ . x . sol . Vast fuit.

In *WILENDONE* . Goda tenuit dim v̆ . Ibi hr̃ Reinbr̃

uñ cot redd xii . den . Tc̃ 7 m̃ . xii . den . Vast fuit.

In *RADETONE* Goda tenuit unā v̆ . Ibi hr̃ Reinbr̃ . iiii.

uill cũ . iii . car̃ . Tc̃ 7 post 7 m̃ . x . solid.

In *RIPE* Goduin un lib hõ tenuit unā v̆ . Ibi hr̃ Reinbr̃

uñ uill cũ . i . car̃ . Tc̃ 7 post 7 m̃ . iiii . sol.

Osbñ fili Goisfridi ten de comite dimid hid in *WILLE*

DONE . Goda comitissa tenuit . Ibi m̃ . ii . car̃ in dñio . cũ . i . cot.

Tc̃ 7 post 7 m̃ . xl . solid.

In *FERLE* tenuit abbatia de Wiltun . unā v̆ . Ibi hr̃ Osbñ

uñ uill cũ . i . car̃ . Tc̃ 7 post 7 m̃ . viii . sol.

In *RADETONE* tenuit Goda comitissa unā v̆ . Ibi hr̃ Eustachi

in dñio . i . car̃ . cũ uno uillo . Tc̃ 7 post . v . sol . M̊ . vi . sol.

In *LOVINGETONE* tenuit Goda unā v̆ . Ibi hr̃ Hugo de com̃

uñ uill cũ . i . car̃ . Tc̃ 7 post 7 m̃ . v . sol.

[In the Rape of PEVENSEY]

61 In CHALVINGTON 2 free men, Leofwin and Edward, held 1 virgate. The Count has
    2 villagers with 1 plough.
    [Value] then, later and now 40d.

62 In SHERRINGTON Leofwin, a free man, held 1 virgate. The Count has
    2 villagers with 1 plough.
    [Value] then, later and now 6s.

63 In ALCISTON Wilton Abbey held 1 virgate. The Count has
    1 villager with 1 plough.
    [Value] then, later and now 5s.

64 Reinbert holds 1 virgate from the Count in RATTON. Ulf, a free man, held it. In lordship 1 plough.
    Meadow, 15 acres; 3 cottagers pay 2s.
    [Value] then, later and now 5s.

65 In ALCISTON Wilton Abbey held 1 virgate. Reinbert has 2 ploughs and
    3 cottagers.
    Woodland, 2 pigs.
    [Value] then, later and now 5s.

66 In WINTON Countess Goda held 1 virgate. Reinbert has in lordship 1 plough, with
    1 cottager.
    [Value] then 5s; now 10s; it was waste.

67 In WILLINGDON Countess Goda held ½ virgate. Reinbert has
    1 cottager who pays 12d.
    [Value] then and now 12d; it was waste.

68 In RATTON Countess Goda held 1 virgate. Reinbert has
    4 villagers with 3 ploughs.
    [Value] then, later and now 10s.

69 In RIPE Godwin, a free man, held 1 virgate. Reinbert has
    1 villager with 1 plough.
    [Value] then, later and now 4s.

70 Osbern son of Geoffrey holds ½ hide from the Count in WILLINGDON. Countess Goda held it. Now in lordship 2 ploughs, with
    1 cottager.
    [Value] then, later and now 40s.

71 In (WEST) FIRLE Wilton Abbey held 1 virgate. Osbern has
    1 villager with 1 plough.
    [Value] then, later and now 8s.

72 In RATTON Countess Goda held 1 virgate. Eustace the cleric has in lordship 1 plough, with
    1 villager.
    [Value] then and later 5s; now 6s.

73 In JEVINGTON Countess Goda held 1 virgate. Hugh has from the Count
    1 villager with 1 plough.
    [Value] then, later and now 5s.

In *RIPE* tenuit Herald unā hđ . Ibi Walter fili Lanɓti hŧ

in dñio . ii . car̃ . 7 iii . uiłł cū . ii . car̃ . 7 ii . acs p̃ti . Tc 7 poſt.' xx . ſoł.

Modo.' xxx . ſoliđ.

In *FERLE* tenuit abbatia de Wiltun unā hiđ 7 unā v

7 dim . Ibi hŧ Walteri . ix . uiłłos cū . v . car̃ . Tra . ē . vi . car̃.

T . R . E . 7 poſt . uał . iii . liɓ . Modo.' iiii . liɓ.

In *ESCHINTONE* tenuit Agemund un liɓ hō dimiđ' hiđ' 7 unā v . Ibi

hŧ Walteri . iii . uiłłos cū . ii . car̃ . Tc 7 poſt . 7 m̃.' xx . ſoliđ.

In *SIRINTONE* tenuit Aluuin un liɓ hō dimiđ hiđ . Ibi hŧ

Walteri in dñio . i . car̃ . 7 ii . uiłłos cū . i . car̃ . Tc 7 poſt.' x . ſoł . M.' v.

In *LESTONE* tenuit Goda . unā v . Walteri nil ibi hŧ . niſi . ii . ſoł.

In *BVRGELSTALTONE* . tenuit Vlſi unā v . liɓ hō fuit . Ibi

hŧ Walteri . ii . uiłłos cū . i . car̃ . Tc 7 poſt 7 m̃.' v . ſoł.

In *DENE* tenuit Goda dim hiđ . Ibi hŧ Walteri in dñio

ii . car̃ . cū . iii . cot . Tc 7 poſt.' x . ſoł . Modo.' xx . ſoł.

In *ALSITONE* tenuit abbatia de Wiltun unā v . Ibi hŧ

Walteri . iii . uiłłos cū . ii . car̃.

ESSEWELDE HVND NVNQ GELDV REDDIDIT.

IN HENHERT HVND.

comitiſſa

Reinɓt ten de comite *SALHERT* . Goda tenuit.

Tc 7 m̃ p dimiđ hida ſe defđ . Tra . ē . iiii . car̃ . In dñio

eſt una . 7 vii . uiłłi 7 viii . cot cū . vi . car̃ . Ibi æccła

7 xvi . ac p̃ti . T . R . E.' uałeɓ . xx . ſoł . Modo.' xxx . ſoł . Vaſt fuit.

Aluric ten de com *DRISNESEL* . Cane qđā liɓ hō

7 una uirga tenuit . 7 tc 7 m̃ p . iii . hiđ 7 dim ſe defđ . Tra . ē . viii . car̃.

In dñio ſunt . ii . 7 xviii . uiłłi 7 vi . cot h̃nt . xii . car̃.

Ibi . x . ac p̃ti . 7 ſilua . xx . porc . T . R . E . uałeɓ . iii . liɓ.

Modo.' iiii . liɓ . Vaſtatū fuit.

74 In RIPE Earl Harold held 1 hide. Walter son of Lambert
has in lordship 2 ploughs;
   3 villagers with 2 ploughs.
   Meadow, 2 acres.
   [Value] then and later 20s; now 30s.

75 In (WEST) FIRLE Wilton Abbey held 1 hide and 1½ virgates.   19 c
Walter has
   9 villagers with 5 ploughs.
   Land for 6 ploughs.
Value before 1066 and later £3; now £4.

76 In ECKINGTON Agemund, a free man, held ½ hide and 1 virgate.
Walter has
   3 villagers with 2 ploughs.
   [Value] then, later and now 20s.

77 In SHERRINGTON Alwin, a free man, held ½ hide. Walter has
in lordship 1 plough;
   2 villagers with 1 plough.
   [Value] then and later 10s; now 5[s].

78 In LAUGHTON Goda held 1 virgate. Walter has nothing but 2s.

79 In BURGELSTALTONE Wulfsi held 1 virgate. He was a free man. Walter has
   2 villagers with 1 plough.
   [Value] then, later and now 5s.

80 In (EAST) DEAN Goda held ½ hide. Walter has in lordship 2 ploughs, with
   3 cottagers.
   [Value] then and later 10s; now 20s.

81 In ALCISTON Wilton Abbey held 1 virgate. Walter has
   3 villagers with 2 ploughs.
   [Value ...]

SHOYSWELL HUNDRED NEVER PAID TAX

In HENHURST Hundred

82 Reinbert holds SALEHURST from the Count. Countess Goda
held it. Then and now it answered for ½ hide. Land for 4 ploughs.
In lordship 1;
   7 villagers and 8 cottagers with 6 ploughs.
   A church; meadow, 16 acres.
Value before 1066, 20s; now 30; it was wasted.

83 Aelfric holds 'DRIGSELL' from the Count. One Cana, a free man,
held it. Then and now it answered for 3½ hides and 1 virgate.
Land for 8 ploughs. In lordship 2.
   18 villagers and 6 cottagers have 12 ploughs.
   Meadow, 10 acres; woodland, 20 pigs.
Value before 1066 £3; now £4; it was wasted.

Wills ten de com dimiđ hiđ in hoc hunđ . Leueua
tenuit . T . R . E . 7 tc̃ 7 m̃ p̃ dim̃ hida ſe defđ . Tra . ē
In dñio . ē una car̃ . 7 vi . ãc p̃ti . 7 ſilua. vi . porc̃ .
T . R . E . 7 m̃. ual . xx . ſol . Q̃do recep. x . ſol.

Reinbt ten de com unã hiđ in iſto hđ . Cane q̃dã
lib hõ tenuit s; n̄ geldauit . Ibi m̃ . viii . uilli . iii . cot
eũ vi . car̃ . Tc̃ 7 m̃. xxx . ſoliđ . Vaſt fuit .

In iſto hunđ Normann tenuit . dimidiã hiđ . lib hõ fuit . nunq;
geldauit . Ibi hr̃ Reinbt . i . car̃ cũ . i . cot . 7 i . moliñ
de . ii . ſoliđ . 7 iii . ãc p̃ti . 7 ſilua . i . porc̃ . Tc̃ 7 m̃. xx . ſoliđ .

In iſto hunđ tenuit Azor un lib hõ unã v̄ . s; n̄ geldau .
Ibi hr̃ Reinbt . i . car̃ in dñio . cũ uno uillo . Ibi . x . ãc p̃ti .
Tc̃ 7 m̃ . x . ſol . Q̃do recep. v . ſoliđ .

In BVRNE . tenuit rex . E . unã hiđ . Nunq geldauit .
Ibi hr̃ Reinbt . iiii . uill cũ . iii . car̃ . Tc̃ 7 poſt 7 m̃. xx . ſol .

In BEREWICE tenuit rex . E . dimiđ hiđ . Nunq geldau .
Ibi hr̃ Reinbt un uill 7 iiii . cot cũ . i . car̃ . 7 i . moliñ
de . x . ſol . 7 xi . ãcs p̃ti . 7 ſiluã. vi . porc̃ . 7 ii as . piſcar̃ de
vi . den . T . R . E . vallb xxx . ſol . 7 poſt. x . ſol . M̃. xxxv . ſol .

In BORNE tenuit rex . E . dimiđ hiđ . Nunq geldauit . Ibi hr̃
Reinbt in dñio . iii . car̃ . cũ . v . cot . 7 una piſcar̃ . Tra . ē . ii . car̃ .
T . R . E. uallb . xx . ſol . 7 poſt. x . ſol . Modo. xlv . ſoliđ .

In eođ hunđ eſt dim̃ hiđ . 7 una v̄ 7 dim̃ . Tra . ē . iii . car̃ . Hæc
tra T . R . E . p̃tinuit tribꝫ m̃ . Ratendone . Willendone . Ferle .
Nunq geld reddiđ . Ibi hr̃ Reinbt . vi . uill cũ . iii . car̃ .

19 d
T . R . E . 7 m̃ ual . xxii . ſol .

84 William holds ½ hide from the Count in this Hundred.
Leofeva held it before 1066. Then and now it answered
for ½ hide. Land for ... In lordship 1 plough.
  Meadow, 6 acres; woodland, 6 pigs.
Value before 1066 and now 20s; when acquired 10s.

85 Reinbert holds 1 hide from the Count in this Hundred.
One Cana, a free man, held it but it did not pay tax.
  Now 8 villagers and 3 cottagers with 6 ploughs.
[Value] then and now 30s; it was waste.

86 In this Hundred Norman held ½ hide. He was a free man.
It never paid tax. Reinbert has 1 plough, with
  1 cottager.
  1 mill at 2s; meadow, 3 acres; woodland, 1 pig.
[Value] then and now 20s.

87 In this Hundred Azor, a free man, held 1 virgate, but it
did not pay tax. Reinbert has 1 plough in lordship, with
  1 villager.
  Meadow, 10 acres.
[Value] then and now 10s; when acquired 5s.

[In the Rape of PEVENSEY]

88 In (EAST?) BOURNE King Edward held 1 hide. It never paid tax.
Reinbert has
  4 villagers with 3 ploughs.
[Value] then, later and now 20s.

89 In BERWICK King Edward held ½ hide. It never paid tax. Reinbert has
  1 villager and 4 cottagers with 1 plough.
  1 mill at 10s; meadow, 11 acres; woodland, 6 pigs;
    2 fisheries at 6d.
Value before 1066, 30s; later 10s; now 35s.

90 In (EAST?)BOURNE King Edward held ½ hide. It never paid tax.
Reinbert has in lordship 3 ploughs, with
  5 cottagers.
  1 fishery.
  Land for 2 ploughs.
Value before 1066, 20s; later 10s; now 45s.

91 In the same Hundred is ½ hide and 1½ virgates. Land for 3
ploughs. Before 1066 this land belonged to the three manors of
RATTON, WILLINGDON and (FROG) FIRLE. It never paid tax. Reinbert has
  6 villagers with 3 ploughs.
Value before 1066 and now 22s.   19 d

In *SIELMESTONE* . tenuit Elfer de rege . E . dim hiđ . Ibi hŧ Reinƀt Nūg geldauit .

unā car . cū uno uitto . Ibi . III . aͨ p̃ti . 7 filua . I . porc . Vat 7 ualuit . x . fot .

In *BVRGEHĀ* . tenuit Vlgar de rege . E . dim hiđ . Nunɋ geldauit .

Ibi hŧ Reinƀt . II . uittos cū . II . car . T . R . E . 7 m̃Ꞌ uat . XII . fot .

Ifdē Reinƀt ten de com dim hiđ quæ p̃tinuit T . R . E . duob̃ m̃ .

BERVICE 7 *CLAVREHĀ* . Vn̄ tenuit Rex . 7 at tenuit Ofward de rege . E .

Nunɋ geldauit . Ibi m̃ un uitt 7 I . cot . Valuit . v . fot . m̃ . VII . fot .

Ifdē Reinƀt ten unā v quā tenuit Cole de rege . E . Nunɋ geldau .

Ibi un uitts cū . I . car . Valuit 7ꞏ uat . v . fot .

In *WILENDONE* tenuit Goda de com dim hiđ . Nunɋ geldauit .

Tra . e̅ . II . car . Ibi hŧ Reinƀt . II . car in dn̄io . 7 IIII . uitt 7 II . cot

cū . II . car . Ibi . v . aͨ p̃ti . 7 filua . II . porc . 7 un feru . T . R . E . uatƀ

xx . fot . 7 poft꞉ x . fot . Modo꞉ xxx . fot .

In *ALCHITONE* tenuit Azor un lib̄ hō unā v . Nunɋ geldauit .

Ibi hŧ Reinƀt . III . uittos cū . I . car 7 dim . Tc 7 m̃Ꞌ vi . foliđ .

In *SEGNESCOME* tenuit Leuuin un lib̄ hō dimiđ hidā . Nunɋ

geldauit . Ibi hŧ com . II . uittos . cū . v . boƀ . 7 I . cot . Tc 7 m̃Ꞌ v . fot .

In *ALSITONE* tenuit Goda comitꞋ . II . v 7 dimiđ . Nunɋ geldaueꞃ .

Tra . e̅ . III . car . Ibi hŧ Roƀt . IIII . uitt 7 v . boƀ . Valuit . xxx . fot . M̊ xx .

In *ALSISTONE* tenuit Goda dimiđ v . Nunɋ geldauit . Ibi hŧ

Hugo de com un uittm . Tc . v . fot . m̃ . II . fot .

92 In SELMESTON Alfhere held ½ hide from King Edward. It never
paid tax. Reinbert has 1 plough, with
  1 villager.
  Meadow, 3 acres; woodland, 1 pig.
The value is and was 10s.

93 In BURGHAM Wulfgar held ½ hide from King Edward. It never
paid tax. Reinbert has
  2 villagers with 2 ploughs.
Value before 1066 and now 12s.

94 Reinbert also holds from the Count ½ hide which belonged
before 1066 to the two manors of BERWICK and CLAVERHAM.
The King held one; Osward held the other from King
Edward. It never paid tax.
  Now 1 villager and 1 cottager.
The value was 5s; now 7s.

95 Reinbert also holds 1 virgate, which Cola held from King
Edward. It never paid tax.
  1 villager with 1 plough.
The value was and is 5s.

96 In WILLINGDON Goda held ½ hide from the Count. It never
paid tax. Land for 2 ploughs. Reinbert has 2 ploughs in lordship;
  4 villagers and 2 cottagers with 2 ploughs.
  Meadow, 5 acres; woodland, 2 pigs; 1 slave.
Value before 1066, 20s; later 10s; now 30s.

97 In ECKINGTON Azor, a free man, held 1 virgate. It never paid tax.
Reinbert has
  3 villagers with 1½ ploughs.
[Value] then and now 6s.

98 In SEGNESCOMBE Leofwin, a free man, held ½ hide. It never paid tax.
The Count has
  2 villagers with 5 oxen and 1 cottager.
[Value] then and now 5s.

99 In ALCISTON Countess Goda held 2½ virgates. They never
paid tax. Land for 3 ploughs. Robert has
  4 villagers and 5 oxen.
The value was 30s; now 20[s].

00 In ALCISTON Goda held ½ virgate. It never paid tax.
Hugh has from the Count
  1 villager.
[Value] then 5s; now 2s.

In *WILENDONE* tenuit Goda . I . v̷ ⁊ dimiđ . Nunⱥ geldauit.

Ibi h̄t Hugo . II . uiłł cū . I . car̄ . T.R.E. ⁊ poſt:́ x . ſol . M̊:́ v . ſol.

In *FERLE* tenuit abbatia de Wiltun̷ dim v̷ . Nunⱥ geldau.́

Ibi hn̄t monachi de Vltreſport . II . uiłł ⁊ II . cot cū una car̷ .

Tc̄ ⁊ poſt ⁊ m̊:́ v . ſol.   IN *BABINRERODE HVNĎ.*

Rainer⁹ ten̷ de comite *CHECEHA̷* . Edric⁹ tenuit T.R.E. liƀ

h̄o fuit . Tc̄ ⁊ m̊ ⱶ dim hida ſe defđ . Tra . ē . I . car̄ . ⁊ ibi . ē in

dn̄io . cū . III . cot . ⁊ II . ac̄ p̃ti . T.R.E. ⁊ poſt:́ ualuit . x . ſol . M̊:́ xx.ᵗⁱ

Reinƀt ten̷ de com̷ *DODIMERE* . Algar tenuit de Goduino

Tc̄ ⁊ m̊ ⱶ . vI . hiđ ſe defđ . Tra , ē . x . car̄ , In dn̄io eſt una.

⁊ xxII . uiłłi hn̄t . xv . car̷ . Ibi æccła . ⁊ II . ac̄ p̃ti . T.R.E. ⁊ m̊

vIII . liƀ . Ꝗdo recep:́ xxx . ſol.   IN *GESTELINGES HVNĎ.*

Goiſfrid⁹ de Floc ten̷ de com̷ *GESTELINGES* . Vlbalđ

tenuit de rege . E . Tc̄ ⁊ m̊ ⱶ . IIII . hiđ ⁊ dim ſe defđ.

Tra . ē . vII . car̄ . In dn̄io . II . car̄ . ⁊ xII . uiłłi cū . v . cot hn̄t

IIII . car̷ . Ibi . v . ac̄ p̃ti.

De hac ͭtra ten̷ Roƀt de Ole . cūbe . I . hiđ . ⁊ ibi h̄t . II . car̄ in dn̄io.

⁊ II . uiłł ⁊ II . cot cū . I . car̷ . T.R.E. ⁊ m̊:́ c . ſoliđ . Vaſtaꝛ fuit.

Witłs de Septmuels ten̷ *LVET* . Leuret tenuit de Goduino

Vna hida|Nunⱥ geldau.́ Tra . ē . II . car̄ . In dn̄io . ē una . ⁊ un̄ uiłłm

⁊ III . cot cū . II . car̷ . Ibi . III . ac̄ p̃ti . T.R.E. ⁊ m̊:́ xx . ſol . Vaſtaꝛ fuit.

01   In WILLINGDON Goda held 1½ virgates. It never paid tax. Hugh has
     2 villagers with 1 plough.
    Value before 1066 and later 10s; now 5s.

02   In (WEST) FIRLE Wilton Abbey held ½ virgate. It never paid tax.
    The monks of Treport have
     2 villagers and 2 cottagers with 1 plough.
    [Value] then, later and now 5s.

   In GOSTROW Hundred

03   Rainer holds KITCHENHAM from the Count. Edric held it before 1066.
    He was a free man. Then and now it answered for ½ hide.
    Land for 1 plough. It is there, in lordship, with
     3 cottagers.
     Meadow, 2 acres.
    Value before 1066 and later 10s; now 20[s].

04   Reinbert holds UDIMORE from the Count. Algar held it from
    Earl Godwin. Then and now it answered for 6 hides.
    Land for 10 ploughs. In lordship 1.
     22 villagers have 15 ploughs.
     A church; meadow, 2 acres.
    [Value] before 1066 and now £8; when acquired 30s.

   In GUESTLING Hundred

05   Geoffrey of Flocques holds GUESTLING from the Count.
    Wulfbald held it from King Edward. Then and now it answered
    for 4½ hides. Land for 7 ploughs. In lordship 2 ploughs.
     12 villagers with 5 cottagers have 4 ploughs.
     Meadow, 5 acres.
    Robert of Ulcombe holds 1 hide of this land. He has 2 ploughs
    in lordship;
     2 villagers and 2 cottagers with 1 plough.
    [Value] before 1066 and now 100s; it was wasted.

06   William of Sept-Meules holds LIDHAM. Leofred held it
    from Earl Godwin. 1 hide. It never paid tax.
    Land for 2 ploughs. In lordship 1. [He has]
     1 villager and 3 cottagers with 2 ploughs.
     Meadow, 3 acres.
    [Value] before 1066 and now 20s; it was wasted.

In eod *HVND* . ten Robt de com uñ Ferlang . Vlmer tenuit.

de Goduino . Tc p . vi . hid . se defd . m p . ii . hid , Tra . e . xii . car .

In dnio sunt . iiii . car . 7 xiiii . uill 7 v . cot cu . viii . car . Ibi æccla

T.R.E. ualb . c . sot . 7 post: xl . sot . Modo: vi . lib . *In COLESPORE HD.*

In *EVEBENTONE* . tenuit Goduin dimid hid . 7 p tanto se defd .

Tra . e . i . car . Ibi ht comes . ii . uill cu . i . car 7 dim . Tc 7 m: xii . sot .

Ipse com ten *PLEIDENA* . Siulf tenuit de rege . E . Tc 7 m

20 a

p . iiii , hid se defd . Tra . e . vii . car . Hanc ten de comite isti hoes .

Ednod . i . hid . Walterius . i . hid . Remir . i . hid . Goisfrid dim hid .

Tetbald . iii . uirg . 7 i . æcclam 7 in dnio . i . car .

Int oms hnt . xxii . uill 7 xv . cot cu . x . car 7 dim . 7 in dnio . i . car .

Ibi . v . ac pti . Totu M T.R.E. ualb . vi . lib . Modo . c . sot 7 xii . sot .

Comes inde ht qd ual . vii . lib 7 iii . solid .

Goisfrid 7 Leuuin ten de comite *IDENE* . Ednod un lib ho

tenuit . T.R.E. 7 tc 7 m se defd p . iii . v . Tra . e . ii . car . 7 ibi sux

in dnio . cu . i . uillo . 7 vii . cot . Ibi . vi . ac pti . T.R.E. 7 m: xxx . sot .

GLESHAM ten de comite . iii . hoes . qui 7 T.R.E. tenuer .

7 qlibet cu ipsa tra ire potuer . Tc 7 m p una hid 7 dim se defd .

Tra . e . ii . car . Ipsi hnt in dnio . iii . car . 7 i . uill 7 ii . cot . Ibi . viii .

ac pti . 7 silua . x . porc . T.R.E: xl . sot . 7 post: xx . sot . Modo: xxx , sot .

In eod *HVND* ten Aluuin de com una v . Edward un lib ho

tenuit . 7 p una v se defd . Ibi . ii . ac pti . Tc 7 post . 7 m: v . sot .

In *LVET* tenuit Leuric . una v . lib ho fuit .   *In BADESLEI HVND*

Nunq geldauit . Tc ualuit . iii . sot . Modo . xii . denar . Wilts ten .

In *CLAVESHA* tenuit Osuuard lib ho , ii . v . Nunq geldau .

Ibi ht Wilts . ii . cot . Valuer . v . sot . Modo . iii sot .

07 In the same Hundred Robert holds 1 Quarter from the Count.
Wulfmer held it from Earl Godwin. Then it answered for 6 hides;
now for 2 hides. Land for 12 ploughs. In lordship 4 ploughs;
   14 villagers and 5 cottagers with 8 ploughs.
   A church.
Value before 1066, 100s; later 40s; now £6.

In GOLDSPUR Hundred

08 In *EVEBENTONE* Earl Godwin held ½ hide. It answered for
as much. Land for 1 plough. The Count has
   2 villagers with 1½ ploughs.
[Value] then and now 12s.

09 The Count holds PLAYDEN himself. Siwulf held it from King Edward.
Then and now it answered for 4 hides. Land for 7 ploughs.   20 a
These men hold it from the Count: Ednoth 1 hide; Walter 1 hide;
Remir 1 hide; Geoffrey ½ hide; Theobald the priest 3 virgates
and 1 church; in lordship 1 plough. Between them they have
   22 villagers and 15 cottagers with 10½ ploughs.
   In lordship 1 plough.
   Meadow, 5 acres.
Value of the whole manor before 1066 £6; now 100s and 12s;
value of what the Count has from it £7 3s.

10 Geoffrey, 1 virgate, and Leofwin, 2 virgates, hold IDEN from the
Count. Ednoth, a free man, held it before 1066. Then and now
it answered for 3 virgates. Land for 2 ploughs. They are there,
in lordship, with
   1 villager and 7 cottagers.
   Meadow, 6 acres.
[Value] before 1066 and now 30s.

11 Three men hold GLOSSAMS from the Count; they also held it
before 1066; they could go wherever they would with their
land. Then and now it answered for 1½ hides. Land for 2
ploughs. They have 3 ploughs themselves in lordship;
   1 villager and 2 cottagers.
   Meadow, 8 acres; woodland, 10 pigs.
[Value] before 1066, 40s; later 20s; now 30s.

12 In the same Hundred Alwin holds 1 virgate from the Count.
Edward, a free man, held it. It answers for 1 virgate.
   Meadow, 2 acres.
[Value] then, later and now 5s.

In BALDSLOW Hundred

13 In LIDHAM Leofric held 1 virgate. He was a free man. It never paid tax.
Value then 3s; now 12d.
   William holds it.

14 In CLAVERHAM Osward, a free man, held 2 virgates. It never paid tax.
   William has 2 cottagers.
Their value was 5s; now 3s.

In CALVINTONE tenuit Godo un̅ lib̅ h̅o̅ IN AILESALTEDE H̅D̅.
ii . v . Nunꝗ geldau̅ . Ibi h̅t Reinb̅t un̅ uitt 7 i . cot cu̅ . i . car̅.
T̅c̅ . ii . ſot . m̅ . iiii . ſot.

In HECTONE tenuit Goduin un̅ lib̅ h̅o̅ . ii . v . Nunꝗ geldau̅.
Ibi h̅t Osb̅n . ii . uitt cu̅ . i . car̅ . T̅c̅ 7 m̅ . iiii . ſot.

In HECTONE . tenuit Goduin un̅ lib̅ h̅o̅ una̅ v Nunꝗ geldau̅.
Ibi h̅t Hugo un̅ cot . T̅c̅ . ii . ſot . M̅ . xii . ſot.

In HECTONE Goduin tenuit una̅ v . Nunꝗ geldau̅ . Ibi h̅t
Hugo . i . uittm cu̅ . v . bob . Vat 7 ualuit . ii . ſot.

In eod̅ HVND ten Saſuualo de com̅ una̅ v . Hanc un̅ lib̅ h̅o̅
tenuit . Nunꝗ geldau̅ . T̅c̅ . xv . den̅ . M̅ . xii . denar̅.

IN STAPLE HVND.

Ipſe comes ten̅ in d̅n̅io WERSTE . Ælfer tenuit de rege . E . T̅c̅
ſe deſd̅ ꝑ . vi . hid̅ . M̅ ꝑ . iiii . hid̅ 7 iii . v . 7 q̅nꝗ ſunt retro . ꝗa una
hida̅ . e̅ in rapo comit̅ de moriton . Tra . e̅ . xx . car̅ . In d̅n̅io ſunt
iiii . car̅ . 7 xii . uitti 7 x . bord̅ cu̅ . vi . car̅ . Ibi . iiii . ſerui . 7 xii . a̅c̅
p̅ti . 7 Silua . x . porc̅.

De t̅ra huj̅ M̅ ten̅ Osb̅n . i . hid̅ 7 iii . v in BODEHA̅ . 7 ſep̅ ja
cuit in WERSTE . 7 illuc fuit Halla . Rogeri dim̅ hid̅ . Radulf̅ . ii . v.
In d̅n̅io . i . car̅ 7 dim̅ . 7 vii . uitt 7 x . bord̅ cu̅ . iiii . car̅ 7 dim̅.
Tot̅ M̅ T.R.E. uatb̅ . x . lib̅ . 7 poſt . vi . lib̅ . m̅ . ix . lib̅.

Ipſe comes ten̅ HIHAM . Goduin tenuit . T.R.E . fuer̅ . ii . hidæ
7 dim̅ . ſed ꝑ . ii . hid̅ ſe deſd̅ ſi̅c̅ dicunt . 7 m̅ ꝑ . ii . hid̅ . Tra . e̅ . xvi.
car̅ . In d̅n̅io . e̅ una . 7 xxx . uitt 7 x . bord̅ cu̅ xix . car̅ . Ibi vi.
a̅c̅ p̅ti . 7 ſilua . ii . porc̅ . T.R.E . uatb̅ . c . ſot . M̅ . vi . lib̅ . Vaſt fuit.

Walter fili̅ Lanb̅ti ten̅ de com̅ SALESCOME . Lefſin tenuit
de Goda̅ ꝑ una hid̅ 7 iii . v foris rap̅ ſe deſd̅ . Tra . e̅ . iiii . car̅.
In d̅n̅io . e̅ una . 7 vi . uitt cu̅ . ii . bord̅ h̅n̅t . v . car̅ . Ibi . vii . a̅c̅
p̅ti . 7 ſilua . vi . porc̅ . Ibi æceleſiola . T.R.E . Lx . ſot . 7 poſt . xx.
ſot . Modo . xL . ſot.

In NETHERFIELD Hundred
115 In CHALVINGTON Godo, a free man, held 2 virgates.
It never paid tax. Reinbert has
  1 villager and 1 cottager with 1 plough.
[Value] then 2s; now 4s.
116 In 'HEIGHTON' Godwin, a free man, held 2 virgates.
It never paid tax. Osbern has
  2 villagers with 1 plough.
[Value] then and now 4s.
117 In 'HEIGHTON' Godwin, a free man, held 1 virgate.
It never paid tax. Hugh has
  1 cottager.
[Value] then 2s; now 12s.
118 In 'HEIGHTON' Godwin held 1 virgate. It never paid tax. Hugh has
  1 villager with 5 oxen.
The value is and was 2s.
119 In the same Hundred Saswalo holds 1 virgate from the Count.
A free man held it. It never paid tax.
[Value] then 15d; now 12d.
In STAPLE Hundred
120 The Count holds EWHURST himself, in lordship. Alfhere held
it from King Edward. Then it answered for 6 hides; now
for 4 hides and 3 virgates; 5 virgates are foregone
because 1 hide is in the Count of Mortain's Rape.
Land for 20 ploughs. In lordship 4 ploughs;
  12 villagers and 10 smallholders with 6 ploughs.
  4 slaves; meadow, 12 acres; woodland, 10 pigs.
Osbern holds 1 hide and 3 virgates of this manor's land
in Bodiam; it always lay in Ewhurst (lands); the Hall was there.
Roger ½ hide; Ralph 2 virgates. In lordship 1½ ploughs;
  7 villagers and 10 smallholders with 4½ ploughs.
Value of the whole manor before 1066 £10; later £6; now £9.
121 The Count holds HIGHAM himself. Earl Godwin held it. Before 1066
there were 2½ hides, but it answered for 2 hides, as they state;
now for 2 hides. Land for 16 ploughs. In lordship 1;
  30 villagers and 10 smallholders with 19 ploughs.
  Meadow, 6 acres; woodland, 2 pigs.
Value before 1066, 100s; now £6; it was wasted.
122 Walter son of Lambert holds SEDLESCOMBE from the Count. Leofsi
held it from Countess Goda. It answered for 1 hide
and 3 virgates outside the Rape; now for 1 hide.
Land for 4 ploughs. In lordship 1 .
  6 villagers with 2 smallholders have 5 ploughs.
  Meadow, 7 acres; woodland, 6 pigs; a small church.
[Value] before 1066, 60s; later 20s; now 40s.

ħec q̃libet ire þotuit. Tc 7 m̃ .p una hida ſe defd . Tra . e

iii . car . In dñio . e una . 7 iiii . uiłłi 7 iii . bord . cũ . ii . car .

Ibi . i . ac pti . 7 ſilua . i . porc . T . R . E . 7 poſt . xiiii . ſoł . M̊ . xx .

In *BELLEST* tenuit Ældret . ii . v in paragio . 7 .p tanto

ſe defd . tc 7 m̃ . Ibi ħt Wiłłs in dñio . i . car . 7 uñ uiłł

cũ . i . car . Vał . 7 ualuit . vii . ſoł .

In *SELESCOME* ten Walter fili Lãbti unã v Nunq̃ geldau .

7 ſep fuit foris rap . Tra . e . i . car . Ibi . e in dñio . 7 iii .

ac pti . 7 ſilua . i . porc . Tc 7 poſt . x . ſoł . M̊ . xx . ſoł .

Ibidẽ ten Goisfrid canonic dimid hidã . In Seleſcome

jacuit . p dimid hid ſe defd . Ibi . ii . bord cũ una car .

7 ſilua . iii . porc . Vał x . ſoł . Waſta fuit .

Ipſe comes ten in ſuo dñio uñ uiłłm . qui jacuit

in Seleſcome . 7 ten unã v foris rap . Vał . v . ſolid .

In eod *HVND* tenuit Weneſtan dim hid . *FODILANT* .

7 potuit ire q̃libet . .p . ii . uirg ſe defd . Ibi ħt Anſchitil

unã car cũ uno uiłło . 7 ſilua . iiii . porc . Vał . x . ſoł .

In *HERSTE* . tenuit Vluuin dimid hidã . T . R . E .

.p . ii . v ſe defd . 7 m̃ facit . Ibi ħt Ednod in dñio . i . car .

7 unã ac pti . Vał 7 ualuit . x . ſoł .

WALILAND ten de comite . v . hões . Vna hida . e

Hanc tenuer . iiii . frs . 7 potuer ire quo uoluer . Non

fuit niſi una haula . T . R . E . 7 m̃ ſe defd .p una hida .

De hac hida ten Aluuold . ir . v . Anſchitil . iii . v .

Roger . v . uirg . Hugo . unã v . Osbn . ii . v . Tra . e

In dñio . i . car . 7 vii . uiłłi 7 i . bord hñt . iiii . car

7 dim . Ibi . v . ac pti . 7 ſilua . xx . porc . T . R . E . 7 m̃ .

lxvi . ſoł .

123 Wibert holds LORDINE from the Count. Winstan held it from Osward.
He could not go wherever he would. Then and now it answered   20 b
for ½ hide. Land for 3 ploughs. In lordship 1;
  4 villagers and 3 smallholders with 2 ploughs.
  Meadow, 1 acre; woodland, 1 pig.
[Value] before 1066 and later 14s; now 20[s].

124 In BELLHURST Aldred held 2 virgates, jointly. Then and now
it answered for as much. William has 1 plough in lordship;
  1 villager with 1 plough.
The value is and was 7s.

125 In SEDLESCOMBE Walter son of Lambert holds 1 virgate. It never
paid tax; it was always outside the Rape. Land for 1 plough.
It is there, in lordship.
  Meadow, 3 acres; woodland, 1 pig.
[Value] then and later 10s; now 20s.

126 There also Canon Geoffrey holds ½ hide. It lay in Sedlescombe (lands).
It answered for ½ hide.
  2 smallholders with 1 plough.
  Woodland, 3 pigs.
Value 10s; it was waste.

127 The Count himself holds in his lordship a villager who(se land) lay
in Sedlescombe, and who holds 1 virgate outside the Rape.
Value 5s.

128 In the same Hundred Winstan held ½ hide, FOOTLAND. He could go
wherever he would. It answers for 2 virgates. Ansketel has 1 plough, with
  1 villager.
  Woodland, 4 pigs.
Value 10s.

129 In HURST Wulfwin held ½ hide. Before 1066 it answered
for 2 virgates and does so now. Ednoth has in lordship 1 plough.
  Meadow, 1 acre.
The value is and was 10s.

130 Five men hold WELLHEAD from the Count. There is 1 hide. 4 brothers
held it. They could go where they would. There was nothing there
but a hall. Before 1066 and now it answered for 1 hide. Of this hide
Alfwold holds 2 virgates; Ansketel 3 virgates; Roger 5 virgates; Hugh
1 virgate; Osbern 2 virgates. Land for....In lordship 1 plough.
  7 villagers and 1 smallholder have 4½ ploughs.
  Meadow, 5 acres; woodland, 20 pigs.
[Value] before 1066 and now 66s.

Basingehā ten Osbñ de comite . Aluiet tenuit
in paragio.tc 7 m̃ se defð p . ii . v̆ . Ibi . ē uñ uitts.
Vat . viii . sot.

.X. TERRA COMITIS MORITONIENS̃.

In Bvrgo Pevenesel . T . R . E . fuer̆ xxiiii . burg̃ses.
in dñio regis . 7 reddeð de gablo xiiii . sot 7 vi . den.

De theloneo . xx . sot . De portu . xxxv . sot . De pastura
vii . sot 7 iii . den̆.

E̅p̅s de Cicestre habeð . v . burg̃ses . Edmer^{pbr} . xv . Ormer^{pbr} . v.
Doda^{pbr} . iii.

Quando com de moritonio recep̆ . nisi . xx.vii . burg̃ses.

Modo h̄t ipse in dñio . lx . burg̃ses . reddt̄es xxxix.

sot de gablo . Theloneŭ . iiii . lib̄ . Monetă . xx . sot.

Monachi de moriton̆ . viii . burg̃ses . de . lxvi . den̆.

Gislebt^{vicecom̃ 9} . i . burg̃se . de . xx . den . Witts de Cahainges̆.

ii . burg̃ses . de . ii . sot . Boselin̆^9 . v . de . ii . sot . Witts̆.

.iiii . de . ii . sot . Ansfrid̆^9 iiii . de . ii . sot . Girold̆ . ii . de

vi . sot . Ansgot̆^9 iii . de . xii . den̆ . Bernard̆ . ii . de

vii . den̆ . Radulfus̆ . ii . de . xii . den̆ . Alan̆^9 vi . de . iiii.

sot . Radulf̆ . iii . de . liii . den̆ . Azelin̆ . iii . de . iiii.

sot . Ipse ten̆ una̅ domu̅ de . xxxii . den̆ . 7 paru̅ træ

de . iii . sot . Walterĭ^9 ii . burg̃ses de xvi . den̆ . Rogerĭ^9

ii . de . xii . den̆ . Hugŏ . i . de . viii . denar̆.

Vñ moliñ h̄t comes de . xx . sot . Alured̆^9 h̄t de herbağ.

xv . sot 7 iiii . denar̆.

In Borne Hvnd̆.

Comes de Moritonio ten̆ in dñio *Borne* . Rex . E.
tenuit . Ibi . xlvi . hidæ fuer̆ 7 sunt . Tra . ē . xxviii^{to} . car̆.

In dñio sunt . iiii . car̆ . 7 lxviii . uitti 7 iii . borð cu̅ . xxviii^{to}.

car̆ . Ibi . i . moliñ de . v . solid̆ . 7 xvi . salinæ de . iiii . lib̄

7 xl . den̆ . 7 xxv . ac̆ p̃ti . De pastură vi . lib̄.

131 Osbern holds 'BASSINGHAM' from the Count. Alfgeat held
it, jointly. Then and now it answered for 2 virgates.
    1 villager.
Value 8s.

10   LAND OF THE COUNT OF MORTAIN   20 c

(Pevensey Rape)

In the Borough of PEVENSEY
1 Before 1066 there were 24 burgesses in the King's lordship.
They paid 14s 6d in tribute; 20s from toll; 35s from
port dues; 7s 3d from pasture.
The Bishop of Chichester had 5 burgesses; Edmer the priest 15;
Ordmer the priest 5; Doda the priest 3.
When the Count of Mortain acquired it, only 27 burgesses.
Now he has 60 burgesses himself in lordship, who pay 39s in tribute;
toll £4; the mint 20s. The monks of Mortain, 8 burgesses at 66d;
Gilbert the Sheriff 1 burgess at 20d; William of Keynes 2 burgesses
at 2s; Boselin 5 at 2s; William 4 at 2s; Ansfrid 4 at 2s;
Gerald 2 at 6s; Ansgot 3 at 12d; Bernard 2 at 7d;
Ralph 2 at 12d; Alan 6 at 4s; Ralph 3 at 53d;
Azelin 3 at 4s; he holds 1 house himself at 32d and a bit of land at 3s;
Walter 2 burgesses at 16d; Roger 2 at 12d; Hugh 1 at 8d.
The Count has 1 mill at 20s. Alfred has 15s 4d from grazing.

In EASTBOURNE Hundred
2 The Count of Mortain holds EASTBOURNE in lordship. King Edward
held it. There were and are 46 hides. Land for 28 ploughs.
In lordship 4 ploughs;
    68 villagers and 3 smallholders with 28 ploughs.
    1 mill at 5s; 16 salt-houses at £4 40d; meadow, 25 acres;
      from pasture £6.

De tra huj ꝉ M̄ funt . II . hidæ 7 una v̇ in rapo de Hafting.

De ead̄ tra ten Wilts . I . hid̄ . Alured . I . hid̄ . Cuftodes

caftelli . II . hid̄ . Rogeri . III . uirg. cleric'

In dn̄io . I . car̄ 7 dim . 7 II . uilti 7 VI . bord̄ cū diṁ car̄.

T.R.E. reddeb̄ firmā uni noctis . Q̇do coṁ receṗ xxx.

lib̄ . Modo dn̄iū ej̇ XL . lib̄ . Hōum ej̇ LXVII . folid.

Ipfe coṁ ten in dn̄io *BEDDINGHĀ* . **IN TOTENORE HVND**.

Rex . E . tenuit . Tc̄ fe defd̄ ꝑ . LII . hid̄ . 7 dimid̄ . Modo

ꝑ . L . hid̄ . Vna hida 7 diṁ . 7 diṁ v̇ funt in Rap de hafting.

Tra . ē . xxxIII . car̄ . In dn̄io funt . IIII . car̄ . 7 LXVIII . uilti

7 VI . bord̄ cū . xxxIIII . car̄ . Ibi . v . ferui . 7 IIII . falinæ de . XL .

deṅ . 7 L . ac̊ p̊ti . 7 filua . xxx . porc de pafnaġ . De herbaġ.

xxxv . fol.

De tra huj ꝉ M̄ ten Godefrid . IIII . hid̄ . Gislebt̄ . I . hid̄

7 dim . In dn̄io hn̄t . III . car̄ 7 diṁ . 7 xv . bord̄ cū diṁ car̄.

7 uñ molin de . vIII . fol.

T.R.E. reddeb̄ firmā uni noctis . Q̇do coṁ receṗ xx . lib̄.

Modo . xxx . lib̄ qd̄ ht̄ coṁ . Qd̄ hōeṡ vI . lib̄.

Walteri ten de coṁ *ESHALLE* . Duo libi hōes tenuer̄

7 q̇libet ire potuer̄ . Tc̄ 7 m̊ fe defd̄ ꝑ . III . hid̄ . Tra . ē . III . car̄.

In dn̄io eft una car̄ . cū uno uilto 7 vIII . bord̄ q̇ hn̄t . I . car̄.

Ibi . II . ac̊ p̊ti . T.R.E. ualeb̄ . L . fol . 7 pofṫ xxx . Modȯ xL . fol̇

Ifd̄ Walteri ten *BEVRINGETONE* . Duo hōes tenuer̄ de rege . E .

7 potuer̄ ire quo uoluer̄ . ꝑ . III . hid̄ fe defd̄ tc̄ 7 m̊ . Tra . ē . III .

car̄ . In dn̄io funt . II . 7 II . bord̄ hn̄t dim car̄ . T.R.E. ualeb̄ . L . fol

7 pofṫ xxx . fol . Modȯ xL . fol . **IN TOTENORE HVND**.

Haiminc ten de coṁ *CLOTINTONE* . 7 ipfe tenuit de rege . E . 7 po

tuit ire quo uoluit . Tc̄ 7 m̊ ꝑ . II . hid̄ fe defd̄ . Tra . ē . II . car̄ . In

dn̄io eft . I . car̄ . 7 vn uilts 7 v . bord̄ cū una car̄ . T.R.E. ualeb̄ . xL . fol̇

7 pofṫ xvI . fol 7 vIII . den . Modȯ xxx . fol.

2 hides and 1 virgate of this manor's land are in the Rape of
Hastings. William holds 1 hide of this land; Alfred 1 hide;
the Castle Wardens 2 hides; Roger the cleric 3 virgates.
In lordship 1½ ploughs;
   2 villagers and 6 smallholders with ½ plough.
Before 1066 it paid one night's revenue; when the Count
acquired it £30; now, his lordship £40, his men's 67s.

In TOTNORE Hundred

3 The Count holds BEDDINGHAM himself, in lordship.
King Edward held it. Then it answered for 52½ hides;
now for 50 hides; 1½ hides and ½ virgate are in the Rape
of Hastings. Land for 33 ploughs. In lordship 4 ploughs;
   68 villagers and 6 smallholders with 34 ploughs.
   5 slaves; 4 salt-houses at 40d; meadow, 50 acres;
     woodland, 30 pigs from pasture; from grazing 35s.
Godfrey holds 4 hides of this manor's land; Gilbert 1½ hides.
They have in lordship 3½ ploughs and
   15 smallholders with ½ plough.
   1 mill at 8s.
Before 1066 it paid one night's revenue; when the Count
acquired it £20; now, what the Count has £30; what his
men have £6.

[In EASTBOURNE Hundred]

4 Walter holds EASTHALL from the Count. Two free men held it;
they could go wherever they would. Then and now it answered
for 3 hides. Land for 3 ploughs. In lordship 1 plough, with
  1 villager and 8 smallholders who have 1 plough.
  Meadow, 2 acres.
Value before 1066, 50s; later 30[s]; now 40s.

20 d

5 Walter also holds 'BEVERINGTON'. Two men held it from King
Edward; they could go where they would. Then and now it
answered for 3 hides. Land for 3 ploughs. In lordship 2.
   2 smallholders have ½ plough.
Value before 1066, 50s; later 30s; now 40s.

In TOTNORE [EASTBOURNE] Hundred

6 Heming holds CHOLLINGTON from the Count. He held it from
King Edward; he could go where he would. Then and now it
answered for 2 hides. Land for 2 ploughs. In lordship 1 plough;
   1 villager and 5 smallholders with 1 plough.
Value before 1066, 40s; later 16s 8d; now 30s.

BEVRINGETONE 7 *LOVRINGETONE* ten Wilłs de cahainges.

Duo hões tenuer̃ de rege . E . Tc̃ 7 m̃ſᵉ|deſdr̃ .p . ii . hiđ . Tra . ē . iii . caɾ̃.

In dñio . ē dim caɾ̃ . cũ . iii . borđ . 7 ii . ãc p̃ti . T . R . E . uałɓ . xxx . ſoł.

7 poſt. xv . ſoł . M̃. xxiiii . ſoł.

Ibiđ ten̊ Hugo 7 Morin̊ . ii . hiđ 7 dim̃ . Cana 7 Frane de rege . E.

7 q̊libet ire potuer̃ . Tra . ē . ii . caɾ̃ . Ibi ſunt cũ . vi . uittis 7 i . borđ.

7 ibi . i . ãc p̃ti . hec tra ap̃pciata . ē in ꝏ de Willendone.

Radulf̊ fili̊ Gunfridi ten̊ in *ESHALLE* i . hiđ . Edmund̊ tenuit

de rege . E . 7 q̊libƺ ire potuit . .p . i . hida ſe deſđ tc̃ 7 m̃ . T . R . E . uałɓ

xv . ſoł . Poſt . 7 m̃. x . ſoł.

In eod̃ *HVND* ten̊ Rannulf̊ unã v de com̃ . 7 .p tanto ſe deſđ.

Vlfer tenuit de rege . E . Tra . ē dim̃ caɾ̃ . Ibi . ē un̊ uittſ.

Tc̃ 7 poſt 7 m̃ . uał . iiii . ſoł.

LITELFORDE ten̊ Wilłs de com̃ . Brixi tenuit de rege . E . 7 potuit

ire quo uoluit . Tc̃ 7 m̃ .p . iiii . hiđ ſe deſđ . Tra . ē . iiii . caɾ̃ . In dñio

ſunt . ii . 7 iiii . uitt 7 ii . ſerui cũ . i . caɾ̃ . 7 l . ãc p̃ti.

T . R . E . 7 m̃ . uał iiii . liɓ . Q̊do recep̃. xl . ſoł.

PRESTETONE ten̊ Radulf̊ de com̃ . Cola tenuit de rege . E . Tc̃ 7 m̃

.p iiii . hiđ ſe deſđ . Tra . ē . iii . caɾ̃ . In dñio . ē una . 7 v . uitti cũ . ii . boɓ.

T . R . E . uałɓ . iiii . liɓ 7 poſt. xxx . ſoł . Modo. xl . ſoł.

In eod̃ *HVND* ten̊ ipſe com̃ . viii . hiđ . ſed ap̃pciatæ ſunt in alio *HVND*.

Aɓɓ de Greſtain ten̊ de com̃ . ii . hiđ in *BEDINGHĀ* . Vlnod tenuit

de rege . E . 7 .p . ii . hiđ tc̃ 7 m̃ ſe deſđ . Tra . ē . ii . caɾ̃ . In dñio . ē una.

7 ii . uitt 7 ii . borđ cũ . i . caɾ̃ . T . R . E . 7 m̃ uałɓ xl . ſoł . Q̊do recep̃. xxx.

Durand̊ ten̊ de com̃|CERLOCESTONE . vi . hiđ . Tres liɓi hões tenuer̃

de rege . E . .p . iii . ꝏ . Tc̃ 7 m̃ .p . vi . hiđ ſe deſđ . Tra . ē . v . caɾ̃ . In

dñio dimiđ caɾ̃ . 7 i . uittſ 7 i . borđ cũ . ii . boɓ.

7 William of Keynes holds 'BEVERINGTON' and YEVERINGTON. Two free
  men held them from King Edward. Then and now they answered
  for 2 hides. Land for 3 ploughs. In lordship ½ plough, with
   3 smallholders.
   Meadow, 2 acres.
   Value before 1066, 30s; later 15s; now 24s.

8 Hugh and Morin also hold 2½ hides there. Cana and Fran
  [held] from King Edward; they could go wherever they
  would. Land for 2 ploughs. They are there, with
   6 villagers and 1 smallholder.
   Meadow, 1 acre.
  This land is assessed in the manor of Willingdon.

9 Ralph son of Gunfrid holds 1 hide in EASTHALL. Edmund held
  it from King Edward; he could go wherever he would. Then
  and now it answered for 1 hide.
  Value before 1066, 15s, later and now 10s.

10 In the same Hundred Ranulf holds 1 virgate from the Count.
   It answers for as much. Wulfhere held it from King Edward.
   Land for ½ plough.
    1 villager.
   Value, then, later and now 4s.

   [In TOTNORE Hundred]

11 William holds ITFORD from the Count. Brictsi held it from
   King Edward; he could go where he would. Then and now it
   answered for 4 hides. Land for 4 ploughs. In lordship 2;
    4 villagers and 2 slaves with 1 plough.
    Meadow, 50 acres.
   Value before 1066 and now £4; when acquired 40s.

12 Ralph holds PRESTON from the Count. Cola held it from
   King Edward. Then and now it answered for 4 hides.
   Land for 3 ploughs. In lordship 1;
    5 villagers with 2 oxen.
   Value before 1066 £4; later 30s; now 40s.

13 In the same Hundred the Count holds 8 hides himself; but they
   are assessed in another Hundred.

14 The Abbot of Grestain holds 2 hides in BEDDINGHAM from the Count.
   Wulfnoth the priest held it from King Edward. Then and now
   it answered for 2 hides. Land for 2 ploughs. In lordship 1;
    2 villagers and 2 smallholders with 1 plough.
   Value before 1066 and now 40s; when acquired 30[s].

15 Durand holds 6 hides in CHARLESTON from the Count. Three free
   men held it from King Edward as three manors. Then and now
   it answered for 6 hides. Land for 5 ploughs. In lordship ½ plough;
    1 villager and 1 smallholder with 2 oxen.

De hac tra ten Roger.ii.hiđ.Gislebt.ii.hiđ.Hi hñt in dñio.ii.car.
7 ii.uilt.7 ii.borđ cũ.i.car.

T.R.E.ualb.lx.sot.7 post.xl.sot.Modo.c.sot int totũ.

Ibidẽ ten Hubt de com.ii.hiđ.Alnod tenuit de rege.E.7 quo
uoluit ire potuit.Tra.ẽ dim car.In dñio.ẽ.i.car.7 ii.uilti 7 ii.borđ
cũ.i.car 7 dim.T.R.E.7 post.ualuit.x.sot.Modo.xx.sot.

In TELENTONE ten Wilts de cahanges.ii.hiđ de com.Elfer tenuit
de rege.E.Tra.ẽ.ii.car.Tc 7 m̃.p.ii.hiđ se defđ.In dñio.ẽ una.car.
7 ii.uilti cũ dim car.Tc 7 post 7 m̃.xx.solid.

Isđẽ Wilts ten SERINTONE de com.Edward tenuit de rege.E.
7 quo uot ire pot.Tra.ẽ.v.car.Tc se defđ p.v.hiđ.m̃ est dimiđ
hida in Rap de Hastinges.In dñio.ẽ.i.car.7 ii.borđ.

T.R.E.ualb.lx.sot.7 post xxv.sot.M̃.xl.sot.p dimidia hiđa
quæ ñ est ibi.decidunt.xx.sot.

21 a

Ibiđ ten Haminc de com.v.hiđ.7 ipse tenuit de rege.E.
Tc se defđ p.v.hiđ.m̃ est dimiđ hida in Rap de Hastinges.
Tra.ẽ.iiii.car.In dñio.i.car 7 dim.7 ii.uilti cũ dim car.
7 iii.borđ.T.R.E.ualb.lx.sot.7 post.xxv.sot.Modo.xl.sot.

Osbn ten de com.iiii.hiđ in TELENTONE.Goduin tenuit
de rege.E.p M̃.Tc se defđ p.iiii.hiđ.M̃.p.ii.hiđ 7 una v.
Tra.ẽ.iiii.car.Ibi nichil m̃ nisi.ii.uilti 7 iiii.ac pti.

T.R.E.ualb.lxx.sot.Modo.xx.sot.

Ibidẽ ht ipse com.i.hiđ.Wilts.i.hiđ.Radulf.i.hiđ.Hanc
tra tenuit Goduin.Tra.ẽ.iiii.car.Valuit xviii.sot.M̃.xv.sot.

Ipse comes ten in dñio FERLE.Abbatia de Wiltun tenuit
T.R.E.7 tc se defđ p.xlviii.hiđ.Modo p nihilo.De hac tra
sunt.vii.hidæ in Rap de Hastinges.Tra.ẽ.xl.car.

In dñio ht com.v.car.7 qt xx.uilti cũ xxx.iiii.car.Ibi.ii.
molini de.xxx.sot.7 lxxii.ac pti.7 silua.xl.porc.

Roger holds 2 hides of this land; Gilbert 2 hides.
They have in lordship 2 ploughs;
  2 villagers and 2 smallholders with 1 plough.
Value before 1066, 60s; later 40s; now in total 100s.

16 Hubert also holds 2 hides there from the Count. Alnoth held
it from King Edward; he could go where he would.
Land for ½ plough. In lordship 1 plough;
  2 villagers and 2 smallholders with 1½ ploughs.
Value before 1066 and later 10s; now 20s.

17 In TILTON William of Keynes holds 2 hides from the Count.
Alfhere held it from King Edward as one manor. Land for 2 ploughs.
Then and now it answered for 2 hides. In lordship 1 plough;
  2 villagers with ½ plough.
[Value] then, later and now 20s.

18 William also holds SHERRINGTON from the Count. Edward
held it from King Edward; he could go where he would.
Land for 5 ploughs. Then it answered for 5 hides; now ½ hide
is in the Rape of Hastings. In lordship 1 plough;
  2 smallholders.
Value before 1066, 60s; later 25s; now 40s;
they deduct 20s for the ½ hide which is not there.

19 Heming holds 5 hides there from the Count. He held it himself, from   21 a
King Edward. Then it answered for 5 hides; now ½ hide is in the
Rape of Hastings. Land for 4 ploughs. In lordship 1½ ploughs;
  2 villagers with ½ plough and 3 smallholders.
Value before 1066, 60s; later 25s; now 40s.

20 Osbern holds 4 hides in TILTON from the Count. Godwin held it from
King Edward as a manor. Then it answered for 4 hides; now
for 2 hides and 1 virgate. Land for 4 ploughs. Now nothing but
  2 villagers.
  Meadow, 4 acres.
Value before 1066, 70s; now 20s.

21 The Count has 1 hide there himself; William 1 hide; Ralph
1 hide; Godwin held this land. Land for 4 ploughs.
Value 18s; now 15s.

22 The Count holds (WEST) FIRLE himself in lordship. Before 1066
Wilton Abbey held it. Then it answered for 48 hides; now
for nothing. 7 hides of this land are in the Rape of Hastings.
Land for 40 ploughs. The Count has in lordship 5 ploughs;
  80 villagers with 34 ploughs.
  2 mills at 30s; meadow, 72 acres; woodland, 40 pigs.

De his hiđ hn̄t clerici S pancratij . 11 . hiđ 7 dim̄ . Roger un̄

molin̄ . Gozelin . 1 . hiđ . Wiłłs . 1 . hiđ . Gisłełł . 11 . hiđ . Cuſtodes

caſtelli . 111 . hiđ 7 xx . ac̄s . In dn̄io . vi . car̄ . 7 111 . uiłłi 7 xi . borđ

cū . 1111 . car̄ . Ibi . vii . ac̄ p̄ti . Itē ten̄ Gisłełł . lx . ac̄s træ uaſtæ.

Totū m̄ T.R.E. ualb̄ . lx . lib̄ . 7 poſt. xxx . lib̄ . Modo . xl . lib̄

qđ com̄ h̄ . Qđ alij hōes. 1111 . lib̄ 7 x . soł.

In CONTONE ten̄ ipſe com̄ . 1111 . hiđ . Herald tenuit de rege . E.

Tc̄ 7 m̄ p . 1111 . hiđ se defđ . H̄ tra ap̄pciata . ē in LESTONE.

Walteri ten̄ de comite   IN WILENDONE HVND.

in ESSETE . 11 . hiđ 7 dim̄ . Doda tenuit de rege . E . 7 po

tuit ire quo uoluit . Tc̄ 7 m̄ p . 11 . h̄d 7 dim̄ se defđ . Tra . ē . 11 . car̄.

In dn̄io . ē una . 7 vii . borđ cū . 1 . car̄ . T.R.E. 7 m̄. xl . soł.

Ibidē ten̄ Wiłłs de com̄ . 111 . hiđ . Edward 7 Aluuin tenueř

de rege . E . 7 q̊ uolueř ire potueř . Tc̄ 7 m̄ p . 111 . h̄d se defđ . Tra . ē

111 . car̄ . In dn̄io . ē una car̄ . cū . vii . borđ.

T.R.E. ualb̄ . l . soł . 7 poſt. xxx . soł . Modo. xl . soł.

Radulf ten̄ de com̄ vii . h̄d 7 dimiđ in LOVRINGETONE.

Cola tenuit de rege . E . p m̄ . Tc̄ 7 m̄ p . vii . hiđ se defđ . Tra.

xiiii . car̄ . In dn̄io . ē una car̄ . 7 xvi . uiłłi cū . v . borđ hn̄t

1111 . car̄ . Ibi . 1 . seru 7 un̄ molin de . viii . soliđ.

T.R.E. ualb̄ . vi . lib̄ . 7 poſt. 111 . lib̄ . Modo. 1111 . lib̄ 7 x . soliđ.

Ipſe com̄ ten̄ in dn̄io WILENDONE . Goduin tenuit.

Tc̄ se defđ p l . hiđ 7 dimiđ . M p nichilo . De hac tra suɴ

in Rapo de Haſtinges . xiiii . hiđ 7 dim̄ . Tra . ē . xxx.vi . car̄.

In dn̄io sunt . vi . car̄ . 7 lxxv . uiłłi 7 xxiiii . borđ cū . xxvi.

car̄ . Ibi . lx . ac̄ p̄ti . 7 xi . salinæ de . xxxv . soliđ . Ibi un̄ seru.

7 Silua . 111 . porc.

De hac tra ten̄ Osb̄n de com̄ . 1111 . hiđ . Wiłłs . 1 . h̄d . Gozelin

11 . hiđ . Gisłełł . 1 . h̄d . Aluuin . 1 . h̄d . Ansgot . 11 . h̄d . Godefrid

The clergy of St. Pancras have 2½ of these hides; Roger 1 mill;
Jocelyn 1 hide; William 1 hide; Gilbert 2 hides; the Castle
Wardens 3 hides and 20 acres. In lordship 6 ploughs;
  3 villagers and 11 smallholders with 4 ploughs.
  Meadow, 7 acres.
  Gilbert also holds 60 acres of waste land.
Value of the whole manor before 1066 £60; later £30;
now, what the Count has £40, what the other men have £4 10s.

23 In COMPTON the Count holds 4 hides himself. Harold held
   it from King Edward. Then and now it answered for 4 hides.
   This land is assessed in Laughton.

In WILLINGDON Hundred

24 Walter holds 2½ hides from the Count in EXCEAT. Doda held it
   from King Edward; he could go where he would. Then and now it
   answered for 2½ hides. Land for 2 ploughs. In lordship 1;
     7 smallholders with 1 plough.
   [Value] before 1066 and now 40s.

25 There William also holds 3 hides from the Count. Edward
   and Alwin held it from King Edward; they could go where they
   would. Then and now it answered for 3 hides.
   Land for 3 ploughs. In lordship 1 plough, with
     7 smallholders.
   Value before 1066, 50s; later 30s; now 40s.

26 Ralph holds 7½ hides in JEVINGTON from the Count. Cola held it
   from King Edward as a manor. Then and now it answered
   for 7 hides. Land for 14 ploughs. In lordship 1 plough.
     16 villagers with 5 smallholders have 4 ploughs.
     1 slave; 1 mill at 8s.
   Value before 1066 £6; later £3; now £4 10s.

27 The Count holds WILLINGDON in lordship, himself. Earl Godwin
   held it. Then it answered for 50½ hides; now for nothing. 14½ hides
   of this land are in the Rape of Hastings. Land for 36 ploughs.
   In lordship 6 ploughs;
     75 villagers and 24 smallholders with 26 ploughs.
     Meadow, 60 acres; 11 salt-houses at 35s. 1 slave;
      woodland, 3 pigs.
   Osbern holds 4 hides of this land from the Count; William 1 hide;
   Jocelyn 2 hides; Gilbert 1 hide; Alwin 1 hide; Ansgot 2 hides;
   Godfrey the priest 1 hide and 1 virgate.

. 1 . ħd 7 unā v̇ . In dñio . 111 . car̄ 7 dim̐ . 7 . 11 . uiłłi 7 1111 . borđ

cū una car̄.   Tot̄ Ⓜ T.R.E. uałb . lx . liƀ.

7 poſt . xxx . liƀ. Modo qđ com̄ ten̐ . xl . liƀ . Qđ hōēs̐ . v11 . liƀ.

Iſe com̄ ten̐ in dñio *WESTBORTONE* . Aluric 7 Goluin⁹

tenuer̄ de rege . E . 7 potuer̄ ire quo uoluer̄ . Tc̄ ꝓ . 11 . ħd

m̄ꝓ nichilo . ꝓ defđ . Tra . ē . 11 . car̄ . Ibi . 111 . uiłłi cū . 1 . car̄ 7 dim̐ . Vał . xx1111 .

21 b   *Ʀ* ſolđ.

Haminc ten̐ de com̄ *ESSETE* . 7 ipſe tenuit de rege. E.

Tc̄ 7 m̐ ſe defđ ꝓ . 1111 . hid 7 dimiđ . Tra . ē . 1111 . car̄ . In dñio

una car̄ 7 dim̐ . 7 111 . uiłł 7 v1 . borđ ħnt dim̐ car̄ . 7 1 . ſeru⁹

ibi . T . R . E . uałb . 1111 . liƀ . Modo . 111 . liƀ.

Ʀadulf⁹ ten̐ de com̄ *CERLETONE* . Vluric tenuit de

rege . E . Tc̄ ſe defđ ꝓ . x . hid . Modo . 11 . ħd 7 dim̐ ſunt in

Rap de Haſtinges . Tra . ē . v111 . car̄ . In dñio . ē una .

v1 . uiłłi 7 v111 . borđ cū . 1111 . car̄ . Ibi . 111 . ſerui . 7 111 . ſalinæ

de . x . ſoł 7 1111 . den̐ . 7 xx . ac̄ ꝓti .

T . R . E . uałb . 1x . liƀ . Modo . 1111 . liƀ ⁒ x . ſolđ .

Gozelin⁹ ten̐ de com̄ *RADETONE* . Vłfon tenuit de Goduino com̄

ꝓ v1 . hid tc̄ ſe defđ . 7 m̐ ꝓ . 1111 . ħd . In Rap de Haſtinges ſuɴ

11 . hidæ . una v̇ min . Tra . ē . v11 . car̄ . In dñio . 1 . car̄ . 7 v111 .

uiłłi 7 v . borđ cū . 11 . car̄ 7 dim̐ . Ibi . 1 . moliñ de . 1111 . ſoł .

7 v1 . ac̄ ꝓti .

De tra huj⁹ Ⓜ ten̐ Azelin⁹ . 1 . hid in elemoſinā de comite.

Rannulf⁹ dim̐ ħd . Ansfriđ dim̐ ħd .

Totū Ⓜ T . R . E . uałb . v1 . liƀ . Modo . 1111 . liƀ 7 x . ſoł.

Ʀadulf⁹ ten̐ de com̄ in eođ *HVND* uñ Ⓜ . qđ Vłmar

tenuit de rege . E . Tc̄ ſe defđ ꝓ . 1111 . hid 7 dim̐ . Modo eſt

dim̐ ħd in rap de Haſtinges . Tra . ē . v1 . car̄ . Ibi . ē un̐ uiłłs

7 11 . borđ 7 11 . ſerui . T . R . E . uałb . 1111 . liƀ . 7 poſt 7 m̐ . xxx . ſoł.

In lordship 3½ ploughs;
  2 villagers and 4 smallholders with 1 plough.
Value of the whole manor before 1066 £60; later £30;
now what the Count holds £40, what the men hold £7.

28 The Count holds 'WEST BURTON' himself, in lordship. Aelfric
and Goldwin held it from King Edward; they could go where
they would. Then it answered for 2 hides; now for nothing.
Land for 2 ploughs;
  3 villagers with 1½ ploughs.
Value 24s.

29 Heming holds EXCEAT from the Count. He held it from King   21 b
Edward. Then and now it answered for 4½ hides.
Land for 4 ploughs. In lordship 1½ ploughs.
  3 villagers and 6 smallholders have ½ plough; 1 slave.
Value before 1066 £4; now £3.

30 Ralph holds CHARLSTON from the Count. Wulfric held it from King
Edward. Then it answered for 10 hides; now 2½ hides are in the
Rape of Hastings. Land for 8 ploughs. In lordship 1;
  6 villagers and 8 smallholders with 4 ploughs.
  3 slaves; 3 salt-houses at 10s 4d; meadow, 20 acres.
Value before 1066 £9; now £4 10s.

31 Jocelyn holds RATTON from the Count. Wulfhun held it from Earl
Godwin. Then it answered for 6 hides; now for 4 hides. 2 hides
less 1 virgate are in the Rape of Hastings. Land for 7 ploughs.
In lordship 1 plough;
  8 villagers and 5 smallholders with 2½ ploughs.
  1 mill at 4s; meadow, 6 acres.
  Azelin holds 1 hide of this manor's land from the Count in alms;
  Ranulf ½ hide; Ansfrid ½ hide.
Value of the whole manor before 1066 £6; now £4 10s.

32 In the same Hundred Ralph holds a manor from the Count which
Wulfmer held from King Edward. Then it answered for 4½ hides;
now ½ hide is in the Rape of Hastings. Land for 6 ploughs.
  1 villager, 2 smallholders and 2 slaves.
Value before 1066 £4; later and now 30s.

Osbn ten de com *DENE* . Eduuin tenuit de rege ꝑ M̃.

Tc 7 m̃ se defd ꝑ.ii.hid. Tra.ē.i.car.7 dim. Ibi.v.uilti
7 iiii.bord cū.ii.car. T.R.E. ualb.xxx.fot.7 poft 7 m̃. xx.folid.

In *DENE* ten Radulf de com.viii.hid. Azor tenuit
de rege.E.ꝑ M̃.Tc 7 m̃ se defd ꝑ.viii.hid.Tra.ē.viii.car.
In dñio funt.ii.car.7 xi.uilti 7 iiii.bord cū.iii.car.
Ibi.iii.ferui.7 iiii.falinæ de.viii.fot.

T.R.E.ualb.vii.lib.7 poft.lx.fot.Modo.c.folid.

Radulf ten de com *RADETONE*. *IN WILEDENE HVND*.
Ofuuard tenuit de rege.E.ꝑ M̃.Tc se defd ꝑ.v.hid.M̃
eft una in Rap de Hafting.Tra.ē.v.car.In dñio funt.ii.
7 iiii.uilt 7 iiii.bord cū dim car.Ibi.iiii.ac pti.Paftura
de xxviii.fot.T.R.E.ualb.c.fot.Modo.iiii.lib.

In *RADETONE* ten Morin de com. iii. hid. Cana tenuit de rege.E.ꝑ M̃
Tc se defd ꝑ.iii.hid.m̃ dimid hd.ē in Rap de Haftinges.
Tra.ē.vii.car.In dñio.ē una.7 vi.uilti 7 iii.bord cū.i.car.
Ibi.ii.ac pti.7 q́rta pars falinæ.de.x.den.

T.R.E.ualb.lx.fot.7 poft.xx.fot.Modo.xl.folid.

In *RADETONE*.ten Hugo de com.iii.hid.Frano tenuit
de rege.E.ꝑ M̃.Tc se defd ꝑ.iii.hd.M̃ eft dim hd in Rap
de Hafting.Tra.ē.vii.car.In dñio.ē dim car.7 v.uilti
7 iii.bord cū.ii.car.Ibi.ii.ac pti.7 iiii.pars falinæ de
x.denar.T.R.E.ualb.lx.fot.Modo.xl.fot.

Witts ten de com *WALNOCH*.Norman tenuit de rege.E.
ꝑ M̃.Tc 7 m̃ se defd ꝑ.vi.hid.Tra.ē.viii.car.In dñio
funt.iii.car.7 iii.uilti cū.i.car.Ibi.iiii.ac pti.

T.R.E.ualb c.7 x.fot.7 poft.xl.fot.Modo.iiii.lib.7 x.fot.

IN AVRONEHELLE HVND.

Abb de Greftain ten de com *WINELTONE*.Alnod
tenuit de Goduino.Tc 7 m̃ se defd.ꝑ.viii.hid.Tra.ē
ix.car.Vna de his hid jacet in Rap de Hafting.

33 Osbern holds (WEST?) DEAN from the Count. Edwin held it from the
King as a manor. Then and now it answered for 2 hides.
Land for 1½ ploughs.
  5 villagers and 3 smallholders with 2 ploughs.
Value before 1066, 30s; later and now 20s.

34 In (WEST?) DEAN Ralph holds 8 hides from the Count. Azor held it
from King Edward as a manor. Then and now it answered
for 8 hides. Land for 8 ploughs. In lordship 2 ploughs;
  11 villagers and 4 smallholders with 3 ploughs.
  3 slaves; 4 salt-houses at 8s.
Value before 1066 £7; later 60s; now 100s.

In WILLINGDON Hundred

35 Ralph holds RATTON from the Count. Osward held it from King
Edward as a manor. Then it answered for 5 hides; now 1 is in
the Rape of Hastings. Land for 5 ploughs. In lordship 2;
  4 villagers and 4 smallholders with ½ plough.
  Meadow, 4 acres; pasture at 28s.
Value before 1066, 100s; now £4.

36 In RATTON Morin holds 3 hides from the Count. Cana held
it from King Edward as a manor. Then it answered for
3 hides; now ½ hide is in the Rape of Hastings.
Land for 7 ploughs. In lordship 1;
  6 villagers and 3 smallholders with 1 plough.
  Meadow, 2 acres; the fourth part of a salt-house at 10d.
Value before 1066, 60s; later 20s; now 40s.

37 In RATTON Hugh holds 3 hides from the Count. Fran held it
from King Edward as a manor. Then it answered for 3 hides;
now ½ hide is in the Rape of Hastings. Land for 7 ploughs.
In lordship ½ plough;
  5 villagers and 3 smallholders with 2 ploughs.
  Meadow, 2 acres; the fourth part of a salt-house at 10d.
Value before 1066, 60s; now 40s.

38 William holds WANNOCK from the Count. Norman held it from
King Edward as a manor. Then and now it answered for 6 hides.
Land for 8 ploughs. In lordship 3 ploughs;
  3 villagers with 1 plough.
  Meadow, 4 acres.
Value before 1066, 110s; later 40s; now £4 10s.

In LONGBRIDGE Hundred

39 The Abbot of Grestain holds WILMINGTON from the Count.   21 c
Alnoth held it from Earl Godwin. Then and now it answered
for 8 hides. Land for 9 ploughs. 1 of these hides lies
in the Rape of Hastings.

Ibidē ten̄ iſdē abb̄ . iiii . hiđ quas tenuit Vlnod de Go

duino com̄ . Tc̄ 7 m̄ p̄ . iiii . hiđ ſe defđ .

Ibidē ten̄ iſdē abb̄ . ii . hiđ de com̄ . quas tenuit Vlſtan

de Goduino . Tc̄ 7 m̄ p̄ . ii . hiđ ſe defđ .

In dn̄io ſunt . iii . car̄ . 7 xvi . uiłłi 7 x . borđ cū . vi . car̄ .

Ibi . iii . ſerui . T.R.E. 7 m̄ uał . xiii . lib̄ .

FOCHINTONE ten̄ Wiłłs de com̄ . Goda tenuit

de rege . E . 7 q̄ uoluit ire potuit . Tc̄ 7 m̄ ſe defđ

p̄ . vi . hiđ . Tra . ē . v . car̄ . In dn̄io ſunt . iii . car̄ . 7 iiii .

uiłłi 7 vi . borđ cū car̄ 7 dimiđ .

T.R.E. uałb̄ . c . ſoł . 7 poſt: xl . ſoł . Modo: lx . ſoliđ .

Ipſe comes ten̄ in dn̄io *TORINGES* . *IN FLEXEBERGE HĐ* .

Azor tenuit de Goduino . Tc̄ 7 m̄ ſe defđ p̄ . viii .

hiđ . Tra . ē . v . car̄ . In dn̄io ſunt . ii . car̄ . 7 dimidia .

7 xi . uiłłi 7 ix . borđ cū . iii . car̄ . Ibi . iii . ſerui . 7 l .

ac̄ p̄ti . De paſtura: xl . denarij .

T.R.E. uałb̄ . viii . lib̄ . 7 poſt: vi . lib̄ . M̊: x . lib̄ .

Ab̄b̄ de Greſtein ten̄ *FERLES* . de com̄ . Eddid regina

tenuit . 7 S̄ Joħi deđ T.R.E. Tc̄ ſe defđ p̄ . viii . hiđ .

modo p̄ . v . hiđ .

Ibiđ ten̄ iſđe abb̄ . i . hiđ . quā tenuit Goduin̄ com̄ .

Tra . ē . iiii . car̄ . In dn̄io ſunt . ii . 7 iiii . uiłłi cū . ii . car̄ .

7 iii . borđ . T.R.E. 7 poſt . uał . iii . lib̄ . Modo: iiii . lib̄ .

Ibidē ten̄ Haminc de com̄ . ii . hiđ . Ipſe tenuit

de Goduino . Tc̄ 7 m̄ ſe defđ p̄ . ii . hiđ . Tra . ē . i . car̄ .

Ibi . i . uiłłs 7 i . borđ cū . i . car̄ . T.R.E: xxx . ſoł . M̊: xx . ſoł .

ESTONE ten̄ Wiłłs de com̄ . Gundulf̄ tenuit

de rege . E . p̄ uno M̄ . Tc̄ 7 m̄ p̄ . ii . hiđ . Tra . ē . ii . car̄ .

In dn̄io . ē una . 7 ii . uiłł 7 iii . borđ cū . ii . bob̄ .

T.R.E. 7 m̄: xxx . ſoł . Q̇do recep̄: xx . ſoł .

40 The Abbot also holds there 4 hides, which Wulfnoth held
from Earl Godwin. Then and now it answered for 4 hides.

41 The Abbot also holds there from the Count 2 hides, which
Wulfstan held from Earl Godwin. Then and now it answered
for 2 hides. In lordship 3 ploughs;
16 villagers and 10 smallholders with 6 ploughs. 3 slaves.
Value before 1066 and now £13.

42 William holds FOLKINGTON from the Count. Goda held it from
King Edward; he could go where he would. Then and now it
answered for 6 hides. Land for 5 ploughs. In lordship 3 ploughs;
4 villagers and 6 smallholders with [1]½ ploughs.
Value before 1066, 100s; later 40s; now 60s.

In FLEXBOROUGH Hundred
43 The Count holds TARRING (NEVILLE) in lordship, himself. Azor held
it from Earl Godwin. Then and now it answered for 8 hides.
Land for 5 ploughs. In lordship 2½ ploughs;
11 villagers and 9 smallholders with 3 ploughs.
3 slaves; meadow, 50 acres; from pasture 40d.
Value before 1066 £8; later £6; now £10.

44 The Abbot of Grestain holds (FROG) FIRLE from the Count. Queen
Edith held it. Before 1066 she gave it to St. John's.
Then it answered for 8 hides; now for 5 hides.

45 The Abbot also holds 1 hide there, which Earl Godwin held.
Land for 4 ploughs. In lordship 2;
4 villagers with 2 ploughs; 3 smallholders.
Value before 1066 and later £3; now £4.

46 Heming holds 2 hides there from the Count. He held it himself
from Earl Godwin. Then and now it answered for 2 hides.
Land for 1 plough.
1 villager and 1 smallholder with 1 plough.
[Value] before 1066, 30s; now 20s.

47 William holds (SOUTH) HEIGHTON from the Count. Gundulf held it
from King Edward as a manor. Then and now [it answered]
for 2 hides. Land for 2 ploughs. In lordship 1;
2 villagers and 3 smallholders with 2 oxen.
[Value] before 1066 and now 30s; when acquired 20s.

In eod *HVND* ten̄ Durand̄ de com̄ . ı . hid̄ . Aluuard te
nuit de rege . E . p uno m̄ . Tc 7 m̄ p una hd̄ se defd̄ .
Tra . ē dim̄ car̄ . Ibi sunt . ıı . boues . cū . ı . bord̄ . Silua . ı . porc̄ .
T . R . E . ualb̄ . xx . sol̄ . Modo . x . sol̄ .

In *FERLES* ten̄ Alan de com̄ . ıııı . hid̄ . Almer 7 Goduin
tenuer̄ de rege . E . p . ıı . m̄ . Tc 7 m̄ se defd̄ p . ıııı . hid̄ .
Dimid̄ hida . ē ext̄ rap quæ n̄ ptin̄ istis . Tra . ē . ıııı . car̄ .
In dn̄io sunt . ıı . car̄ cū xv . bord̄ .

T . R . E . 7 m̄ ual̄ . lx . solid̄ . 7 post̄ . xxx . solid̄ . *IN LATILLE HD̄ .*

In *PENGEST* hb̄ comes in dn̄io unā v̄ træ . Vluied te
nuit de rege . E . 7 potuit ire quo uoluit . Tc 7 m̄ p una v̄
se defd̄ . Tra . ē . ı . car̄ . Ibi un uills cū dim̄ car̄ .
T . R . E . 7 m̄ . ual̄ . xx . v . denar̄ .

In *HAINGVRGE* . hb̄ com̄ unā hid̄ . sed dim̄ est in rap
de Hastinges . 7 p dim̄ hid̄ se m̄ defd̄ . Bristui tenuit in
alodiū . Tra . ē . ıı . car̄ . Ibi un uills cū . ıı . car̄ . 7 silua . ıııı .
porc̄ de pasnag . T . R . E . ualb̄ . xx̄ . sol̄ . 7 post̄ . x . sol̄ . Modo .

In *HENDENE* hb̄ com̄ dim̄ hid̄ . 7 p tanto se defd̄ . Almar tenuit
in alodiū . Tra . ē . ıı . car̄ . Ibi un uills cū una car̄ 7 ıı . bord̄ .
T . R . E . ualb̄ . ıx . sol̄ . 7 post̄ . ıııı . sol̄ . Modo . v . solid̄ .

Wi ts ten̄ de com̄ *SELMESTONE* *IN WANDELMESTREI*
7 *SIDENORE* . Alfer tenuit in alodiū . Tc 7 m̄ se defd̄ p . ıııı .
hid̄ . 7 dim̄ . Tra . ē . vıı . car̄ . In dn̄io sunt . ııı . car̄ . 7 ıııı . uilli
7 ııı . bord̄ cū . ıııı . car̄ . Ibi æccia 7 pbr 7 . v . serui .
T . R . E . 7 m̄ . ual̄ . lxx . sol̄ . Qdo recep̄ . xl . solid̄ .

Radulf ten̄ de com̄ unā hid̄ in *SIDENORE* . 7 p tanto se defd̄ .
Vlmar tenuit in alodiū . Tra . ē . ı . car̄ . 7 ibi . ē cū uno uillo .
T . R . E . ualb̄ . vııı . sol̄ . 7 post̄ . vı . sol̄ . Modo . x . sol̄ .

48 In the same Hundred Durand holds 1 hide from the Count.
Alfward held it from King Edward as a manor. Then and now
it answered for 1 hide. Land for ½ plough. 2 oxen there, with
  1 smallholder.
  Woodland, 1 pig.
Value before 1066, 20s; now 10s.

49 In (FROG) FIRLE Alan holds 4 hides from the Count. Aelmer and
Godwin held it from King Edward as two manors. Then and now it
answered for 4 hides. ½ hide which does not belong to them is
outside the Rape. Land for 4 ploughs. In lordship 2 ploughs, with
  15 smallholders.
Value before 1066 and now 60s; later 30s.

In DILL Hundred
50 In *PENGEST* the Count has 1 virgate of land in lordship. Wulfgeat
held it from King Edward; he could go where he would.
Then and now it answered for 1 virgate. Land for 1 plough.
  1 villager with ½ plough.
Value before 1066 and now 25d.

51 In HAWKRIDGE the Count has 1 hide, but half is in the Rape of
Hastings. It answers now for ½ hide. Brictwy held it in
freehold. Land for 2 ploughs.
  1 villager with 2 ploughs.
  Woodland, 4 pigs from pasturage.
Value before 1066, 20s; later 10s; now 15s.

52 In 'HENDON' the Count has ½ hide. It answers for as much.   21 d
Aelmer held it in freehold. Land for 2 ploughs.
  1 villager with 1 plough; 2 smallholders.
Value before 1066, 9s; later 4s; now 5s.

In ALCISTON Hundred
53 William holds SELMESTON and 'SIDNOR' from the Count. Alfhere
held them in freehold. Then and now they answered for 4½
hides. Land for 7 ploughs. In lordship 3 ploughs;
  4 villagers and 3 smallholders with 4 ploughs.
  A church and a priest; 5 slaves.
Value before 1066 and now 70s; when acquired 40s.

54 Ralph holds 1 hide in 'SIDNOR' from the Count. It answers
for as much. Young Wulfmer held it in freehold.
Land for 1 plough. It is there, with
  1 villager.
Value before 1066, 8s; later 6s; now 10s.

Ibidē teñ Walter de cõ dim̄ hīd . 7 ꝑ tanto se defđ . Goduiñ
tenuit . Tra . ē dim̄ caʀ . 7 ibi . ē cū . ı . uitto . Val 7 ualuit . ıııı . sot.

Gerold teñ de cõ in SESINGEHA . ı . hīd . Medietas ej est
in rapo de Hastinges . Aluuiñ tenuit sīc alodiū . Tra . ē . vı . caʀ.
7 ibi sunt cū xvı . uittis . 7 uñ molīn de . x . sot 7 q̄ngent
anguitt . T.R.E . 7 m̄ː ᴌx . sot . Q̄do recep̄ː xx . sot.

Gisteʙt teñ ad firmā de cõ in ALVRICESTONE . uñ hidā.
Aluric tenuit sīc alodiū . Tra . ē . ı . caʀ . Ibi m̄ uñ borđ.

T.R.E . 7 post . 7 m̄ː vıı ı . sot.

In ipsa ALVRICESTONE . teñ de cõ Rannulf . ı . hīd . Radulf
dim̄ hīd . Witts dim̄ hīd . Radulf . ı . hīd . Walteri . ıı . hīd.
Int totū . v . hīd . 7 ꝑ tanto se defđ . Hanc trā tenueʀ Leuuiñ
Aluuold Alnod 7 Goduiñ sīc alodia . Tra . ē . v . caʀ.

In dñio m̄ . ııı . caʀ 7 dim̄ . 7 ıı . uitti 7 vı . borđ . arant ad mediet̄.
T.R.E ː ualeʙ totū . xx . sot . m̄ . ᴌıııı . sot . IN HERTEÑEL HVND.

Ipse cõ teñ in dñio WILDENE . Herald tenuit . Tc 7 m̄ ꝑ . ıı.
hīd se defđ . Tra . ē . vıı . caʀ . In dñio sunt . ıı . 7 vıı . uitti 7 ııı . borđ
hñt . v . caʀ . T.R.E . 7 post . ualuit . ᴌx . sot . Modoː ᴌxx . sot.

In HERTEVEL . teñ Walter de cõ . ı . hīd . 7 ꝑ tanto se defđ.
Carle tenuit sīc alodiū . Tra . ē . ııı . caʀ . In dñio . ē una caʀ
7 dim̄ . 7 vı . uitti 7 ıı . serui cū . ı . caʀ 7 dim̄ . Ibi . ı . molīn de . ıııı.
sot . 7 ccc.ᴌ . anguitt . 7 ııı . ac̄ p̄ti . 7 silua . ııııı porc̄ de pasnag.
T.R.E . 7 m̄ː xᴌ . sot . Q̄do recep̄ː xx . solid.

In eođ HVND hễ cõ unā hīd 7 dim̄ ext̄ rap̄ . 7 p̄tiñ CO de
Ramelle . Goduiñ tenuit . 7 nunꝗ geld . Tra . ē . vı . caʀ . Ibi sunt
vıı . uitti 7 ı . borđ cū . v . caʀ . Ibi silua de . xᴌ . porc̄.
T.R.E . 7 m̄ː xᴌ . sot . Q̄do recep̄ː xxx . sot.

In eođ HVND teñ Radulf ad firmā de cõ . ı . hīd . ext̄ rap̄ū.
Azor tenuit sīc alodiū . 7 nunꝗ geldau . Tra . ē . ıı . caʀ.
Ibi sunt . ııı . uitti cū . ıı . caʀ . T.R.E . 7 post . 7 m̄ː x . solid.

55 Walter also holds ½ hide there from the Count. It answers for as
much. Godwin held it. Land for ½ plough. It is there, with
　1 villager.
The value is and was 4s.

56 Gerald holds 1 hide in SESSINGHAM from the Count. Half of
it is in the Rape of Hastings. Alwin held it as freehold.
Land for 6 ploughs. They are there, with
　16 villagers.
　1 mill at 10s and 500 eels.
[Value] before 1066 and now 60s; when acquired 20s.

57 Gilbert holds 1 hide from the Count in ALFRISTON at a revenue.
Aelfric held it as freehold. Land for 1 plough.
　Now 1 smallholder.
[Value] before 1066, later and now 8s.

58 In ALFRISTON itself Ranulf holds 1 hide from the Count;
Ralph ½ hide; William ½ hide; Ralph 1 hide; Walter 2 hides;
5 hides in total. It answers for as much. Leofwin, Alfwold,
Alnoth and Godwin held this land as freehold. Land for
5 ploughs. Now in lordship 3½ ploughs.
　2 villagers and 6 smallholders plough the half.
Total value before 1066, 20s; now 54s.

　In HARTFIELD Hundred
59 The Count holds WILDENE in lordship, himself. Earl Harold held it.
Then and now it answered for 2 hides. Land for 7 ploughs.
In lordship 2.
　7 villagers and 3 smallholders have 5 ploughs.
Value before 1066 and later 60s; now 70s.

60 In HARTFIELD Walter holds 1 hide from the Count. It answers
for as much. Karl held it as freehold. Land for 3 ploughs.
In lordship 1½ ploughs;
　6 villagers and 2 smallholders with 1½ ploughs.
　1 mill at 4s and 350 eels; meadow, 3 acres; woodland,
　　5 pigs from pasturage.
　[Value] before 1066 and now 40s; when acquired 20s.

61 In the same Hundred the Count has 1½ hides outside the Rape.
They belong to the manor of Rodmell. Earl Godwin held them.
They never paid tax. Land for 6 ploughs.
　7 villagers and 1 smallholder with 5 ploughs.
　Woodland for 40 pigs.
[Value] before 1066 and now 40s; when acquired 30s.

62 In the same Hundred Ralph holds 1 hide from the Count at
a revenue outside the Rape. Azor held it as freehold.
It never paid tax. Land for 2 ploughs.
　　3 villagers with 2 ploughs.
[Value] before 1066, later and now 10s.

In *APEDROC* ten ipſe com̄ dim̄ hiđ . Nunꝗ głdauit . Ext̄ rap̄ . ē.

Eddid regina tenuit . Tra . ē . ɪɪ . car̄ . Ibi ſunt . ɪɪ . uiłłi cū . ɪ . car̄

⁊ dim̄ . Silua . xʟ . porc̄ . ⁊ xɪɪ . ſoł . Ibi . ē una v̄ ubi com̄ h̄t aulā

ſuā . Similit Herald habuit . ⁊ abſtulit Ꞩ Joħi.

T.R.E. ⁊ poſt . ⁊ m̄ː ʟɪɪ . ſoliđ . ɪN *FRAMELLE HVND*.

Ibi ten̄ Wiłłs de comite . unā v̄ . ext̄ rap̄ . Nunꝗ geldauit.

Leuuin tenuit ſic alodiū . Tra . ē dim̄ car̄ . ⁊ ibi . ē cū . ɪɪɪ . borđ.

Silua . ɪ . porc̄ᷓ de paſnaḡ . T.R.Eː x . ſoliđ . ⁊ poſt ⁊ m̄ː v . ſoliđ.

Radulf ten̄ de com̄ in *GORDE* unā hiđ ⁊ unā v̄ . ⁊ ꝓ tanto

22 a

ſe defđ . Helghi tenuit de rege . E . ⁊ q̄ uoluit ire potuit . Tra . ē

vɪ . car̄ . In dn̄io . ē . una car̄ ⁊ dim̄ . ⁊ vɪɪɪ . uiłłi ⁊ ɪ . borđ cū . ɪɪ . car̄.

Ibi . ɪ . moliñ de . ɪx . ſoł . ⁊ ɪɪ . ac̄ pti . ⁊ ſilua . vɪ . porc̄.

T.R.E. ⁊ m̄ː ʟ . ſoliđ . Q̄do recep̄ː xxx . ſoliđ.

Rannulf ten̄ de com̄ in *HORSTEDE* . v . hiđ ⁊ ɪɪɪ . v̄ ، ⁊ ꝓ

tanto ſe defđ . Vlfer tenuit de rege . E . ⁊ quo uoluit ire potuit.

Tra . ē . vɪɪ . car̄ ⁊ dim̄ . In dn̄io ſunt . ɪɪ . ⁊ ɪx . uiłłi ⁊ vɪ . borđ cū

ɪɪɪɪ . car̄ ⁊ dimiđ . ⁊ ɪ . moliñ de . vɪɪɪ . ſoliđ.

De hac tra jacet una hida in rapo de Lewes . ⁊ aliā hiđ ten̄

Azelin in Bechingetone . ⁊ Grento ten̄ unā v̄ ⁊ dimiđ.

Hi hn̄t . ɪ . car̄ ⁊ dim̄ in dn̄io.

Tot̄ T.R.E. ualeb̄ . c . ſoł . ⁊ poſtː ʟ . ſoł . Modoː ʟx . ſoliđ.

Ipſe com̄ ten̄ ad *LODINTONE* . ɪN *PEVENESEL HVND*.

ɪɪɪɪ . hiđ ⁊ dim̄ . ⁊ ꝓ tanto ſe defđ . Hanc trā tenuer̄ . vɪ . teigni

ſic alodiū . Tra . ē . v . car̄ . In dn̄io ſunt . ɪɪ . car̄ . ⁊ v . uiłł cū . v .

car̄ . ⁊ uñ moliñ de . xx . ſoł . ⁊ paſtura de . xx . ſoł . ⁊ v . ſalinæ de

xʟɪ . ſoł ⁊ vɪɪɪ . ſoł . T.R.E. ualuit . xxx . ſoł . m̄ . vɪ . lib̄ ⁊ xɪ . ſoł.

Wiłłs ten̄ de com̄ ad *HAMELESHĀ* unā hiđ ⦗ ⁊ vɪɪɪ . den̄.

⁊ dim̄ . ⁊ ꝓ tanto ſe defđ . Alnod tenuit ſic alodiū . Tra . ē . ɪɪɪɪ.

car̄ . Ibi ſunt . ɪɪɪɪ . borđ cū uno boue . ⁊ ɪɪ . ſalinæ de vɪɪ . ſoł.

T.R.E. ualeb̄ c ⁊ x . ſoł . Modoː xx . ſoliđ.

In hoc ꝏ retinuit com̄ . xɪ . ſalinas . quæ uał . xxɪɪɪɪ . ſoł . ⁊ vɪ . den̄.

63 In PARROCK the Count holds ½ hide, himself. It never paid tax.
It is outside the Rape. Queen Edith held it. Land for 2 ploughs.
 2 villagers with 1½ ploughs.
 Woodland, 40 pigs and 12s too.
There is 1 virgate where the Count has his hall. Earl Harold
had it likewise; he took it from St. John's.
[Value] before 1066, later and now 52s.

In FRAMFIELD Hundred

64 William holds 1 virgate from the Count outside the Rape.
It never paid tax. Leofwin held it as freehold.
Land for ½ plough. It is there, with
 3 smallholders.
 Woodland, 1 pig from pasturage.
[Value] before 1066, 10s; later and now 5s.

65 Ralph holds 1 hide and 1 virgate from the Count in WORTH.
It answers for as much. Helgi held it from King Edward; he could   22 a
go where he would. Land for 6 ploughs. In lordship 1½ ploughs;
 8 villagers and 1 smallholder with 2 ploughs.
 1 mill at 9s; meadow, 2 acres; woodland, 6 pigs.
[Value] before 1066 and now 50s; when acquired 30s.

66 Ranulf holds 5 hides and 3 virgates in (LITTLE) HORSTED from the Count.
It answers for as much. Wulfhere held it from King Edward;
he could go where he would. Land for 7½ ploughs. In lordship 2;
 9 villagers and 6 smallholders with 4½ ploughs.
 1 mill at 8s.
 1 hide of this land lies in the Rape of Lewes. Azelin holds
 another hide in 'Bechington'. Grento holds 1½ virgates.
 These men have 1½ ploughs in lordship.
Total value before 1066, 100s; later 50s; now 60s.

In PEVENSEY Hundred

67 The Count holds 4½ hides at WOOTTON himself. It answers
for as much. Six thanes held this land as freehold.
Land for 5 ploughs. In lordship 2 ploughs;
 5 villagers with 5 ploughs.
 1 mill at 20s; pasturage at 20s; 5 salt-houses at 41s and 8[d?].
Value before 1066, 30s; now £6 11s 8d.

68 William holds 1½ hides at HAILSHAM from the Count. It answers
for as much. Alnoth held it as a freehold. Land for 4 ploughs.
 4 smallholders with 1 ox.
 2 salthouses at 7s.
Value before 1066, 110s; now 20s.
In this manor the Count kept 11 salt-houses, value 24s 6d.

Ansfrid ten de com ad *CHENENOLLE* . II . hiđ . Tra . e . II . car.

Tochi tenuit sic alodiū . In dnio . e dim car . 7 I . uitł cū dim car.

7 v . ačs pti . T.R.E. uatł . XL . sot . m̄ xv . sot.

Isđē Ansfrid ten de com jn *WILENDONE* | 7 p̄ tanto se defđ. dimiđ hidă.

Leuuard tenuit sic alodiū . Tra . e dim car . Tc 7 m̄ uał . x . sot.

Godefrid cleric ten in elemosina in Palinges . I . hidā . 7 ibi h̄t

II . borđ reddt . VIII . denar . Vał 7 ualuit . III . soliđ.

Roger cleric ten . I . hiđ ad *COONARE* . in elemosina . Tra . e . I.

car . 7 ibi . e in dnio . cū uno borđ . 7 uno boue . Bricuin tenuit.

Idē Roger ten ad Horselie . I . hiđ in elemosina S Michaelis.

Clerici tenueř cōmunit . Tra . e . I . car . Ibi . e un̄ uitłs cū . I . car.

Iste . II . hidæ tc 7 m̄ p̄ tanto se defđ . Tc: x . sot . M: xxII . soliđ.

Walteri ten de com . I . hiđ . 7 p̄ tanto se defđ . Bricuin

tenuit ad *COONORE* . Tra . e dim car . 7 ibi . e in dnio . Vał . v . sot.

Ansfrid ten de com ad *ORNE* . II . hiđ . 7 p̄ tanto se defđ.

Tres hōes tenueř sic alodiū . Ibi sunt . II . borđ . 7 VIII . ač pti.

T.R.E. uatł xxv . sot . modo: x . soliđ.

Rannulf ten de com ad *ORNE* . I . hiđ.

Tra . e . II . car . Ibi . e un̄ borđ . Tc uatł . xIII . sot . M . LxIII . den.

In *HOV* . ten com . IIII . salinas in dnio . quæ uał . xx . soliđ.

In *REMECINGES* . ten Witłs 7 Radulf 7 alt Radulf

de com . II . hiđ . 7 p̄ tanto se defđ . Duo libi hōes tenueř sic

alodiū . Tra . e . IIII . car . Ibi . II . uitłi 7 I . borđ . 7 II . bou arantes.

T.R.E: uatł . xvI . sot . Modo: xv . sot.

In *PELLINGES* ten Alan 7 Godefrid 7 Ansfrid 7 Rogeri

. IIII . hiđ de com . 7 p̄ tanto se defđ . Tra . e . IIII . car . Aluuard

7 Algar tenueř de rege p̄ . II . m̄ . in alodia . Ibi m̄ . I . uitł . 7 I . borđ.

69 Ansfrid holds 2 hides at *CHENENOLLE* from the Count. Land for 2 ploughs.
   Toki held it as freehold. In lordship ½ plough;
     1 villager with ½ plough.
     Meadow, 5 acres.
   Value before 1066, 40s; now 15s.

70 Ansfrid also holds ½ hide in WILLINGDON from the Count.
   It answers for as much. Leofward held it as freehold.
   Land for ½ plough.
   Value then and now 10s.

71 Godfrey the cleric holds 1 hide in PEELINGS in alms. He has
     2 smallholders who pay 8d.
   The value is and was 3s.

72 Roger the cleric holds 1 hide at 'CUDNOR' in alms. Land for 1 plough.
   It is there, in lordship, with
     1 smallholder and 1 ox.
     Brictwin held it.

73 Roger also holds 1 hide at HORSEY of St. Michael's, in alms.
   The clergy held it in common. Land for 1 plough.
     1 villager with 1 plough.
   These 2 hides answered for as much then and now.
   [Value] then 10s; now 22s.

74 Walter holds 1 hide from the Count. It answers for as much.
   Brictwin held it at 'CUDNOR'. Land for ½ plough. It is there,
   in lordship.
   Value 5s.

75 Ansfrid holds 2 hides at HORNS from the Count. It answers
   for as much. Three men held it as freehold.
     2 smallholders.
     Meadow, 8 acres.
   Value before 1066, 25s; now 10s.

76 Ranulf holds 1 hide at HORNS from the Count. Land for 2 ploughs.
     1 smallholder.
   Value then 13s; now 63d.

77 In HOOE the Count holds 4 salt-houses in lordship, value 20s.

78 In 'RENCHING' William, Ralph and another Ralph hold
   2 hides from the Count. It answers for as much. Two free
   men held it as freehold. Land for 4 ploughs.
     2 villagers and 1 smallholder; 2 ploughing oxen.
   Value before 1066, 16s; now 15s.

79 In PEELINGS Alan, Godfrey, Ansfrid and Roger hold 4 hides
   from the Count. It answers for as much. Land for 4 ploughs.
   Alfward and Algar held it from the King as 2 manors, in freehold.
     Now 1 villager and 1 smallholder.

In *LANGELIE* ten Rannulf de com̄ . I . hidā . 7 p̄ tanto ſe deſd̄

Lemar 7 Bricſtan tenuer̄ ſic̄ alodiū . Ibi ſunt . II . bord̄ .

Ibid̄ ten Witts . I . hid̄ . 7 p̄ tanto ſe deſd̄ . Alfec tenuit .

Ibi ſunt . II . bord̄ . T . R . E . uateb . XVI . ſot . 7 VIII . den̄ . Modo . x . ſot .

Witts ten de com̄ ad *HENECHĀ* . II . hid̄ . quæ jacuer̄
in ꝏ de *BORNE* . Tra . ē . III . car̄ . Ibi ſunt . IIII . bord̄ .

T . R . E . ualeb . xv . ſot . Modo . VIII . ſot .

In *HENECHĀ* hc̄ com̄ unā hid̄ 7 dim v . Rex . E . tenuit .

Tra . ē . I . car̄ . Inde nullū reſponſū .   Vat . IX . ſot .

Ibid̄ ten Anſgot de com̄ dim hid̄ . quæ jacuit in *BVRNE* .

In *BOGELIE* ten Witts de com̄ dim hid̄ . Herald tenuit .

Tra . ē . II . car̄ . 7 ibi ſunt cū . II . uittis . 7 I . bord̄ . 7 VIII . ac̄ p̄ti .

7 IIII . ſalinæ de . XXII . ſot 7 IIII . den̄ . T . R . E . uat . xv . ſot . M . xxx . ſot .

In *LODIVTONE* deb mitti . XIII . ſolid de paſtura q̄ com̄ ded̄ ei .

Ipſe com̄ ten *RIPE* . Herald tenuit . *IN EDLVESTONE HD* .

Tc̄ 7 m̄ p̄ . xxII . hid̄ ſe deſd̄ . Ex his jaceN . VIII . in rapo
de Haſtinges . Tra . ē . x . car̄ . In dn̄io ſunt . II . car̄ . 7 xvi .

uitti 7 VIII . bord̄ cū . VIII . car̄ . Ibi . XII . ac̄ p̄ti . 7 VIII .

ſalinæ de . xx . ſot . T . R . E . uateb . XII . lib . Modo . VIII . lib .

Ipſe com̄ ten *CLAVEHĀ* . Oſuuard tenuit de rege . E .

Tc̄ 7 m̄ p̄ . IIII . hid̄ ſe deſd̄ . Tra . ē . IIII . car̄ . In dn̄io . ē una .

7 II . uitti 7 II . bord̄ 7 II . ſerui cū dim car̄ .

De his . IIII . hid̄ eſt dimid̄ hida in Rapo de Haſtinges .

7 Alured ten . I . hidā . 7 ibi hc̄ un̄ uittm .

Tot T . R . E . uateb . xl . ſot . Modo . xxxvi . ſolid̄ .

In *CLAVEHĀ* ten | Morin' de com̄ . I . hid̄ 7 unā v . Hugo . III . hid̄
una v min . Cane 7 Frane tenuer̄ p̄ . II . ꝏ de rege . E .

Tc̄ 7 m̄ p̄ . IIII . hid̄ ſe deſd̄ . Tra . ē . III . car̄ 7 dim . In dn̄io
ē una car̄ 7 dim . 7 I . uitts 7 v . bord̄ .

T . R . E . uateb . xlv . ſot . Modo . xl . ſolid̄ .

Ibid̄ ten Anſgot de . Co.
dimid̄ hid̄ . q̄ jacuit
in *BORNE* . Val . IX .

10

80 In LANGNEY Ranulf holds 1 hide from the Count. It answers
for as much. Leofmer and Brictstan held it as freehold.
  2 smallholders.
William also holds 1 hide there. It answers for as much.
Alfheah held it.
  2 smallholders.
Value before 1066, 16 8d; now 10s.

81 William holds 2 hides from the Count at HANKHAM which lay
in the (lands of the) manor of Eastbourne. Land for 3 ploughs.
  4 smallholders.
Value before 1066, 15s; now 8s.

82 In HANKHAM the Count has 1 hide and ½ virgate. King Edward
held it. Land for 1 plough. No return from it.
  Ansgot also holds there from the Count ½ hide which lay
in Eastbourne (lands).
Value 9s.

83 In BOWLEY William holds ½ hide from the Count. Earl Harold
held it. Land for 2 ploughs. They are there, with
  2 villagers and 1 smallholder.
  Meadow, 8 acres; 4 salt-houses at 22s 4d.
Value before 1066, 15s; now 30s.

84 Ansgot also holds there from the Count ½ hide which lay
in Eastbourne (lands).
Value 9s.

85 In WOOTTON 13s should be placed, from the pasture
which the Count gave him (William).
  In SHIPLAKE Hundred

86 The Count holds RIPE himself. Earl Harold held it. Then and now
it answered for 22 hides. 8 of these lie in the Rape of Hastings.
Land for 10 ploughs. In lordship 2 ploughs;
  16 villagers and 8 smallholders with 8 ploughs.
  Meadow, 12 acres; 8 salt-houses at 20s.
Value before 1066 £12; now £8.

87 The Count holds CLAVERHAM himself. Osward held it from
King Edward. Then and now it answered for 4 hides.
Land for 4 ploughs. In lordship 1;
  2 villagers, 2 smallholders and 2 slaves with ½ plough.
Of these 4 hides, ½ hide is in the Rape of Hastings.
Alfred holds 1 hide. He has
  1 villager.
Total value before 1066, 40s; now 36s.

88 In CLAVERHAM Morin holds 1 hide and 1 virgate from the Count;
Hugh 3 hides less 1 virgate. Cana and Fran held it as two
manors from King Edward. Then and now it answered for 4 hides.
Land for 3½ ploughs. In lordship 1½ ploughs;
  1 villager and 5 smallholders.
Value before 1066, 45s; now 40s.

Wilts ten *ACHINTONE* de com̄. Agemund tenuit

de rege. E. Tc̄ ſe deſđ p̄. v. hiđ. m̄ p̄. iii. q̄a. ii. jaceℵ

in Rapo de Haſtinges. Tra. ē. iiii. car̄. In dn̄io ſunt. ii.

car̄. 7 viii. borđ cū. i. car̄. Ibi ſilua de x. porc̄.

De hac tra ten un̄ hō ej dimiđ hiđ. 7 ibi hł. i. car̄ in dn̄io.

T.R.E. ualeb̄. c. ſoł. Modo. lx. ſoliđ.

In *ACHILTONE* 7 *CALVINTONE* ten ipſe com̄ in dn̄io. v. hiđ.

7 p̄ tanto ſe deſđ. Eddiđ regina tenuit. p̄. ii. Maner̄.

Tra. ē. vi. car̄. Ibi ſunt. vii. uilti cū. ii. car̄.

T.R.E. uałb̄. xl. ſoł. Modo. xxx. ſoł.

In *CALVINTONE* ten Anſfriđ de com̄. iiii. hiđ. 7 p̄ tanto

ſe deſđ. Oſuuarđ 7 Toti teneb̄ p̄. ii. m̄. ſic alodiū.

Tra. ē. i. car̄ 7 dim. In dn̄io. ē una car̄. cū. ii. borđ 7 ii. ſeruis.

De hac tra jacet dim hida in Rapo de Haſtinges.

7 Hunfriđ ten. i. hiđa. 7 ibi hł dimiđ car̄ in dn̄io

T.R.E. 7 m̄. xl. ſoliđ.

In *WALDRENE*. ten Anſfriđ de com̄. i. hiđ. 7 p̄ tanto

ſe deſđ. Ælueua tenuit de rege. E. ſic alodiū. Tra. ē

iii. car̄ 7 dim. In dn̄io. ē una car̄ cū. i. uilto. Tc̄ 7 m̄. xx. ſoł.

Ipſe com̄ ten in dn̄io *LESTONE*. Goduin tenuit.

Tc̄ ſe deſđ. p̄ x. hiđ. m̄ p̄. vi. q̄a. iiii. jaceℵ in rapo de

22 c   Haſtinges.

Tra. ē. xvi. car̄. In dn̄io ſunt. iii. car̄. 7 xiiii. uilti

7 iii. borđ cū. x. car̄ 7 dim. Ibi. xvi. ſalinæ de. xxv. ſoł.

T.R.E. uałb̄. xv. liɓ. Modo. x. liɓ. 7 v. ſoliđ.

Ipſe com̄ ten *ESTOCHINGEHĀ*. Leuenot tenuit de

rege. E. Tc̄ 7 m̄ ſe deſđ p̄. x. hiđ. Tra. ē. viii. car̄.

In dn̄io. ē una car̄. 7 x. uilti cū. iiii. car̄ 7 dimidia.

De herbagio. xii. porc̄. T.R.E. 7 m̄. lx. ſoł.

89 William holds ECKINGTON from the Count. Agemund held it from King Edward. Then it answered for 5 hides; now for 3, because 2 lie in the Rape of Hastings. Land for 4 ploughs. In lordship 2 ploughs;
    8 smallholders with 1 plough.
    Woodland at 10 pigs.
    A man of his holds ½ hide of this land. He has 1 plough in lordship.
Value before 1066, 100s; now 60s.

90 In ECKINGTON and CHALVINGTON the Count holds 5 hides in lordship himself. It answers for as much. Queen Edith held it as two manors. Land for 6 ploughs.
    7 villagers with 2 ploughs.
Value before 1066, 40s; now 30s.

91 In CHALVINGTON Ansfrid holds 4 hides from the Count. It answers for as much. Osward and Toti held it as two manors as freehold. Land for 1½ ploughs. In lordship 1 plough, with
    2 smallholders and 2 slaves.
    Of this land, ½ hide lies in the Rape of Hastings.
    Humphrey holds 1 hide. He has ½ plough in lordship.
[Value] before 1066 and now 40s.

92 In WALDRON Ansfrid holds 1 hide from the Count. It answers for as much. Aelfeva held it from King Edward as freehold. Land for 3½ ploughs. In lordship 1 plough, with
    1 villager.
[Value] then and now 20s.

93 The Count holds LAUGHTON in lordship himself. Earl Godwin held it. Then it answered for 10 hides; now for 6, because 4 lie in the Rape of Hastings. Land for 16 ploughs. In lordship 3 ploughs;
    14 villagers and 3 smallholders with 10½ ploughs.
    16 salt-houses at 25s.
Value before 1066 £15; now £10 5s.

22 c

94 The Count holds 'STOCKINGHAM' himself. Leofnoth held it from King Edward. Then and now it answered for 10 hides. Land for 8 ploughs. In lordship 1 plough;
    10 villagers with 4½ ploughs.
    From grazing 12 pigs.
[Value] before 1066 and now 60s.

In CETELINGEI teñ Radulf⁹ 7 Goduin⁹ de com⁷ unã . v̄ .

Ælmar tenuit de rege ſic alodiũ . Tc̄ 7 m̃ p̄ una v̄ ſe defđ

T̃ra . ē . III . cař . In dño . ē una cař . 7 II . uitti cũ . I . cař .

7 I . moliñ cũ molinario de . IIII . ſot . In rapo de Haſtinges

T . R . E . uatb . xx . ſot . m̃ ſimilit⁷ .   [jacet alia v̄ .

In CALVRESTOT hab com⁷ . I . hiđ . IN GRENESTEDE HĐ .

quæ jacuit in Rapo de Leuues . Nc̄ ext rap̃ . ē . Ñ geldat .

Alnod tenuit de rege . E . T̃ra . ē . II . cař⁷ . Ibi ſuɴ⁷ . cũ

uno uitto 7 III . borđ . De herbagio⁷ III . porc̃ . De ſilua⁷ v̄ .

T . R . E . 7 m̃⁷ uat . xx . ſot .

In CELRESTVIS teñ Anſfrid de com⁷ unã v̄ ext rap̃ .

Nunq geldaũ . Ælmar tenuit de rege . E . T̃ra . ē . I . cař .

Ibi . ē cũ . I . uitto . Silua 7 Herbag⁷ . II . porc̃ .

T . R . E⁷ uatb . v . ſot . Modo⁷ VII . ſoliđ .

In FELESMERE teñ com̃ . I . hiđ 7 dimiđ ext⁷ rap̃ .

Non geldauit . Vitti tenuer⁷ . 7 ē ap̄ciata in Manerio .

In BERCHELIE teñ Witts . I . hiđ 7 dim⁷ . de com⁷ . Ext⁷ rap̃ . ē .

Non geldaũ . T . R . E . Alfer tenuit de S ḰINIꞍ in c̃ō de

ODETONE . ut hunđ teſtificat⁷ . T̃ra . ē . IIII . cař . Ibi ſunt

. III . uitti cũ . I . cař⁷ . T . R . E . uatb . xx . ſot . m̃ . x . ſot .

Iſđe Witts teñ de com WARLEGE . Ibi ſunt . II . hidæ

Nunq geldaũ . Ext⁷ rap̃ . ē . Vlueua tenuit de rege . E

p̄ uno c̃ō . T̃ra . ē . v . cař . Ibi . III . uitti cũ . III . cař . De

herbagio . v . porc̃⁷ . 7 ſilua . II . porc̃⁷ . Tc̄ . xx . ſot . m̃ . xv . ſot .

Iſđ Witts teñ⁷ de com⁷ ext⁷ rap̃ unã⁷ v̄ . ſpchedene .

In Wildetone jacuit . 7 nunq geldaũ . Cano tenuit de

rege E . T̃ra . ē dim⁷ cař . Tc̄ uat . III . ſot . m̃ . II . ſot .

Anſfrid⁹ teñ de com⁷ ext⁷ rap̃ . II . hidas unã⁷ v̄ min⁹ .

Rex . ē . tenuit in c̃ō diceninges jacuer⁷ . 7 ñ geldauer⁷ .

95 In CHIDDINGLY Ralph and Godwin hold 1 virgate from the Count.
Aelmer held it from the King as freehold. Then and now it
answered for 1 virgate. Land for 3 ploughs. In lordship 1 plough;
  2 villagers with 1 plough.
  1 mill, with a miller, at 4s.
  Another virgate lies in the Rape of Hastings.
Value before 1066, 20s; now the same.

In (EAST) GRINSTEAD Hundred

96 In SHOVELSTRODE the Count has 1 hide which lay in the Rape of
Lewes. Now it is outside the Rape. It does not pay tax. Alnoth
held it from King Edward. Land for 2 ploughs. They are there, with
  1 villager and 3 smallholders.
  From grazing 3 pigs; from the woodland 5 [pigs].
Value before 1066 and now 20s.

97 In SHOVELSTRODE Ansfrid holds 1 virgate outside the Rape
from the Count. It never paid tax. Aelmer held it from
King Edward. Land for 1 plough. It is there, with
  1 villager.
  Woodland, and grazing 2 pigs.
Value before 1066, 5s; now 7s.

98 In FELESMERE the Count holds 1½ hides outside the Rape. It did not
pay tax. The villagers held it. It is assessed in the manor.

99 In BURLEIGH William holds 1½ hides from the Count. It is
outside the Rape. It did not pay tax. Before 1066 Alfhere
held it from Holy Trinity in the manor of Wootton, as the
Hundred testifies. Land for 4 ploughs.
  3 villagers with 1 plough.
Value before 1066, 20s; now 10s.

100 William also holds 'WARLEY' from the Count. 2 hides.
They never paid tax. It is outside the Rape. Wulfeva held
it from King Edward as one manor. Land for 5 ploughs.
  3 villagers with 3 ploughs.
  From grazing 5 pigs; woodland, 2 pigs.
[Value] then 20s; now 15s.

101 William also holds 1 virgate outside the Rape from the Count in
SPERCHEDENE. It lay in *WILDETONE* (lands). It never paid tax.
Cana held it from King Edward. Land for ½ plough.
Value then 3s; now 2s.

102 Ansfrid holds 2 hides less 1 virgate from the Count outside
the Rape. King Edward held them; they lay in the (lands of the)
manor of Ditchling. They did not pay tax. Land for 6 ploughs.

Tra . ē . vi . car̄ . De ſilua 7 herbag̋ . vi . porc̋ . Ibi . i . ac̄
p̄ti . 7 una ferraria . Ibi . vi . uilli cū . ii . car̄.

T.R.E. ualb̄ . xv . ſol . m̄ ꞉ xx . ſol.

Iſdē Anſfrid ten ext̋ rap̄ dim̄ hid̄ . Halſeeldene . Vluuard
tenuit de rege . E . In Alitone jacuit . 7 nunꝗ geldauit.

Tra . ē . ii . car̄ . Valuit . x . ſol . m̄ . v . ſol.

Iſd̄ Anſfrid ten de com̄ ext̋ rap̄ dim̄ hid̄ . Biocheſt . Frane
tenuit de rege . E . In Waningore jacuit . Nunꝗ geldaű.

Tra . ē . i . car̄ . 7 ibi . ē cū uno uilto . Valuit . xv . ſol . m̄ . v . ſol.

Radulf̋ ten de com̄ BRANBERTEI . Cola tenuit de
rege . E . Tc̄ 7 m̄ ꝑ una hida ſe defd̄ . Tra . ē . i . car̄ 7 dim̄.
Ibi . ē p̄br cū uno uilto . 7 i . car̄ 7 dim̄ . 7 xiiii . bord̄.
De ſilua 7 Herbagio . xii . porc̋ . 7 v . ac̄ p̄ti . 7 i . molin̄ . ii . ſot.

T.R.E. ualb̄ . xxx . ſot . m̄ . xx . ſolid̄.

Iſd̄ Radulf̋ ten de com̄ ext̋ rap̄ WASLEBIE . Ibi . ē . i . hida . Fulchi
tenuit de rege . E . Ad LOVINTVNE jacuit . Nunꝗ geldaű . Tra . ē
iii . car̄ . Ibi ſunt . ii . uilti cū dim̄ car̄ . Valuit . xxx . ſot . m̄ . xx . ſot.

Ipſe com̄ ten ext̋ rap̄ unā v̄ 7 dim̄ . Standene . Azor tenuit
de rege . E . Ad Beuedene jacuit . Nunꝗ geldaű . Cōputat̋ 7 ap
p̄ciat̋ . ē in ꝏ de Toringes.

Ipſe com̄ ten FERLEGA . ꝑ una v̄ . Ext̋ rap̄ . ē . in rapo de Leuues.
Ad DICELINGES jacuit . Nunꝗ geldaű . Tra . ē dim̄ car̄ . Ibi . ē
un̋ uilts cū . i . car̄ . Valuit . x . ſot . m̄ ꞉ v . ſolid̄.

Wilts ten de com̄ HORSTEDE . IN RISTONE HVND̄.

Ext̋ rap̄ . ē . Vlueue tenuit de rege . E . In HAME jacuit . Nunꝗ
geldaű . Ibi . iiii . hidæ . Tra . ē . viii . car̄ . In dñio . ē una . 7 ix . uilti
cū . iii . car̄ . Ibi . i . molin̄ de . ii . ſolid̄ . 7 iii . bord̄.

T.R.E. ualb̄ . lx . ſot . m̄ . xl . ſot.

Iſdē Wilts ten de com̄ ext̋ rap̄ unā v̄ in Bontegraue . Goda
tenuit de rege . E . ſic alodiū . Ad Bergcinere jacuit . Nunꝗ geldaű.
Tra . ē dim̄ car̄ . Val 7 ualuit . ii . ſolid̄ . Ibi . ē un̋ uilts.

From the woodland and grazing 6 pigs; meadow, 1 acre; a forge.
6 villagers with 2 ploughs.
Value before 1066, 15s; now 20s.

103 Ansfrid also holds ½ hide outside the Rape. It is called
HAZLEDEN. Wulfward held it from King Edward. It lay in
Allington (lands). It never paid tax. Land for 2 ploughs.
The value was 10s; now 5s.

104 Ansfrid also holds ½ hide, BROCKHURST, from the Count, outside
the Rape. Fran held it from King Edward. It lay in Warningore
(lands). It never paid tax. Land for 1 plough. It is there, with
1 villager.
The value was 15s; now 5s.

105 Ralph holds BRAMBLETYE from the Count. Cola held it from
King Edward. Then and now it answered for 1 hide.
Land for 1½ ploughs.
A priest with 1 villager; 1½ ploughs; 14 smallholders.
From woodland and grazing 12 pigs; meadow, 5 acres; 1 mill, 2s.
Value before 1066, 30s; now 20s.

106 Ralph also holds WHALESBEECH from the Count, outside the Rape.   22 d
1 hide. Fulk held it from King Edward. It lay in Lavant
(lands). It never paid tax. Land for 3 ploughs.
2 villagers with ½ plough.
The value was 30s; now 20s.

107 The Count holds 1½ virgates, STANDEN, himself, outside the Rape.
Azor held it from King Edward. It lay in Bevendean (lands).
It never paid tax. It is accounted and assessed in the manor
of Tarring (Neville).

108 The Count holds FAIRLIGHT himself for 1 virgate. It is outside the
Rape, in the Rape of Lewes. It lay in Ditchling (lands). It never
paid tax. Land for ½ plough.
1 villager with 1 plough.
The value was 10s; now 5s.

In RUSHMONDEN Hundred
109 William holds HORSTED (KEYNES) from the Count. It is outside the
Rape. Wulfeva held it from King Edward. It lay in Hamsey (lands).
It never paid tax. 4 hides. Land for 8 ploughs. In lordship 1;
9 villagers with 3 ploughs.
1 mill at 2s; 3 smallholders.
Value before 1066, 60s; now 40s.

110 William also holds 1 virgate in BIRCHGROVE from the Count, outside
the Rape. Goda held it from King Edward as freehold.
It lay in Balmer (lands). It never paid tax. Land for ½ plough.
The value is and was 2s.
1 villager.

Ipſe com̄ ten̄ *SIFELLE* . Goduin tenuit de rege . E . in alodiū.

Tc̄ 7 m̄ ꝓ . vi . hiđ . Tra . ē . xi . car̄ . In dn̄io . ē una car̄ . 7 ix . uiłłi

7 v . borđ cū . vii . car̄ . Ibi . i . molin̄ de . xl . den̄ 7 q̄ngent anguiłł.

7 x . ãc p̄ti . De ſilua 7 herbagioꞏ xxxii . porc̄.

T . R̄ . E . uałb . c . ſoł . m̄ . iiii . lib̄.

Anſfrid ten̄ de com̄ in *FLESCINGE* . i . hiđ . 7 ꝓ tanto ſe defđ.

Leuuin tenuit ꝓ M̄ de rege . E . Tra . ē . iii . car̄ . Ibi ſunt . iiii . uiłłi

7 iii . borđ cū . ii . car̄ . De ſilua 7 herbagio . vi . porc̄ . 7 ibi . i . ãc p̄ti.

T . R . E . uałb . xl . ſoł . m̄ꞏ xx . ſoł.

FLESCINGES ten̄ de com̄ Morin 7 Hugo . Cano tenuit de rege . E.

Tc̄ 7 m̄ ſe defđ ꝓ . ii . hiđ . Tra . ē . v . car̄ . In dn̄io . i . car̄ . 7 xi . uiłłi

7 v . borđ cū . iiii . car̄ . Ibi . vi . ãc p̄ti . 7 dē ſilua . xxx . porc̄.

T . R . E . uałb . iiii . lib̄ . m̄ , l . ſoliđ.

Giſlebt ten̄ de com̄ exẗ rap̄ dim̄ hiđ . ad Berchehā . Carlo

tenuit de rege . E . Nunꝗ geldau̇ . Tra . ē . i . car̄ . 7 ibi . ē cū . iii . uiłłis.

Valuit . vii . ſoł . m̄ . ix . ſoliđ.

Warneri ten̄ de com̄ . In *BERCHEHĀ* . iii . uirḡ . 7 ꝓ tanto ſe defđ.
Goduin tenuit de rege . E . ꝓ M̄ ſic alodiū . Tra . ē . iii . car̄ . In dn̄io

ē una car̄ . 7 iiii . uiłłi 7 v . borđ cū . ii . car̄ . Ibi . vi . ãc p̄ti . De ſilua

7 herbaḡ . ix . porc̄ . T . R . E . 7 poſt . 7 m̄ . uał . xx . ſoliđ.

Alan ten̄ de com̄ unā v̇ . jnode . Exẗ rap̄ . ē . Ad Neumonaſteriū

jacuit . 7 nunꝗ geldau̇ . Elmær tenuit ꝓ M̄ de rege . E . Tra . ē . i . car̄

7 dimiđ . In dn̄io . ē una . 7 ii . uiłłi 7 ii . borđ cū dim̄ car̄.

T . R . E . uałb . xv . ſoliđ . m̄ x . ſoliđ . *IN REREDFELLE HVND.*

Ipſe com̄ ten̄ . ii . hiđ . q̄s tenuer̄ de rege . E . Aluuard 7 Vluuard.

ꝓ . ii̇ . M̄ . Tra . ē . vi . car̄ . De hac tra ten̄ Anſfrid . i . hiđ de com̄.

Hunfrid . unā v̇ . Wiłłs unā v̇ 7 un̄ ferdinc . 7 q̄dā anglic̄ unā v̇.

In dn̄io ſunt . iiii . car̄ 7 dim̄ . 7 vi . uiłłi 7 viii . borđ . cū . vi . car̄ . Ibi un̄

ſeru̇ . 7 i . molin̄ de xxx . den̄ . T . R . E . uałb xxx . ſoł . Modo . lxxiii . ſoł.

22 d

111 The Count holds SHEFFIELD himself. Godwin held it from
King Edward in freehold. Then and now [it answered] for 6 hides.
Land for 11 ploughs. In lordship 1 plough;
  9 villagers and 5 smallholders with 7 ploughs.
  1 mill at 40d and 500 eels; meadow, 10 acres;
   from woodland and grazing 32 pigs.
Value before 1066, 100s; now £4.

112 Ansfrid holds 1 hide in FLETCHING from the Count. It answers
for as much. Leofwin held it as a manor from King Edward.
Land for 3 ploughs.
  4 villagers and 3 smallholders with 2 ploughs.
  From woodland and grazing 6 pigs; meadow, 1 acre.
Value before 1066, 40s; now 20s.

113 Morin and Hugh hold FLETCHING from the Count. Cana held
it from King Edward. Then and now it answered for 2 hides.
Land for 5 ploughs. In lordship 1 plough;
  11 villagers and 5 smallholders with 4 ploughs.
  Meadow, 6 acres; from woodland 30 pigs.
Value before 1066 £4; now 50s.

114 Gilbert holds ½ hide at BARKHAM from the Count, outside
the Rape. Karl held it from King Edward. It never paid
tax. Land for 1 plough. It is there, with
  3 villagers.
The value was 7s; now 9s.

115 Warner holds 3 virgates in BARKHAM from the Count. It
answers for as much. Earl Godwin held it from King Edward
as a manor, as a freehold. Land for 3 ploughs.
In lordship 1 plough;
  4 villagers and 5 smallholders with 2 ploughs.
  Meadow, 6 acres; from woodland and grazing 9 pigs.
Value before 1066, later and now 20s.

116 Alan holds 1 virgate, 'INWOOD', from the Count. It is outside
the Rape. It lay in (the lands of) the New Minster. It never paid tax.
Aelmer held it as a manor from King Edward. Land for 1½ ploughs.
In lordship 1;
  2 villagers and 2 smallholders with ½ plough.
Value before 1066, 15s; now 10s.

In ROTHERFIELD Hundred
117 The Count holds 2 hides himself which Alfward and Wulfward held
from King Edward as 2 manors. Land for 6 ploughs. Ansfrid
holds 1 hide of this land from the Count; Humphrey 1 virgate;
William 1 virgate and 1 furlong; an Englishman 1 virgate.
In lordship 4½ ploughs;
  6 villagers and 8 smallholders with 6 ploughs.
  1 slave; 1 mill at 30d.
Value before 1066, 30s; now 73s.

Ipse com̃ teñ *MESEWELLE* . Goduiñ tenuit . Tc̃ 7 m̃ p̃ . IIII . hiđ.

Tra . ẽ . II . car̃ . 7 ibi fuñ cũ . IIII . uiℓℓis . 7 v . borđ . In dñio . ẽ una car̃.

De filua: xxx . porc̃ . T.R.E. uaℓℬ . IIII . liℬ . m̃: xL . foliđ.

De hac t̃ra . teñ Wiℓℓs de Warene . III . uirg t̃ræ . 7 uñ moliñ.

TERRA COMITIS ROGERII.

XI. *IN GICESTRE* Ciuitate . T . R . E . erant . c . hagæ . II . 7 dim̃ miñ.

7 . III . croftæ . 7 reddeℬ . xLIX . foliđ . uñ denar̃ miñ.

Modo eft ipfa ciuitas in manu comitis Rogerii . 7 funt in

eifdẽ mafuris . Lx . dom̃ plufquã antea fuerant : 7 ibi uñ

moliñ de . v . foliđ . Reddeℬ . xv . liℬ . Regi: x . liℬ . comiti: c . foℓ:

Modo uaℓ xxv . liℬ : 7 tam̃ redd . xxxv . liℬ.

Hunfrid h̄t ibi . I . hagā de . x . foliđ.

CASTRU HARUNDEL . T . R . E . reddeℬ de q̃dā molino . xL.

foliđ . 7 de . III . conuuiis . xx . foliđ . 7 de uno pafticio . xx . foℓ.

Modo int̃ burgũ 7 portũ aquæ 7 c̃fuetudinẽ nauiũ redđ

XII . liℬ . 7 tam̃ uaℓ . XIII . liℬ . de his h̄t S̃ Nicolaus xxIIII.

foliđ . Ibi una pifcaria de . v . foliđ . 7 uñ moliñ reddę S

x . modia frum̃ti . 7 x . modia groffæ annonæ . Infup̃ . IIII . modia.

Hoc app̃ciat̃ . ẽ . xIIII . liℬ.

Rob̃t fili̾ Tetbaldi h̄t . II . hagas de . II . foliđ . 7 de hōibȝ

extneis h̄t fuũ theloneũ.

Moriñ h̄t ibi c̃fuetuđ de . II . burg̃fibȝ . de . xII . denar̃.

Ernalđ uñ burg̃fe de . xII . deñ . S̃cs Martiñ . I . burg̃fe de . xII . deñ.

Radulf̃ unā hagā de . xII . deñ . Wiℓℓs . v . hagas de . v . foliđ.

Nigellus . v . hagas quæ faciunt feruitiũ.

118 The Count holds MAYFIELD (?) himself. Godwin held it. Then and
now for 4 hides. Land for 2 ploughs. They are there, with
   4 villagers and 5 smallholders. In lordship 1 plough.
   From woodland 30 pigs.
Value before 1066 £4; now 40s.
   Of this land, William of Warenne holds 3 virgates of land and 1 mill.

11   LAND OF EARL ROGER   23 a
(Chichester and Arundel Rapes)

1 In the City of CHICHESTER before 1066 there were 100 sites
less 2½ and 3 crofts. They paid 49s less 1d. This city is now
in Earl Roger's hands. In the same dwelling-sites there
are 60 more houses than there were before.
   A mill at 5s.
They paid £15; £10 to the King, 100s to the Earl;
value now £25; however they pay £35.
   Humphrey Flambard has 1 site there at 10s.

2 ARUNDEL CASTLE before 1066 paid 40s from a mill; 20s for 3
banquets; and 20s for 1 entertainment. Now the Borough and the
harbour and the ship customs between them pay £12;
value, however, £13, of which St. Nicholas' has 24s.
   A fishery at 5s; a mill which pays 10 measures of wheat
      and 10 measures of rough corn; 4 measures in addition.
This is assessed at £14.
   Robert son of Theobald has 2 sites at 2s; he has his tolls
from strangers. Morin has customs dues there from
2 burgesses at 12d; Arnold 1 burgess at 12d; St. Martin's 1 burgess
at 12d; Ralph 1 site at 12d; William 5 sites at 5s; Nigel 5 sites
which do service.

Comes Rogerius ten in dñio *Silletone* . Goduin tenuit.
Tc̄ se defđ p . c . hiđ . ii . 7 dim min . Modo p . xlvii . hiđ.
Tra . ē . xl . car̄ . In dñio sunt . vii . car̄ . 7 qt xx 7 vi . uitti
7 lii . borđ cū . xxxiii . car̄ . Ibi . xvii . serui . 7 ii . molini
de . xii . sot 7 vii . denar̄ . 7 lx . ac̄ pti . de silua . cl . porc̄.
Ibi æcct̃a . in q̃ jaceͫ de hac tra . iii . hidæ 7 una v̄ . Clerici
hn̄t . ii . car̄ 7 v . borđ.

De tra huj M̃ ten Pagen de com̃ . i . hiđ . Witts . i . hiđ . Goisfrid
ii . hiđ . In dñio . i . car̄ . 7 iii . uitti 7 i . borđ . 7 iii . serui . cū dim car̄.
Ad hoc M̃ ptin̄ . ix . hage in Cicestre . redđt . vii . soliđ 7 iiii . den.
7 un̄ molin̄ de . xl . den̄ . 7 de herbagio . xv . soliđ.
Vn̄ monach de S̄ Ebrulfo tęn . i . hidā de tra huj M̃ . Vat . x . sot.
Totū M̃ T.R.E. ualeb qt xx 7 ix . lib̄ . 7 post . lvii . lib̄.
Modo appͨciat qt xx 7 xiii . lib̄ . 7 unā mark auri . Tam
redđ . cxx . lib̄ 7 unā mark auri . qđ ad comitē ptinet.
Qđ clerici ten̄ . viii . lib̄ . 7 tam hn̄t x . lib̄ . Qđ milites . xiiii . lib̄.

Ipse com̃ ten̄ *Bertredtone* . Gida comitissa tenuit.
Tc̄ se defđ p . vii . hiđ . m̊ p . iii . hiđ . Tra . ē . iiii . car̄ . In dñio
sunt . ii . car̄ . 7 viii . uitti 7 ix . borđ cū . ii . car̄ . Ibi . iiii . ac̄ pti.
Ibi æcct̃a . T.R.E. uatb̄ . c . sot . 7 post . lx . sot . Modo . vii . lib̄.

Loventone ten̄ Iuo de com̃ . Goduin tenuit de Goduino.
Tc̄ 7 m̊ se defđ p . ix . hiđ . Tra . ē . v . car̄ . In dñio sunt . ii,
7 x . uitti 7 x . borđ cū . iii . car̄ . Ibi un̄ molin̄ de . vii . sot.
7 in Cicestre . i̊ . haga de . v . denar̄ . T.R.E. 7 m̊ . viii . lib̄.
Ibi ten̄ Wido . i . hidā 7 p tanto se defđ . Aluuard tenuit
de Goduino . p M̃ . nichil . ē ibi . tam uat 7 ualuit . xx . sot.

In SINGLETON Hundred

3 Earl Roger holds SINGLETON in lordship. Earl Godwin held it.
   Then it answered for 100 hides less 2½; now for 47 hides.
   Land for 40 ploughs. In lordship 7 ploughs;
     86 villagers and 52 smallholders with 33 ploughs.
     17 slaves; 2 mills at 12s 7d; meadow, 60 acres; from the
       woodland 150 pigs. A church in whose (lands) lie 3 hides
       and 1 virgate of this land. The clergy have 2 ploughs and
       5 smallholders.
   Payne holds 1 hide of this manor's land from the Earl;
   William 1 hide; Geoffrey 2 hides. In lordship 1 plough;
     3 villagers, 1 smallholder and 3 slaves with ½ plough.
   To this manor belong 9 sites in Chichester which pay 7s 4d.
     1 mill at 40d; from grazing 15s.
   A monk of St. Evroul's holds 1 hide of this manor's land. Value 10s.
   Value of the whole manor before 1066 £89; later £57;
   now it is assessed at £93 and 1 gold mark; however what belongs
   to the Earl pays £120 and 1 gold mark; what the clergy hold £8;
   however, they have £10; what the men-at-arms hold £14.

4 The Earl holds BINDERTON himself. Countess Gytha held it.
   Then it answered for 7 hides; now for 3 hides.
   Land for 4 ploughs. In lordship 2 ploughs;
     8 villagers and 9 smallholders with 2 ploughs.
     Meadow, 4 acres. A church.
   Value before 1066, 100s; later 60s; now £7.

5 Ivo holds LAVANT from the Earl. Godwin held it from
   Earl Godwin. Then and now it answered for 9 hides.
   Land for 5 ploughs. In lordship 2;
     10 villagers and 10 smallholders with 3 ploughs.
     1 mill at 7s; 1 site in Chichester at 5d.
   [Value] before 1066 and now £8.
     Guy holds 1 hide; it answers for as much. Alfward
     held it from Earl Godwin as a manor. Nothing there.
   The value however is and was 20s.

Ipſe cõm teñ in dñio *Hertinges*. Gida comitiſſa
tenuit de rege. E. Tc ſe deſd ꝓ qt xx. hið. modo
ꝓ xl.viii. hið. Tra é. lx.iiii. car. In dñio ſunt. x.c
car. 7 cxxviii. uitti 7 xxxv. bord cũ. li. car.
Ibi. xx. ſerui. 7 ix. molini de iiii. lib 7 xviii. den.
De herbagio. xviii. ſolid. 7 xxx. ac ꝑti. Silua. c. porc.
In Ciceſtre. xi. hagæ de. xv. ſolid.
De tra huj ꝳ teñ clerici de S Nicolao. vi. hið. 7 ibi hñt
vi. uittos 7 vii. bord. cũ. iii. car. 7 ſic fuit T.R.E.
Totũ ꝳ T.R.E. uatb qt xx. lib. 7 poſt. lx. lib. Modo. c. lib.
Ipſe cõm teñ in dñio *Kaitone*. Gida comit tenuit de rege. E.
Tc ſe deſd ꝓ. ix. hið. Modo ꝓ. iiii. Tra é. xxxvi. car. In dñio
ſunt. ii. 7 iiii. uitti 7 x. bord cũ. iii. car. Ibi æccła 7 i. moliñ
de. xii. ſot 7 vi. den. 7 v. ac ꝑti. 7 de ſilua. x. porc.
T.R.E. uatb. lx. ſot. 7 poſt. xxx. ſot. Modo. c. ſot. 7 tamen
ħ. ii. ꝳ Hertinges 7 Traitone redd. cxx. lib. 7 i. mark auri.
Rotb fili Tetbaldi teñ de cõm *Keverde*. Ælard te
nuit de Goduino. Tc 7 m ſe deſd ꝓ. xi. hið. Tra é. vi. car.
In dñio ſunt. ii. 7 viii. uitti 7 viii. bord cũ. iiii. car. Ibi. v.
ſerui. 7 i. moliñ de. xxx. den. 7 vi. ac 7 dim ꝑti. 7 ſilua. x. porc.
De tra huj ꝳ ſuŋ. ii. hidæ in ꝓbenda de cicestre. Rotb
teñ de epo. Offa tenuit de epo in feudo ꝓ ꝳ. ꝓ. ii. hið ſe
deſd tc 7 m. Apꝑciat. viii. ſot. ſed tam. xv. ſot redd.
Totũ ꝳ T.R.E. 7 m. uat. c. ſot. Qdo recep. lx. ſolid.
Hoc ꝳ caluniat abb S *Petri* Winton. Teſtat *HVND*
qd T.R.E. teneb eũ de abbe q̃ reneb. tantm tꝑ uitæ ſuæ.

In DUMPFORD Hundred

6 The Earl holds HARTING in lordship himself. Countess Gytha held   23 b
 it from King Edward. Then it answered for 80 hides; now
 for 48 hides. Land for 64 ploughs. In lordship 10 ploughs;
  128 villagers and 35 smallholders with 51 ploughs.
  20 slaves; 9 mills at £4 18d; from grazing 18s; meadow,
    30 acres; woodland, 100 pigs. In Chichester 11 sites at 15s.
 St. Nicholas' clergy hold 6 hides of this manor's land. They have
  6 villagers and 7 smallholders with 3 ploughs; it was so
    before 1066.
 Value of the whole manor before 1066 £80; later £60; now £100.

7 The Earl holds TROTTON in lordship himself. Countess Gytha
 held it from King Edward. Then it answered for 9 hides;
 now for 3. Land for 36 ploughs. In lordship 2;
  4 villagers and 10 smallholders with 3 ploughs.
  A church; 1 mill at 12s 6d; meadow, 5 acres; from woodland 10 pigs.
 Value before 1066, 60s; later 30s; now 100s; however these two
 manors, Harting and Trotton, pay £120 and 1 gold mark.

8 Robert son of Theobald holds TREYFORD from the Earl. Aethelhard
 held it from Earl Godwin. Then and now it answered for 11 hides.
 Land for 6 ploughs. In lordship 2;
  8 villagers and 8 smallholders with 4 ploughs.
  5 slaves; 1 mill at 30d; meadow, 6½ acres; woodland, 10 pigs.
 2 hides of this manor's land are in the prebend of Chichester church.
 Robert holds it from the Bishop. Offa held it from the Bishop
 as a Holding, as a manor. Then and now it answered for 2 hides.
 It is assessed at 8s, but it pays 15s.
 Value of the whole manor before 1066 and now 100s;
 when acquired 60s.
  The Abbot of St. Peter's of Winchester claims this manor.
 The Hundred testifies that before 1066 the holder held it
 from the Abbot, for the term of his life only.

Titeherste ten Moriñ de com̄. Almar tenuit de

Goduino. in alodiū. Tc 7 m̄ se defđ ꝑ. iiii. hiđ. Tra. e̅. ii. car.

In dn̄io. e̅ una. 7 vi. uilti 7 v. borđ cū. ii. car. Ibi ecctola.

7 iii. serui. 7 i. moliñ de. viii. sot. 7 c. anguilt. 7 v. ac̄ pti.

7 de silua. iii. porc. In Cicestre. i. haga de. vi. denar.

T.R.E. uatb. xl. sot. 7 post. xxx. sot. Modo. lx. sot.

R̄obt ten de com̄ *Stedeha*. Eddiua tenuit de Goduino.

Tc 7 m̄ se defđ ꝑ. xiiii. hiđ. Tra. e̅. xv. car. In dn̄io sunt

iiii. car. 7 xxiii. uilti 7 xvi. borđ cū. x. car. Ibi. x. serui.

7 iii. molini de. xxx. soliđ. 7 iiii. ac̄ pti. 7 silua. xl. porc.

Quadraria. de. vi. sot 7 viii. denar. 7 in cicestre. i. haga

de. vi. den. De hac tra ten un francig. i. hiđ 7 iiii. ac̄s.

Tot co̅ T.R.E. uatb xv. lib. 7 post. viii. lib. Modo. xii. lib.

Isđe R̄obt ten de com̄ *Cochinges*. Azor tenuit de

rege. E. Tc 7 m̄ se defđ ꝑ xii. hiđ. Tra. e̅ xi. car 7 dim.

In dn̄io sunt. ii. 7 xviii. uilti 7 viii. borđ cū. ix. car.

Ibi æccta 7 vi. serui. 7 v. molini de. xxxvii. sot. 7 vi. den.

De hac tra ten Turald de R̄obto dimiđ hidā. 7 h̄t dim

car ibi. 7 in Cicestre. i. haga de. xii. den.

T.R.E. 7 m̄. uat. xv. lib. Qdo recep. x. lib.

Isđ R̄obt ten de com̄ *Lince*. Vluric tenuit de rege. E.

Tc 7 m̄ se defđ ꝑ. v. hiđ. Tra. e̅. vi. car. In dn̄io. est uña.

7 vii. uilti 7 v. borđ cū. ii. car. Ibi æccta 7 ii. serui.

7 iii. ac̄ pti. 7 silua. x. porc. In Cicestre. i. haga de. x. den.

T.R.E. uatb. viii. lib. 7 post. iiii. lib. Modo. c. soliđ.

23 c

Isđe R̄obt ten de com̄ *Botintone*. 7 Radulf de eo. Eduiñ

tenuit de Goduino. Tc 7 m̄ se defđ ꝑ una hida. Tra. e̅. iii.

car. In dn̄io. e̅ una. 7 v. uilti 7 iii. borđ cū. ii. car. Ibi. ii.

serui. T.R.E. uatb. xxx. sot. 7 post 7 m̄. xx. sot.

9 Morin holds CHITHURST from the Earl. Aelmer held it from Earl
  Godwin in freehold. Then and now it answered for 4 hides.
  Land for 2 ploughs. In lordship 1;
    6 villagers and 5 smallholders with 2 ploughs.
      A small church; 3 slaves.
    1 mill at 8s and 100 eels; meadow, 5 acres; from the woodland
      3 pigs; in Chichester 1 site at 6d.
  Value before 1066, 40s; later 30s; now 60s.

[In EASEBOURNE Hundred]
10 Robert holds STEDHAM from the Earl. Edeva held it from
  Earl Godwin. Then and now it answered for 14 hides.
  Land for 15 ploughs. In lordship 4 ploughs;
    23 villagers and 16 smallholders with 10 ploughs.
      A church; 10 slaves.
    3 mills at 30s; meadow, 4 acres; woodland, 40 pigs;
      a quarry at 6s 8d; 1 site in Chichester at 6d.
  A Frenchman holds 1 hide and 4 acres of this land.
  Value of the whole manor before 1066 £15; later £8; now £12.

11 Robert also holds COCKING from the Earl. Azor held it from King
  Edward. Then and now it answered for 12 hides. Land for 11½ ploughs.
  In lordship 2;
    18 villagers and 8 smallholders with 9 ploughs.
      A church; 6 slaves.
    5 mills at 37s 6d.
    Thorold holds ½ hide of this land from Robert. He has
    ½ plough and 1 site in Chichester at 12d.
  Value before 1066 and now £15; when acquired £10.

12 Robert also holds LINCH from the Earl. Wulfric held it from King
  Edward. Then and now it answered for 5 hides. Land for 6 ploughs.
  In lordship 1;
    7 villagers and 5 smallholders with 2 ploughs.
    A church; 2 slaves; meadow, 3 acres; woodland, 10 pigs;
      1 site in Chichester at 10d.
  Value before 1066 £8; later £4; now 100s.

13 Robert also holds BUDDINGTON from the Earl and Ralph from him.   23 c
  Edwin held it from Earl Godwin. Then and now it answered for 1 hide.
  Land for 3 ploughs. In lordship 1;
    5 villagers and 3 smallholders with 2 ploughs. 2 slaves.
  Value before 1066, 30s; later and now 20s.

Seleha͞ ten̄ Roƀt de com̄ . 7 Fulcoius de eo . Codulf te

nuit de Goduino . Tc 7 m̄ se defđ ꝓ . iiii . hiđ . Tra . e͞ . iii . car̄.

In dn̄io . e͞ una . 7 ii . uiłłi 7 ii . borđ cū . i . car . Ibi . ii . serui.

7 un̄ molin̄ de . x . sol 7 c . anguiłł . 7 xvii . ac̄ p̄ti . 7 silua

x . porc . In Cicestre . i . haga de . vii . denar̄.

Tot c̄n̄ T.R.E . uałƀ . iiii . liƀ . 7 post . xxx . sol . Modo . lxii . sol.

Goisfriđ ten̄ de com̄ *Babintone* . Wigot tenuit de

rege . E . Tc 7 m̄ se defđ ꝓ . iiii . hiđ . Tra . e͞ . iiii . car . In dn̄io

est una . 7 x . uiłłi 7 x . borđ cū . iii . car . Ibi æccła . 7 iii.

serui . 7 In Cicestre . i . haga de . x . den.

T.R.E . uałƀ . iiii . liƀ . 7 post . xl . sol . Modo . c . solid.

Wiłłs ten̄ de com̄ *Tadeha͞* . Nigell ten̄ de eo . Vlnod tenuit

de Goduino . Tc 7 m̄ se defđ ꝓ . iiii . hiđ . Tra . e͞ . iii . car . In dn̄io

e͞ una . 7 viii . uiłłi 7 iii . borđ . cū . i . car . 7 tcia pars molini.

de . xiiii . denar . Ibi . viii . ac̄ p̄ti . 7 silua . iii . porc.

T.R.E . 7 m̄ ual xl . sol . Q͞do recep̄ . xx . sol.

Grafha͞ ten̄ de com̄ . iiii . francig . Radulf . iiii . hiđ . Rol

land . ii . hiđ 7 dim . Ernald . ii . hiđ . vi . teigni tenueꝛ T.R.E.

ꝓ c̄n̄ in alodia sua . Tc 7 m̄ se defđ ꝓ . x . hiđ . Tra . e͞

In dn̄io sunt . ii . car 7 dim . 7 vii . uiłłi 7 vi . borđ cū . ii . car.

Ibi æccła . 7 de silua . viii . porc.

T.R.E . uałƀ tot c̄n̄ viii . liƀ . 7 post . vii . liƀ . Modo . viii . liƀ.

Roƀt ten̄ de com̄ *Peteorde* . *In Redrebruge Hvnd*.

Eddeua tenuit de rege . E . in alodiū . Tc 7 m̄ se defđ ꝓ . ix.

hiđ . Tra . e͞ . xii . car . In dn̄io sunt . ii . 7 xxii . uiłłi 7 x . borđ

cū . viii . car . Ibi æccła 7 ix . serui . 7 i . molin̄ de xx . sol . 7 ix . anguiłł.

anguiłł . 7 xxix . ac̄ p̄ti . 7 silua . de q̄t xx . porc . In Cicestre

ii . hag de . xvi . den . De hac tra ten̄ . ii . francig . ii . hiđ.

7 ibi . iii . car 7 dim hūt . 7 ii . uiłłos 7 i . borđ.

Tot c̄n̄ T.R.E . uałƀ xviii . liƀ . 7 post . x . liƀ . Modo . xviii . liƀ.

14 Robert holds SELHAM from the Earl, and Fulk from him.
Cuthwulf held it from Earl Godwin. Then and now it answered
for 4 hides. Land for 3 ploughs. In lordship 1;
  2 villagers and 2 smallholders with 1 plough.
  2 slaves; 1 mill at 10s and 100 eels; meadow, 17 acres;
    woodland, 10 pigs; 1 site in Chichester at 7d.
Value of the whole manor before 1066 £4; later 30s; now 64s.

15 Geoffrey holds BEPTON from the Earl. Wigot held it from
King Edward. Then and now it answered for 4 hides.
Land for 4 ploughs. In lordship 1;
  10 villagers and 10 smallholders with 3 ploughs.
    A church; 3 slaves.
  1 site in Chichester at 10d.
Value before 1066 £4; later 40s; now 100s.

16 William holds TODHAM from the Earl. Nigel holds it from
him. Wulfnoth held it from Earl Godwin. Then and now it
answered for 4 hides. Land for 3 ploughs. In lordship 1;
  8 villagers and 3 smallholders with 1 plough.
  The third part of a mill at 14d; meadow, 8 acres;
    woodland, 3 pigs.
Value before 1066 and now 40s; when acquired 20s.

17 Four Frenchmen hold GRAFFHAM from the Earl. Robert 4 hides;
Roland 2½ hides; Arnold 2 hides. Before 1066 6 thanes held it
as a manor in their freeholds. Then and now it answered
for 10 hides. Land for .... In lordship 2½ ploughs;
  7 villagers and 6 smallholders with 2 ploughs.
  A church; from the woodland, 8 pigs.
Value of the whole manor before 1066 £8; later £7; now £8.

In ROTHERBRIDGE Hundred
18 Robert holds PETWORTH from the Earl. Edeva held it from King
Edward in freehold. Then and now it answered for 9 hides.
Land for 12 ploughs. In lordship 2;
  22 villagers and 10 smallholders with 8 ploughs.
    A church; 9 slaves.
  1 mill at 20s and 189 eels; meadow, 29 acres; woodland
    at 80 pigs; 2 sites in Chichester at 16d.
  Two Frenchmen hold 2 hides of this land. They have 3½ ploughs;
    2 villagers and 1 smallholder.
Value of the whole manor before 1066 £18; later £10; now £18.

Tolintone teñ Robt̃ de cõm̃. *IN ESEBVRNE HVND.*

Eddeua tẽnuit de rege . E . Tc̃ 7 m̃ ſe deſd̃ ᵱ . v . hid̃ . Tra . ẽ

vii . car . In dñio ſunt . ii . 7 xxi . uiłł 7 xi . bord̃ cũ ⸴ v . car .

Ibi . viii . ſerui . 7 i . moliñ de xx . ſoł . 7 cxx . anguiłł .

7 In Ciceſtre . i . haga de . viii . den̄ . 7 xii . ac̃ p̃ti . 7 ſilua . xx . porc̃ .

De hac tra teñ . ii . francig . unã v 7 dim̃ . 7 ibi hñt . v . bord̃ .

T . R . E . uałb̃ . viii . łib̃ . 7 poſt ⸴ c . ſoł . Modo . viii . łib̃ . 7 vi . ſoł .

GRETEHÃ teñ Robt̃ de cõm̃ . Duo teigni tenuer̃ de rege . E .

in alodiũ ᵱ . iiii̷ . Ⓜ . Tc̃ 7 m̃ ſe deſd̃ ᵱ . iiii . hid̃ 7 una v . Tra . ẽ . vii .

car̃ . In dñio ſunt . ii . 7 xiiii . uiłłi 7 ix . bord̃ cũ . iii . car̃ . Ibi . v .

ſerui . 7 i . moliñ de . x . ſoł . 7 Quadraria de . x . ſoł . 7 x . denar̃ .

7 xx . ac̃ p̃ti . 7 ſilua . xxx . porc̃ . De iſto Ⓜ teñ Turſtin . dim̃ hid̃

7 i . v . 7 ibi ht̃ . ii . car̃ . cũ . iii . uiłłis 7 iii . bord̃ .

T . R . E . uałb̃ . vi . łib̃ . 7 poſt ⸴ iiii . łib̃ . 7 m̃ . vi . łib̃ 7 v . ſoł .

DONECHITONE teñ Robt̃ de cõm̃ . *IN REDREBRVGE HD̃.*

Leuuiñ tenuit de rege . E . in alodiũ . Tc̃ 7 m̃ ſe deſd̃ ᵱ . v . hid̃ .

23 d

Tra . ẽ . v . car 7 dim̃ . In dñio ſunt ⸴ ii . car̃ . 7 xv . uiłłi 7 viii . bord̃ cũ

iii . car̃ . Ibi æccła 7 ii . ſerui . 7 iiii . molini de . xxxviii . ſolid̃ . 7 ii . piſcariæ

de . ccc . lx . anguiłł . 7 xxxv . ac̃ p̃ti . 7 ſilua . xv . porc̃ . 7 In Ciceſtre

una haga de . ii . ſolid̃ .

De iſto Ⓜ teñ . iiii . francig unã hid̃ 7 dim̃ . 7 unã v 〔7 x . ac̃s træ .

7 ibi hñt . vi . bord̃ cũ dimid̃ car̃ .

To . T . R . E . uałb̃ . vi . łib̃ . 7 poſt . iii . łib̃ . Modo . vii . łib̃ 7 iii . ſolid̃ .

Iſdẽ Robt̃ teñ de cõm *SVDTONE* . 7 v . teigni tenuer̃ ᵱ Ⓜ in

alodiũ . Tc̃ 7 m̃ ſe deſd̃ ᵱ . viii . hid̃ 7 dim̃ . Tra . ẽ . viii . car 7 dim̃ .

In dñio ſunt . ii . 7 xvii . uiłł 7 xi . bord̃ cũ . iiii . car̃ . Ibi . v . ſerui .

7 iii . molini de . xiii . ſolid̃ 7 ix . den̄ . 7 xxii . ac̃ p̃ti . 7 ſilua . xxx .

porc̃ . De iſto Ⓜ teñ . iii . francig . iii . hid̃ 7 uñ ferding . 7 ibi . i . car̃

in dñio . 7 viii . uiłłi 7 vii . bord̃ cũ . ii . car̃ .

T . R . E . uałb̃ 7 m̃ . x . łib̃ 7 poſt ⸴ vi . łib̃ .

23 c, d

In EASEBOURNE Hundred

19 Robert holds TILLINGTON from the Earl. Edeva held it from King
Edward. Then and now it answered for 5 hides. Land for 7 ploughs.
In lordship 2;
   21 villagers and 11 smallholders with 5 ploughs.
   8 slaves; 1 mill at 20s and 120 eels; 1 site in Chichester
   at 8d; meadow, 12 acres; woodland, 20 pigs.
   2 Frenchmen hold 1½ virgates of this land. They have
   5 smallholders.
Value before 1066 £8; later 100s; now £8 6s.

20 Robert holds GRITTENHAM from the Earl. Two thanes held it from King
Edward in freehold as 3 manors. Then and now it answered for 4
hides and 1 virgate. Land for 7 ploughs. In lordship 2;
   14 villagers and 9 smallholders with 3 ploughs.
   5 slaves; 1 mill at 10s; a quarry at 10s 10d;
   meadow, 20 acres; woodland, 30 pigs.
Thurstan holds ½ hide and 1 virgate of this manor.
He has 2 ploughs, with
   3 villagers and 3 smallholders.
Value before 1066 £6; later £4; now £6 5s.

In ROTHERBRIDGE Hundred

21 Robert holds DUNCTON from the Earl. Leofwin held it from King
Edward in freehold. Then and now it answered for 5 hides.
Land for 5½ ploughs. In lordship 2 ploughs;   23 d
   15 villagers and 8 smallholders with 3 ploughs.
   A church; 2 slaves; 4 mills at 38s; 2 fisheries at 360 eels;
   meadow, 35 acres; woodland, 15 pigs; 1 site in
   Chichester at 2s.
Of this manor 4 Frenchmen hold 1½ hides, 1½ virgates
and 10 acres of land. They have
   6 smallholders with ½ plough.
Total value before 1066 £6; later £3; now £7 3s.

22 Robert also holds SUTTON from the Earl. 5 thanes held it as a manor
in freehold. Then and now it answered for 8½ hides.
Land for 8½ ploughs. In lordship 2;
   17 villagers and 11 smallholders with 4 ploughs.
   5 slaves; 3 mills at 13s 9d; meadow, 22 acres; woodland, 30 pigs.
   3 Frenchmen hold 3 hides and 1 furlong of this manor.
   1 plough in lordship;
      8 villagers and 7 smallholders with 2 ploughs.
Value before 1066 and now £10; when acquired £6.

BERLEVENTONE ten Roƀt de com̃ . 7 Corbelin de eo . Frauuin
tenuit de rege . E . in alodiū . Tc 7 m̃ ſe deſđ ꝓ . v . hiđ . Tra . e . vi .
car . In dñio ſunt . ii . 7 viii . uilli 7 viii . borđ cū . iii . car . Ibi
iiii . ſerui . 7 ii . molini   7 vii . ac̃ ꝑti . 7 ſilua . ii . porc̃ .
T.R.E. ualƀ . c . ſol . 7 poſt . lx . ſol . Modo: vii . liƀ .
CLOTINGA ten Roƀt de com̃ 7 Radulf de eo . Quattuor hões
libi tenuer̃ in alodiū . Tc 7 m̃ ſe deſđ ꝓ . iiii . hiđ . Tra . e . iii . car̃ .
In dñio ſunt . ii . 7 iii . uilli 7 ii . borđ cū . i . car . Ibi . vi . ſerui .
T.R.E. ualƀ . lx . ſol . 7 poſt: xl . ſol . Modo: iiii . liƀ .
STOPEHA ten Roƀt de com̃ . Radulf de eo . Quinq̃ libi hões
tenuer̃ in alodiū . Tc ſe deſđ ꝓ . v . hiđ . m̃ ꝓ . iii . hiđ . Tra . e . v . car̃ .
In dñio . e una . 7 iiii . uilli 7 iiii . borđ cū . i . car . Ibi . i . ſeru . 7 viii .
ac̃ ꝑti . 7 iii . piſcariæ . 7 ſilua: x . porc̃ . 7 In Ciceſtre . i . haga de . iii . deñ .
In eod̃ *HVND* ten Turchil de com̃ unā v̄ . 7 ipſe tenuit de Heraldo .
7 ꝑ una v̄ ſe deſđ . Tra . e . i . car . 7 . ibi . e in dñio cū . i . borđ . 7 i . molino .
Tc 7 m̃ ual . x . ſol .
Roƀt ten de com̃ *BOTECHITONE* . 7 hamelin de eo . Vlmer
tenuit de rege . E . ꝓ . ii . M̃ in alodiū . Tc 7 m̃ ſe deſđ ꝓ . v . hiđ .
Tra . e . v . car̃ . In dñio ſunt . ii . 7 viii . uilli 7 iii . borđ cū . ii .
car̃ . Ibi . ii . ſerui . 7 i . moliñ de . xi . ſol . Piſcaria de . c.c.lxxx .
7 iiii . ac̃ ꝑti . 7 ſilua . ii . porc̃ .
T.R.E. 7 poſt: ualuit . xl . ſol . Modo: c . ſolid .
In eod̃ *HVND* ten Hamelin . i . hiđ 7 dim̃ . 7 ꝓ tanto ſe deſđ .
Vluuin tenuit de rege . E . ꝓ M̃ . Tra . e . i . car . 7 ibi . e in dñio
cū . i . uillo 7 iii . borđ . 7 vi . ac̃ ꝑti . T.R.E. 7 m̃ . ual . xx . ſol .

23 Robert holds BARLAVINGTON from the Earl, and Corbelin from him.
Frawin held it from King Edward in freehold. Then and now
it answered for 5 hides. Land for 6 ploughs. In lordship 2;
   8 villagers and 8 smallholders with 3 ploughs.
   4 slaves; 2 mills ... meadow, 7 acres; woodland, 2 pigs.
Value before 1066, 100s; later 60s; now £7.

24 Robert holds GLATTING from the Earl, and Ralph from him.
4 free men held it in freehold. Then and now it answered
for 4 hides. Land for 3 ploughs. In lordship 2;
   3 villagers and 2 smallholders with 1 plough. 6 slaves.
Value before 1066, 60s; later 40s; now £4.

25 Robert holds STOPHAM from the Earl, and Ralph from him.
5 free men held it in freehold. Then it answered for 5 hides;
now for 3 hides. Land for 5 ploughs. In lordship 1;
   4 villagers and 4 smallholders with 1 plough.
   1 slave; meadow, 8 acres; 3 fisheries; woodland, 10 pigs;
      1 site in Chichester at 3d.
[Value ....].

26 In the same Hundred Thorkell holds 1 virgate from the Earl.
He held it from Harold. It answers for 1 virgate.
Land for 1 plough. It is there, in lordship, with
   1 smallholder.
   1 mill.
Value then and now 10s.

27 Robert holds BURTON from the Earl, and Hamelin from him.
Wulfmer held it from King Edward as 2 manors in freehold.
Then and now it answered for 5 hides. Land for 5 ploughs.
In lordship 2;
   8 villagers and 3 smallholders with 2 ploughs.
   2 slaves; 1 mill at 11s; a fishery at 280 [eels ?]; meadow,
      4 acres; woodland, 2 pigs.
Value before 1066 and later 40s; now 100s.

28 In the same Hundred Hamelin holds 1½ hides. It answers
for as much. Wulfwin held it from King Edward as a
manor. Land for 1 plough. It is there, in lordship, with
   1 villager and 3 smallholders.
   Meadow, 6 acres.
Value before 1066 and now 20s.

In eod *HVND* ten Morin uñ m̄ de cõm . Edric tenuit de rege . E.
in alodiũ . Tc̄ 7 m̄ se defđ ꝑ . 1 . hida . Tra . e̅ . 11 . car̄ . 7 ibi sunt
cū . 111 . uiłłis 7 111 . borđ . 7 11 . seruis . T.R.E. 7 m̄ ualꞇ . xx . soł.
Qdo recep̄ꞇ x . soł.   *IN GHIDENETROI HVND.*

Ipse cõm ten in dñio *BORNE* . Goduin tenuit . Ibi . xxxvi .
hidæ . sed ꝑ xii . hiđ se defđ tc̄ 7 m̄ . Tra . e̅ . xxx . car̄ . In dñio
sunt . 11 . car̄ . 7 xxvii . uiłłi 7 xxxi . borđ cū . xv . car̄ . Ibi . vii . serui .
7 1111 . molini de . xl . soliđ . 7 piscaria de . xvi . deñ . 7 silua . 111 . porc̄.
In Cicestre . vi . hagæ de . xxx . denar̄.
Huic m̄ ꝑtiñ Warblitetone in Hantescire . T.R.E. se defđ
ꝑ . xii . hiđ . m̄ ꝑ . 1111 . hiđ . Tra . e̅   In dñio sunt . 11 . car̄.

24 a

7 xvii . uiłłi 7 xii . borđ cū . v . car̄ . Ibi . 11 . æcclæ . 7 vi . serui
7 uñ moliñ de . x . soł.
De hac tra ten Pagan . 1111 . hiđ . Alric tenuit ad mõnaster̄.
In dñio . e̅ una car̄ . 7 viii . uiłłi 7 v . borđ cū . 11 . car̄ . 7 uñ
moliñ de . x . soliđ . 7 11 . ac pti . In Cicestre . 1 . haga de xii .
denar̄ . Toꞇ m̄ T.R.E. ualꞇ . xxx . liḃ . 7 post̄ꞇ x . liḃ . Modo
xl . liḃ qđ cõm ten̄ 7 tam redđ . l . liḃ . Qđ Pagan teñꞇ
uał 7 ualuit . lx . soliđ.

MEREꝒONE ten Roḃt de cõm 7 Corbeliñ de eo . Aluuiñ
7 Aluric tenuer̄ ꝑ . 11 . m̄ in alodiũ . Tc̄ 7 m̄ se defđ ꝑ . v . hiđ .
Tra . e̅ . vi . car̄ . In dñio sunt . 11 . 7 xiii . uiłłi 7 11 . borđ cū . 1111 .
car̄ . Ibi . v . serui . 7 in Cicestre . 1 . haga de xiiii . deñ.
Fulcoius ten dim hiđ quæ ꝑtiñ huic m̄ . Aluric tenuit in alod̄.
Totũ T.R.E. ualꞇ . 1111 . liḃ 7 x . soł . 7 post xlv . soł . Modo̅ ꞇ c̄ . xv . soł.
RACHETONE ten de cõm Iuo . Fulcoius tenuit de rege . E.
Tc̄ 7 m̄ se defđ ꝑ . v . hiđ . Tra . e̅ . 1111 . car̄ . In dñio . e̅ una car̄
7 viii . uiłłi 7 xiii . borđ cū . 11 . car̄ 7 dim . Ibi . 111 . ac pti . 7 silua
1111 . porc̄ . In Cicestre . 1 . haga de . xx . denar̄.
T.R.E. ualꞇ lx . soł . 7 post̄ꞇ xl . soł . Modo . 1111 . liḃ

23 d. 24 a

29 In the same Hundred Morin holds 1 manor from the Earl.
Edric held it from King Edward in freehold. Then and now
it answered for 1 hide. Land for 2 ploughs; they are there, with
    3 villagers, 3 smallholders and 2 slaves.
Value before 1066 and now 20s; when acquired 10s.

In WESTBOURNE Hundred

30 The Earl holds WESTBOURNE in lordship himself. Earl Godwin
held it. 36 hides there, but then and now it answered for 12 hides.
Land for 30 ploughs. In lordship 2 ploughs;
    27 villagers and 31 smallholders with 15 ploughs.
    7 slaves; 4 mills at 40s; a fishery at 16d; woodland, 3 pigs;
    6 sites in Chichester at 30d.
Warblington in Hampshire belongs to this manor.
Before 1066 it answered for 12 hides; now for 4 hides.
Land for .... In lordship 2 ploughs;
    17 villagers and 12 smallholders with 5 ploughs.
    2 churches; 6 slaves.
    1 mill at 10s.
Payne holds 4 hides of this land. Alric held it for
the monastery. In lordship 1 plough;
    8 villagers and 5 smallholders with 2 ploughs.
    1 mill at 10s; meadow, 2 acres; 1 site in Chichester at 12d.
Value of the whole manor before 1066 £30; later £10;
now, what the Earl holds £40; however it pays £50;
the value of what Payne holds is and was 60s.

24 a

31 Robert holds MARDEN from the Earl, and Corbelin from him.
Alwin and Aelfric held it as 2 manors in freehold.
Then and now it answered for 5 hides. Land for 6 ploughs.
In lordship 2;
    13 villagers and 2 smallholders with 4 ploughs.
    5 slaves; 1 site in Chichester at 14d.
Fulk holds ½ hide which belongs to this manor.
    Aelfric held it in freehold.
Total value before 1066 £4 10s; later 45s; now 115s.

32 Ivo holds RACTON from the Earl. Fulk held it from
King Edward. Then and now it answered for 5 hides.
Land for 4 ploughs. In lordship 1 plough;
    8 villagers and 13 smallholders with 2½ ploughs.
    Meadow, 3 acres; woodland, 4 pigs; 1 site in
    Chichester at 20d.
Value before 1066, 60s; later 40s; now £4.

ngeler ten de com̃ *MEREDONE* . Lepſi tenuit de Gida.

Tc̃ 7 m̃ ſe defd̃ p̃ . iii . hid̃ . Tra . ē . iii . car̃ . In dñio . ē dimid̃ car̃.

7 ii . uitti 7 iii . bord̃ cũ . ii . bob . In Ciceſtre . i . haga de . i . den̓.

T . R . E . uatb̃ . L . ſot . 7 poſt : xx . ſot . Modo : xxx . ſot.

Azo ten̓ de com̃ *MEREDONE* . Aluuin̓ tenuit de rege . E.

in alodiũ . Tc̃ 7 m̃ ſe defd̃ p̃ . iiii . hid̃ . Tra . ē . iiii . car̃ . In dñio

ſunt . ii . 7 vi . uitti 7 iiii . bord̃ eũ . i . car̃ . Ibi . iii . ſerui . In

Ciceſtre . iii . hagæ de . xxi . den̓ . T . R . E . 7 m̃ : Lx . ſot . Q̃do recep̃ :

Witts ten̓ de com̃ *HARDITONE* . Vlſtan tenuit ∫ xxx . ſot.

de rege . E . in alodiũ . Tc̃ 7 m̃ ſe defd̃ p̃ . iiii . hid̃ . Tra . ē . iiii . car̃.

In dñio . ē una . 7 viii . uitti 7 vii . bord̃ cũ . ii . car̃ . Ibi . ii . ſerui.

7 molin̄ de xxx . den̓ . 7 ſilua : iii . porc̃.

T . R . E : uatb̃ . L . ſot . 7 poſt : xxx . ſot . Modo : Lxx . ſolid̃.

Goisfrid ten̓ de com̃ *CONTONE* . Sbern tenuit de Goduino.

Tc̃ 7 m̃ ſe defd̃ p̃ . x . hid̃ . Tra . ē . x . car̃ . In dñio . ē una car̃.

7 xviii . uitti 7 v . bord̃ cũ . v . car̃ . Ibi æccta 7 iiii . ſerui.

In Ciceſtre . ii . hagæ de . ii . ſot . Pbr ten̓ dimid̃ hidã.

T . R . E . 7 m̃ uat . viii . lib̃ . Q̃do recep̃ : c . ſot.

Ipſe com̃ ten̓ in dñio *ESTONE* . Goduin̓ tenuit . Ibi ſunt

xxxvi . hidæ . ſed tc̃ 7 m̃ p̃ . xv . hid̃ ſe defd̃ . De his fuer̃ xvi.

hidæ miſſæ in m̃ *BVRNE* . m̃ iterũ ſunt in *ESTONE* . Tra . ē . xxvi.

car̃ . In dñio ſunt . iii . car̃ . 7 Liiii . uitti 7 xxxv . bord̃ cũ . xxiii.

car̃ . Ibi . v . ſerui . 7 xi . ac pti . 7 ſilua : de . c . porc̃ . In Ciceſtre

xv . hagæ de . vii . ſot 7 viii . den̄ . In hoc m̃ eſt æccta . ad quã

ptin̄ . i . hida 7 dim̃ . 7 ibi ht̃ pbr dim̃ car̃ . Vat hoc . iiii . lib̃.

Tot m̃ T . R . E . uatb̃ xL . lib̃ . 7 poſt : xxx . lib̃ . Modo xL . lib̃ . 7 tam̃

redd̃ . L . lib̃ . ∫ De iſto m̃ eſt una hida in Rapo Witti de braioſe.

7 ſilua mille qñgent porc̃.

33 Engelhere holds MARDEN from the Earl. Leofsi held it
from Countess Gytha. Then and now it answered for 3 hides.
Land for 3 ploughs. In lordship ½ plough;
  2 villagers and 3 smallholders with 2 oxen.
  1 site in Chichester at 1d.
Value before 1066, 50s; later 20s; now 30s.

34 Azor holds MARDEN from the Earl. Alwin held it from King
Edward in freehold. Then and now it answered for 4 hides.
Land for 4 ploughs. In lordship 2;
  6 villagers and 4 smallholders with 1 plough.
  3 slaves; 3 sites in Chichester at 21d.
[Value] before 1066 and now 60s; when acquired 30s.

35 William holds LORDINGTON from the Earl. Wulfstan held it
from King Edward in freehold. Then and now it answered
for 4 hides. Land for 4 ploughs. In lordship 1;
  8 villagers and 7 smallholders with 2 ploughs.
  2 slaves; a mill at 30d; woodland, 3 pigs.
Value before 1066, 50s; later 30s; now 70s.

36 Geoffrey holds COMPTON from the Earl. Esbern held it
from Earl Godwin. Then and now it answered for 10 hides.
Land for 10 ploughs. In lordship 1 plough;
  18 villagers and 5 smallholders with 5 ploughs.
    A church; 4 slaves.
  2 sites in Chichester at 2s.
A priest holds ½ hide.
Value before 1066 and now £8; when acquired 100s.

37 The Earl holds STOUGHTON in lordship himself. Earl Godwin
held it. 36 hides there, but then and now it answered
for 15 hides. 16 of these hides were put in the manor
of Westbourne, but now they are in Stoughton again.
Land for 26 ploughs. In lordship 3 ploughs;
  54 villagers and 35 smallholders with 23 ploughs.
  5 slaves; meadow, 11 acres; woodland at 100 pigs; 15 sites in
    Chichester at 7s 8d.
In this manor is a church, to which 1½ hides belong.
A priest has ½ plough there; value of this £4.
Value of the whole manor before 1066 £40; later £30;
now £40; however, it pays £50.
  1 hide of this manor is in the Rape of William of Braose;
woodland, 1500 pigs.

Aluuin̄ ten̄ de com̄ *MEREDONE* . Goduin tenuit in alodiū.
Tc̄ 7 m̊ se defđ p̄ . II . hiđ . In dn̄io . ē una . cū . VI . borđ.
T.R.E. 7 m̊:´ XL . sol̄ . Q̄do recep̄:´ XX . soliđ.

24 b

Juxta Meredone ten̄ q̄dā Accipitrarius dim̄ hiđ de com̄.
Ipsemet tenuit eā p̄ ꝯ in alodiū. *IN ESTOCBRIGE HVND.*
Eccła S̄ Martini de Sais . ten̄ de com̄ *FISEBORNE*.
Tosti com̄ tenuit . Tc̄ 7 m̊ se defđ p̄ . VI . hiđ . Tra . ē . VI . car̄.
In dn̄io sunt . II . 7 VI . uitti 7 XI . borđ cū . II . car̄ . Ibi un̄
seruus . 7 II . molini de . XL . sol̄ . 7 XXVII . ac̄ p̄ti . In Cicestre
II . hagæ de . XXI . denar̄ . T.R.E.:´ uatb̄ . VI . lib̄ . 7 post . L . sol̄ . M̊:´ VII . lib̄.
Hugo ten̄ de com̄ *WICHE* . 7 Warin̄ de eo . Quinq̄
libi hoēs tenuer̄ p̄ . V . ꝯ . Tc̄ se defđ p̄ . IX . hiđ . Modo
p̄ . VI . hiđ . Tra . ē . IX . car̄ . In dn̄io . ē una car̄ . 7 VI . uitti
7 II . borđ cū . II . car̄ . Ibi . I . seruus . Tc̄ 7 m̊:´ C . sol̄ . Q̄do recep̄:´
Alcher ten̄ de com̄ *MVNDREHĀ* . Gida XL . sol̄.
comitissa tenuit de Goduino . Tc̄ se defđ p̄ . IX . hiđ . m̊
p̄ . VI . hiđ . Tra . ē . VI . car̄ . In dn̄io sunt . II . 7 XIIII . uitti
7 XIII . borđ cū . II . car̄ . Ibi . II . serui . 7 I . molin̄ 7 dimiđ
de . VI . soliđ 7 VIII . den̄ . Ibi eccła . ad quā p̄tin̄ dim̄ hiđ.
Pb̄r h't dim̄ car̄ . T.R.E. 7 m̊:´ uał . VIII . lib̄ . Q̄do recep̄:´ C . sol̄.
In eođ *HVND* ten̄ Chetel tra ad . I . car̄ . Nunq̄ hidata
fuit . Hanc c̄cessit ei . W . rex . Ibi ht̄ . I . molin̄ de . V . sol̄.
7 I . borđ . 7 V . ac̄ p̄ti . Vał . XXV . soliđ.
Wiłłs ten̄ de com̄ *HVNESTAN* . Sex libi hoēs tenuer̄
in alodiū . Tc̄ 7 m̊ se defđ p̄ . IIII . hiđ . Tra . ē . IIII . car̄.
In dn̄io . ē una car̄ . 7 V . uitti 7 XIX . borđ cū . II . car̄.
Ibi un̄ molin̄ de . XX . soliđ . 7 II . salinæ . 7 de . I . haga . VI . den̄.
T.R.E. uatb̄ XL . sol̄ . 7 post:´ XXX . soliđ . Modo:´ IIII . lib̄.

38 Alwin holds MARDEN from the Earl. Godwin held it in freehold.
Then and now it answered for 2 hides. In lordship 1, with
  6 smallholders.
Value before 1066 and now 40s; when acquired 20s.
  Near Marden a falconer holds ½ hide from the Earl.   24 b
He held it as a manor in freehold.

  In STOCKBRIDGE Hundred
39 St. Martin's Church, Sees, holds FISHBOURNE from the Earl.
Earl Tosti held it. Then and now it answered for 6 hides.
Land for 6 ploughs. In lordship 2;
  6 villagers and 11 smallholders with 2 ploughs.
  1 slave; 2 mills at 40s; meadow, 27 acres; 2 sites in Chichester at 21d.
Value before 1066 £6; later 50s; now £7.

40 Hugh holds RUMBOLDSWHYKE from the Earl, and Warin from him.
5 free men held it as 5 manors. Then it answered for 9 hides;
now for 6 hides. Land for 9 ploughs. In lordship 1 plough;
  6 villagers and 2 smallholders with 2 ploughs. 1 slave.
[Value] then and now 100s; when acquired 40s.

41 Alchere holds MUNDHAM from the Earl. Countess Gytha
held it from Earl Godwin. Then it answered for 9 hides; now for 6
hides. Land for 6 ploughs. In lordship 2;
    14 villagers and 13 smallholders with 2 ploughs.
    2 slaves. 1½ mills at 6s 8d. A church, to which ½ hide belongs.
    A priest has ½ plough.
Value before 1066 and now £8; when acquired 100s.

42 In the same Hundred Ketel holds land for 1 plough. It was never
hidated. King William assigned it to him. He has
  1 mill at 5s.
  1 smallholder.
  Meadow, 5 acres.
  Value 25s.

43 William holds HUNSTON from the Earl. 6 free men held
it in freehold. Then and now it answered for 4 hides.
Land for 4 ploughs. In lordship 1 plough;
  5 villagers and 19 smallholders with 2 ploughs.
  1 mill at 20s; 2 salt-houses; from 1 site, 6d.
Value before 1066, 40s; later 30s; now £4.

Iſdē Witts ten̄ de com̄ BRIDEHĀ. IN WESTRINGES HD̄.

7 Nigell de eo . Alnod tēhuit in Alodiū . Tc 7 m̄ ſe defd̄

p . III . hid̄ 7 dim̄ . Tra . ē . v . car̄ . In dn̄io ſunt . ii . 7 v ; uitti

7 VIII . bord̄ cū . III . car̄ . Ibi . I . molin de . xx . ſot . 7 ii . piſcariæ.

7 III . ac̄ p̄ti . De ſilua 7 herbagio . v . porc̄ .   ſ 7 ii . bord̄.

De iſto m̄ ten̄ Anſchitil . I . hid̄ 7 dim̄ . 7 hr̄ ibi ; I . car̄ 7 I . uitt.

Totū T . R . E . uat̄b . xl . ſot . 7 poſt.′ xxx . ſot . Modo .′ LXV . ſolid̄.

Warin ten̄ de com̄ ICENORE . Leuuin tenuit de Go

duino . Tc 7 m̄ ſe defd̄ p una hid̄ . Tra . ē . I . car̄ ; Iñ dn̄io . ē

una car̄ . 7 III . uitti 7 III . bord̄ cū . I . car̄ . Ibi ; I . ac̄ p̄ti.

T . R . E . uat̄b xx . ſot . 7 poſt.′ xv . ſot . Modo .′ xxii . ſolid̄.

Rainald ten̄ de com̄ SVMERLEGE . Helghi tenuit

de rege . E . in alodiū . Tc 7 m̄ ſe defd̄ p . I . hida . Tra . ē . I . car̄.

In dn̄io . ē una . 7 II . uitti 7 III . bord̄ . cū . I . car̄ . Ibi . I , ſeru.

T . R . E . 7 m̄ .′ uat xx . ſolid̄ . Qdo recep̄ .′ xv , ſot.

Radulf ten̄ de Rob̄to 7 Rob̄t de com̄ WESTRINGES.

Duo lib̄i hōes tenuer̄ p . II . m̄ . Tc 7 m̄ ſe defd̄ p . I . hida.

Tra . ē . I . car̄ . Ibi ſunt . IIII . uitti cū . II . car̄ . 7 I . haga de . VI . den.

T . R . E . 7 poſt . 7 m̄ .′ uat . xx . ſolid̄ . IN ISIWIRIDI HVND.

Rob̄t ten̄ de com̄ ESTORCHETONE , 7 Durand ten̄ de eo.

Tc ſe defd̄ p . VI . hid̄ . m̄ p . v . hid̄ 7 dim̄ . Tra . III . car̄.

In dn̄io ſunt . ii . car̄ . 7 VI . uitti 7 VII . cot . cū . I . car̄ . Ibi æccta.

7 II . molini de . xi . ſot . T . R . E . 7 m̄ . uat . IIII . lib̄ . 7 poſt.′ xL . ſot.

Rob̄t ten̄ de com̄ STORCHESTONE . 7 Aluuin de illo.

7 iſtemet tenuit T . R . E . 7 q̄libet ire potuit . Tc 7 m̄ p . III . hid̄.

24 c

Tra . ē . II . car̄ . In dn̄io . ē una car̄ cū . I . uitto 7 v . cot . 7 II.

ſeruis . 7 molin de . v . ſot . T . R . E . 7 poſt . 7 m̄ . uat xxx . ſot.

In WITTERING Hundred

44 William also holds BIRDHAM from the Earl, and Nigel from him.
Alnoth held it in freehold. Then and now it answered for 3½ hides.
Land for 5 ploughs. In lordship 2;
　5 villagers and 8 smallholders with 3 ploughs.
　1 mill at 20s; 2 fisheries; meadow, 3 acres; from
　　woodland and grazing 5 pigs.
　Ansketel holds 1½ hides of this manor. He has 1 plough
　　1 villager and 2 smallholders.
Total value before 1066, 40s; later 30s; now 65s.

45 Warin holds ITCHENOR from the Earl. Leofwin held it
from Earl Godwin. Then and now it answered for 1 hide.
Land for 1 plough. In lordship 1 plough;
　3 villagers and 3 smallholders with 1 plough.
　Meadow, 1 acre.
Value before 1066, 20s; later 15s; now 22s.

46 Reginald holds SOMERLEY from the Earl. Helgi held it
from King Edward in freehold. Then and now it answered
for 1 hide. Land for 1 plough. In lordship 1;
　2 villagers and 3 smallholders with 1 plough. 1 slave.
Value before 1066 and now 20s; when acquired 15s.

47 Ralph holds (WEST?) WITTERING from Robert, and Robert holds it
from the Earl. 2 free men held it as 2 manors.
Then and now it answered for 1 hide. Land for 1 plough.
　4 villagers with 2 ploughs.
　1 site at 6d.
Value before 1066, later and now 20s.

In EASEWRITHE Hundred

48 Robert holds STORRINGTON from the Earl, and Durand holds
from him. Then it answered for 6 hides; now for 5½ hides.
Land for 3 ploughs. In lordship 2 ploughs;
　6 villagers and 7 cottagers with 1 plough.
　A church. 2 mills at 11s.
Value before 1066 and now £4; later 40s.

49 Robert holds STORRINGTON from the Earl, and Alwin from him.
He held it himself before 1066; he could go wherever he would.
Then and now [it answered] for 3 hides. Land for 2 ploughs.　　24 c
In lordship 1 plough, with
　1 villager, 5 cottagers and 2 slaves.
　A mill at 5s.
Value before 1066, later and now 30s.

CODEHÁ teń Rob̃t de com̃ . 7 Alb̃ic de illo . Duo lib̃i

hōes tenueŕ T.R.E.Tc̃ 7 m̃ ſe defd̃ ꝑ.IIII.hid̃ 7 una v́.

Tra.ē.III.car̃. In dñio ſunt.II.7 IIII.uiłłi 7 v.cot̃ cū

dim̃ car̃.T.R.E.7 poſt.7 m̃.⸍uał.III.lib̃.

In eod̃ m̃ teń Rob̃t de com̃.II.hid̃ 7 unā v́.7 ꝑ tantò

ſe defd̃.Duo lib̃i hōes tenueŕ.Tra.ē.II.car̃.7 ibi ſunt

in dñio cū.I.uiłło 7 I.cot̃.T.R.E.7 poſt.7 m̃.⸍uał.xx.ſoł.

PERHAM teń Rob̃t de com̃.Toui q̃dā lib̃ hō tenuit

Tc̃ 7 m̃ ſe defd̃ ꝑ.III.hid̃.Tra.ē.II.car̃.In dñio eſt una

7 dim̃.7 II.uiłłi 7 I.cot̃ cū dim̃ car̃.7 I.moliñ de.xxx.deń.

T.R.E.7 poſt.7 m̃.⸍uał.III.lib̃.

NORDBORNE teń idē Rob̃t de com̃.Wariń de eo.

Duo lib̃i hōes tenueŕ T.R.E.Tc̃ 7 m̃ ſe defd̃ ꝑ.VI.hid̃.

Tra.ē.VI.car̃.In dñio.ē una 7 xx.uiłłi 7 IIII.cot̃ cū

VII.car̃.7 II.molini de.xxv.ſoł.Ibi ⸗VII.ac̃ ꝑti.Silua⸍

de.XII.porc̃.T.R.E.7 m̃.⸍uał.VII.lib̃.Q̃do recep⸍VI.lib̃.

ROgeri teń de com̃ NITINBREHÁ.7 Aluuard̃ de eo.

Leuuiñ tenuit T.R.E.7 q̃ uoluit ire potuit.Tc̃ 7 m̃ ſe defd̃

ꝑ.IIII.hid̃.Tra.ē.v.car̃.7 xvi.uiłłi 7 III.cot̃ cū.IIII.car̃.

7 III.ac̃ ꝑti.7 ſilua⸍de.x.porc̃.T.R.E.7 poſt.7 m̃.⸍uał.III.lib̃.

ROt̃b̃t teń de com̃ POLEBERGE.Vluric̃ tenuit.T.R.E.

Tc̃ 7 m̃ ſe defd̃ ꝑ.xvi.hid̃.Tra.ē.xvIII.car̃.In dñio

ſunt.IIII.car̃.7 xxxv.uiłłi 7 xv.cot̃ cū xIII.car̃.

Ibi.Ix.ſerui.7 II.molini de.xI.ſoł.7 xxx.ac̃ ꝑti.7 ſilua⸍

de.xxv.porc̃.7 II.piſcariæ de.III.ſoł.Ibi.II.æccłæ.

De tra huj̃ m̃ teń Tetbald̃ 7 Iuo.II.hid̃ 7 dim̃ virgā.

7 ibi in dñio.I.car̃.7 III.uiłłi 7 IIII.cot̃ cū.I.car̃.

Totū m̃ T.R.E.uałb̃.xvI.lib̃.7 poſt⸍xvI.lib̃.Modo⸍

dñium Rob̃ti⸍xxII.lib̃.Hominū⸍xxxv.ſoł.

50 Robert holds COOTHAM from the Earl, and Aubrey from him.
2 free men held it before 1066. Then and now it answered
for 4 hides and 1 virgate. Land for 3 ploughs. In lordship 2;
  4 villagers and 5 cottagers with ½ plough.
Value before 1066, later and now £3.

51 In the same manor Robert holds 2 hides and 1 virgate from the Earl.
It answers for as much. 2 free men held it. Land for 2 ploughs.
They are there, in lordship, with
  1 villager and 1 cottager.
Value before 1066, later and now 20s.

52 Robert holds PARHAM from the Earl. Tovi, a free man, held it.
Then and now it answered for 3 hides. Land for 2 ploughs.
In lordship 1½;
  2 villagers and 1 cottager with ½ plough.
  1 mill at 30d.
Value before 1066, later and now £3.

53 Robert holds NUTBOURNE from the Earl, and Warin from him.
2 free men held it before 1066. Then and now it answered
for 6 hides. Land for 6 ploughs. In lordship 1;
  20 villagers and 4 cottagers with 7 ploughs.
  2 mills at 25s; meadow, 7 acres; woodland at 12 pigs.
Value before 1066 and now £7; when acquired £6.

54 Roger holds NYETIMBER from the Earl, and Alfward from him.
Leofwin held it before 1066; he could go where he would.
Then and now it answered for 4 hides. Land for 5 ploughs.
  16 villagers and 3 cottagers with 4 ploughs.
  Meadow, 3 acres; woodland at 10 pigs.
Value before 1066, later and now £3.

55 Robert holds PULBOROUGH from the Earl. Wulfric held it
before 1066. Then and now it answered for 16 hides.
Land for 18 ploughs. In lordship 4 ploughs;
  35 villagers and 15 cottagers with 13 ploughs.
  9 slaves; 2 mills at 11s; meadow, 30 acres; woodland at 25 pigs;
    2 fisheries at 3s. 2 churches.
    Theobald and Ivo hold 2 hides and ½ virgate of this
      manor's land. In lordship 1 plough;
    3 villagers and 4 cottagers with 1 plough.
Value of the whole manor before 1066 £16; later £16;
now, Robert's lordship £22; the mens' 35s.

GRETHA ten Ernucion de com̄. Azor tenuit .de rege . E.

Tc̄ ſe deſđ ꝓ . v . hiđ . M̄ eſt . i . hida in Rapo Witti de braioſ.

Tra . ē . iii . car̄ . In dn̄io ſunt . ii . 7 x . uilti 7 vii . cot cū

ii . car̄ . 7 iiii . piſcariæ de . v . ſoliđ.

T.R.E. ualb̄ . vi . lib̄ . 7 poſt . 7 m̄ . c . ſol.

Rotb̄t ten de com̄ CILLETONE . 7 Oſulf de eo . Azor tenuit

de rege . E . Tc̄ ſe deſđ ꝓ . vi . hiđ . m̄ ſunt . iii . hidæ in rapo

Witti de braioſe . Tra . ē . iii . car̄ . In dn̄io . ē una car̄ . 7 iiii.

uilti 7 ii . cot cū . i car̄ . Ibi æccta . Tc̄ 7 poſt . 7 m̄ . xxx . ſot.

In SILLINTONE ten Rotb̄ unā v̄ . Vluuard tenuit de

rege . E . Ibi . ē un uilts cū dim car̄ . Vat 7 ualuit . ii . ſot.

Ipſe com̄ ten in dn̄io LOLINMINSTRE . IN RISBERG HĐ.

Rex . E . tenuit in dn̄io . Ibi . xx . hidæ . Nunq geldau.

Tra . ē . xl.iiii . car̄ . In dn̄io ſunt . iiii . car̄ . 7 lxviii . uilti

7 xl.iii . cot . cū xl . car̄ . Ibi æccta . 7 molin de . v . ſoliđ.

7 ii . ſalinæ de . xx . deñ . 7 viii . ac̄ p̄ti . 7 ſilua . xxx . porc̄.

T.R.E. 7 poſt . 7 m̄ . uat . l . lib̄.

Ibiđ ten Rotb̄ . i . hiđ de com̄ . Azor tenuit . Nūq geldau.

Ibi . vi . ac̄ p̄ti . 7 lx . ac̄ paſturæ . Vat 7 ualuit . x . ſoliđ.

24 d

TOTINTONE ten Rotb̄ de com̄ . Azor tenuit de regē . E.

Tc̄ 7 m̄ ſe deſđ ꝓ . iiii . hiđ . Tra . ē . iiii . car̄ . In dn̄io ſunt . ii . car̄.

7 x . uilti 7 xi . cot . cū . ii . car̄ . 7 vi . ac̄ p̄ti . 7 un ſeruus

T.R.E. 7 poſt . uat . lx . ſot . m̄ . lxx . ſoliđ.

Nigellus ten WARNECHA . Turgot tenuit de rege . E . Tc̄

7 m̄ ſe deſđ ꝓ . iiii . hiđ . Tra . ē . iii . car̄ . In dn̄io . ē una car̄.

7 iii . uilti 7 iii . cot cū . i . car̄ . 7 viii . ac̄ p̄ti.

De hac tra ten Raſin de Nigello . iii . hiđ . 7 ibi . i . car̄ in dn̄io.

7 viii . uilti 7 iii . cot cū . ii . car̄ . Ibi . xxiiii . ac̄ p̄ti . 7 ii . piſcariæ.

de . xviii . denar̄ . Silua de . iii . porc̄

Totū ꝳ T.R.E. ualb̄ . lx . ſot . 7 poſt . xx . ſot . Modo . l . ſot.

56 Ernucion holds GREATHAM from the Earl. Azor held it from King
Edward. Then it answered for 5 hides; now 1 hide is in the Rape
of William of Braose. Land for 3 ploughs. In lordship 2;
   10 villagers and 7 cottagers with 2 ploughs.
   4 fisheries at 5s.
Value before 1066 £6; later and now 100s.

57 Robert holds (WEST) CHILTINGTON from the Earl, and Oswulf from him.
Azor held it from King Edward. Then it answered for 6 hides;
now 3 hides are in the Rape of William of Braose.
Land for 3 ploughs. In lordship 1 plough.
   4 villagers and 2 cottagers with 1 plough.
   A church.
[Value] then, later and now 30s.

58 Robert holds 1 virgate in SULLINGTON. Wulfward held it
from King Edward.
   1 villager with ½ plough.
The value is and was 2s.

In POLING Hundred

59 The Earl holds LYMINSTER himself, in lordship. King Edward
held it in lordship. 20 hides. It never paid tax.
Land for 44 ploughs. In lordship 4 ploughs;
   68 villagers and 43 cottagers with 40 ploughs.
   A church. A mill at 5s; 2 salt-houses at 20d; meadow, 8 acres;
     woodland, 30 pigs.
Value before 1066, later and now £50.

60 Robert also holds 1 hide from the Earl there. Azor held it.
It never paid tax.
   Meadow, 6 acres; pasture, 60 acres.
The value is and was 10s.

61 Robert holds TODDINGTON from the Earl. Azor held it from   24 d
King Edward. Then and now it answered for 4 hides.
Land for 4 ploughs. In lordship 2 ploughs;
   10 villagers and 11 cottagers with 2 ploughs.
   Meadow, 6 acres; 1 slave.
Value before 1066 and later 60s; now 70s.

62 Nigel holds WARNINGCAMP. Thorgot held it from King Edward.
Then and now it answered for 4 hides. Land for 3 ploughs.
In lordship 1 plough;
   3 villagers and 3 cottagers with 1 plough.
   Meadow, 8 acres.
Rafwin holds 3 hides of this land from Nigel. In lordship, 1 plough;
   8 villagers and 3 cottagers with 2 ploughs.
   Meadow, 24 acres; 2 fisheries at 18d; woodland at 3 pigs.
Value of the whole manor before 1066, 60s; later 20s; now 50s.

Abbatia de Almanefches ten de com̃ NONNEMINSTRE.

Efmund tenuit de rege . E . Tc̃ 7 m̃ fe defd̃ p̃ xiii . hid̃ . Tra . e͂ . xii .
car̃ . In dñio funt . iii . car̃ . 7 lix . uilli . 7 xii . cot cũ . xvii . car̃ .
Ibi æccła 7 iiii . ferui . 7 ii . falinæ de xxx . den̄ . Silua ꝰ de xx . porc̃ .
T . R . E . uałb xx . lib̃ . 7 poft ꝰ xvi . lib̃ . Modo ꝰ xxv . lib̃ .

Ibid̄ten̄ Roger de ipfa abbatia . i . hid̃ . Efmeld pb̃r tenuit
7 nũnq geldauit . Tra . e͂ . i . car̃ . Ibi eft in dñio . cũ . ix . cot .
7 xxv . ac̃ p̃ti . 7 i . pifcaria de . ii . folid̃ . 7 lx . ac̃ pafturæ .
7 Adhuc ten̄ Roger de ipfa abbatia . i . hid̃ . Aluuin̄ tenuit
de rege . E . Tra . e͂ . ii . car̃ . p̃ una hida fe defd̃ . Ibi funt . iiii .
uilli 7 vi . cot cũ . ii . car̃ . 7 molin̄ de . xxx . den̄ .
Hæ . ii . hidæ . T . R . E . 7 poft . 7 m̃ uał . lx . folid̃ .

Warin ten de com̃ ANGEMARE . Goduin̄ tenuit . Tc̃ fe
defd̃ p̃ . v . hid̃ . Modo . e͂ una ex his hd̃ in Rapo de braiofe
Tra . e͂ . ii . car̃ . In dñio . e͂ una . 7 vi . uilli 7 iiii . cot cũ . i . car̃ .
T . R . E . 7 poft . 7 m̃ ꝰ uał . xl . folid̃ .

Goisfrid ten̄ de com̃ ANGEMARE . Tres libi ho͂es tenuer̃
T . R . E . Tc̃ fe defd̃ p̃ . v . hid̃ . m̃ una ex his hd̃ e͂ in Rapo Wilłi
de braiofe . Tra . e͂ . ii . car̃ . In dñio . e͂ una . 7 vi . uilli 7 ii . cot
cũ . ii . car̃ . Ibi . iii . ac̃ p̃ti . 7 filua ꝰ de . iii . porc̃ .
T . R . E . 7 poft ꝰ uał , l . fol . m̃ . lx . folid̃ .

Rainald ten de com̃ STOCHES . Brixi tenuit de rege . E .
Tc̃ 7 m̃ fę defd̃ p̃ . viii . hid̃ . Tra . e͂ . vii . car̃ . In dñio funt . iii .
car̃ . 7 xvi . uilli 7 xvi . cot cũ . iiii . car̃ . Ibi æccła . 7 v . ferui .
7 ii . pifcariæ de . x . den̄ . T . R . E . 7 poft . 7 m̃ ꝰ ual . xx . lib̃ .

Rogeri ten de com̃ BERCHEHA . 7 Aluuard de eo . Leuuin̄
tenuit de rege . E . Tc̃ 7 m̃ fe defd̃ p̃ . v . hid̃ . Tra . e͂ . iiii . car̃ .
In dñio funt . iii . car̃ . 7 viii . uilli 7 xii . cot cũ . iii . car̃ . Ibi æccła
7 x . ferui . 7 viii . ac̃ p̃ti . 7 filua ꝰ iii . porc̃ . T . R .
T . R . E . 7 poft . 7 m̃ . uał viii . lib̃ . 7 tam̃ redd . x . lib̃ .

63   Almenesches Abbey holds 'NUNMINSTER' from the Earl. Esmelt
the priest held it from King Edward. Then and now it answered
for 13 hides. Land for 12 ploughs. In lordship 3 ploughs;
    59 villagers and 12 cottagers with 17 ploughs.
   A church; 4 slaves; 2 salt-houses at 30d; woodland
     at 20 pigs.
Value before 1066 £20; later £16; now £25.

64   Roger also holds 1 hide there from the Abbey. Esmelt the priest
held it.. It never paid tax. Land for 1 plough. It is there,
in lordship, with,
    9 cottagers.
    Meadow, 25 acres; 1 fishery at 2s; pasture, 60 acres.
Further, Roger holds 1 hide from the Abbey. Alwin held it
from King Edward. Land for 2 ploughs. It answers for 1 hide.
    4 villagers and 6 cottagers with 2 ploughs.
    A mill at 30d.
Value of these 2 hides before 1066, later and now 60s.

65   Warin holds ANGMERING from the Earl. Earl Godwin held it.
Then it answered for 5 hides; now 1 of these hides is in the
Rape of William of Braose. Land for 2 ploughs. In lordship 1;
   6 villagers and 4 cottagers with 1 plough.
Value before 1066, later and now 40s.

66   Geoffrey holds ANGMERING from the Earl. 3 free men held it
before 1066. Then it answered for 5 hides; now 1 of these hides
is in the Rape of William of Braose. Land for 2 ploughs.
In lordship 1;
    6 villagers and 2 cottagers with 2 ploughs.
    Meadow, 3 acres; woodland at 3 pigs.
Value before 1066 and later 50s; now 60s.

67   Reginald holds (NORTH) STOKE from the Earl. Brictsi held it
from King Edward. Then and now it answered for 8 hides.
Land for 7 ploughs. In lordship 3 ploughs;
    16 villagers and 16 cottagers with 4 ploughs.
    A church; 5 slaves; 2 fisheries at 10d.
Value before 1066, later and now £20.

68   Roger holds BURPHAM from the Earl, and Alfward from him.
Leofwin held it from King Edward. Then and now it answered for 5 hides.
Land for 4 ploughs. In lordship 3 ploughs;
    8 villagers and 12 cottagers with 3 ploughs.
    A church; 10 slaves; meadow, 8 acres; woodland, 3 pigs.
Value before 1066, later and now £8; however it pays £10.

Robtus ten de com *PRESTETVNE* . Vlueua q̄dā lib̃a femina

tenuit . T.R.E. Tc̄ 7 m̃ ſe deſd̃ ꝑ . vII . hid̃ . Tra . ē . IIII . car̃ . Ibi

ſunt . xIIII . uiłłi 7 I . cot cū . IIII . car̃ . 7 III . ſalinæ de . xxx . den̄ . VI . II . lib̃ .

Iſd̃e Robt ten de com *GARINGES* . Bereuuica fuit regis . E.

Ibi . vI . hidæ . Nunꝗ geldau . Tra . ē . vII . car̃ . In dn̄io ſunt . II .

car̃ . 7 xx . uiłłi 7 xII . cot cū . v . car̃ . Val 7 ualuit ſēp . IIII . lib̃ .

Robt ten de com *GARINGES* . Goduin un lib̃ hō te

nuit T.R.E. Tc̄ ſe deſd̃ ꝑ xI . hid̃ . m̃ hт̃ Wiłłs de braioſe

in rapo ſuo . II . hid̃ . Tra . ē . IIII . car̃ . In dn̄io ſunt . II . car̃ .

25 a

7 xIII . uiłłi 7 vIII . cot cū . II . car̃ . T.R.E. 7 poſt 7 m̃ . ual . c . ſol .

Iſd̃e Robt ten de com *GARINGES* . Gondrede tenuit de

rege . E. Tc̄ ſe deſd̃ ꝑ . IIII . hid̃ . m̃ ꝑ . II . 7 dim̃ . ꝗa una 7 dim̃ hт̃

eſt in Rapo Wiłłi de braioſe . Tra . ē . I . car̃ . 7 ibi . ē in dn̄io . cū . II .

uiłłis . 7 ibi . III . ãc p̃ti . T.R.E. 7 poſt . 7 m̃ . ual . xx . ſol .

Id̃e Robt ten de com *GARINGES* . Tres libi hōēs tenuer̃ . T.R.E.

Tc̄ ſe deſd̃ ꝑ vIII . hid̃ . m̃ ꝑ . v . hid̃ 7 dim̃ . Qd̃ reſtat . ē in Rapo

Wiłłi de braioſe . Tra . ē . III . car̃ . In dn̄io ſunt . II . car̃ . 7 vI . uiłłi

7 III . cot cū . I . car̃ . 7 II . ãc p̃ti . Val 7 ualuit ſēp . xL . ſol .

Picotus ten de com *WEPEHÃ* . Duo libi hōēs . tenuer̃ . T.R.E.

Tc̄ 7 m̃ ſe deſd̃ ꝑ . vIII . hid̃ . Tra . ē . vI . car̃ . In dn̄io ſunt . II .

7 molin̄ de . xxx . den̄ . 7 x . ãc p̃ti . Silua . de . III . porc̃ . 7 II . piſ

cariæ de . III . ſol . 7 xvIII . uiłłi 7 Ix . cot cū . IIII . car̃ .

T.R.E. ualb̃ . vIII . lib̃ . 7 poſt . Ix . lib̃ . Modo . x . lib̃ .

CLEPINGES ten abbatia de almaneſches de com in elemoſina.

Goduin tenuit . Tc̄ 7 m̃ ſe deſd̃ ꝑ xI . hid̃ . Tra . ē . Ix . car̃ . 7 xxvI ,

uiłłi 7 xxIIII . cot cū . vII . car̃ . Ibi æccła . 7 xII . ãc p̃ti . Silua . xx .

T.R.E. ualb̃ . xx . lib̃ . 7 poſt . 7 m̃ . xv . lib̃ .   �“ porc̃ .

69 Robert holds (EAST) PRESTON from the Earl. Wulfeva, a free woman, held it before 1066. Then and now it answered for 7 hides.
Land for 4 ploughs.
    14 villagers and 1 cottager with 4 ploughs.
    3 salt-houses at 30d.
Value £4.

70 Robert also holds GORING from the Earl. It was an outlier of King Edward's (lands). 6 hides. It never paid tax. Land for 7 ploughs.
In lordship 2 ploughs;
    20 villagers and 12 cottagers with 5 ploughs.
The value is and always was £4.

71 Robert holds GORING from the Earl. Godwin, a free man, held it before 1066. Then it answered for 11 hides; now William of Braose has 2 hides in his Rape. Land for 4 ploughs. In lordship 2 ploughs.
    13 villagers and 8 cottagers with 2 ploughs.
Value before 1066, later and now 100s.

25 a

72 Robert also holds GORING from the Earl. Gundrada held from King Edward. Then it answered for 4 hides; now for 2½ because 1½ hides are in the Rape of William of Braose. Land for 1 plough.
It is there, in lordship, with
    2 villagers.
    Meadow, 3 acres.
Value before 1066, later and now 20s.

73 Robert also holds GORING from the Earl. 3 free men held it. before 1066. Then it answered for 8 hides; now for 5½ hides. The rest is in the Rape of William of Braose.
Land for 3 ploughs. In lordship 2 ploughs;
    6 villagers and 3 cottagers with 1 plough.
    Meadow, 2 acres.
The value is and always was 40s.

74 Picot holds WEPHAM from the Earl. 2 free men held it before 1066. Then and now it answered for 8 hides.
Land for 6 ploughs. In lordship 2.
    A mill at 30d; meadow, 10 acres; woodland at 3 pigs;
      2 fisheries at 3s.
    18 villagers and 9 cottagers with 4 ploughs.
Value before 1066 £8; later £9; now £10.

75 Almenesches Abbey holds CLIMPING from the Earl in alms.
Earl Godwin held it. Then and now it answered for 11 hides.
Land for 9 ploughs.
    26 villagers and 24 cottagers with 7 ploughs.
    A church; meadow, 12 acres; woodland, 10 pigs.
Value before 1066 £20; later and now £15.

In eod Manerio ten Ŝ Maruɴ de Sais de com in elemoſina
xi . hiđ . 7 ꝑ tanto ſe defđ . T.R.E. 7 m̃ . Goduin tenuit . Ꞇra . ē
ix . car̄ . In dñio ſunt . ii . car̄ . 7 xxvi . uiłłi 7 xxiiii . cot cū . vii .
car̄ . Ibi æccła . 7 xii . ac̃ ꝑti . 7 ſilua . xx . porc̃ .
T.R.E. uałb . xx . lib . 7 poſt 7 m̃ ꞏ xv . lib .
In Hantone ten Wiłłs de com unã hiđ . Goda comitiſſa te
nuit . 7 ꝑ una hđ ſe defđ . Ꞇra . ē . i . car̄ . 7 ibi . ē in dñio . cū . ii . cot .
7 una ac̃ ꝑti . Vał 7 ualuit ſēp . x . ſoliđ ꞏ   _IN BERIE HVND_ .
Roƀt ten de com _BIGENEVRE_ . 7 Radulf de eo . Tres libi
hões tenueꝝ . T.R.E. Ꞇc̃ 7 m̃ ſe defđ ꝑ . iiii . hiđ . Ꞇra . ē . iii . car̄ .
In dñio ſunt . ii . car̄ . 7 ix . uiłłi 7 v . cot cū . ii . car̄ . Ibi æccła .
7 ii . molini de xxviii . ſoł . 7 una molaria de . iiii . ſoliđ .
Ibi . ii . ſerui . 7 ii . ac̃ ꝑti . 7 ſilua . de . iii . porc̃ .
T.R.E. uałb . iii . lib . 7 poſt ꞏ xl . ſoł . Modo ꞏ iiii . lib .
Roƀt ten de com _HERIEDEHĀ_ . Goduin un lib hõ T.R.E.
Ꞇc̃ 7 m̃ ſe defđ ꝑ . v . hiđ . Ꞇra . iiii . car̄ . In dñio ſunt . ii . 7 x . uiłłi
7 iiii . cot cū . iii . car̄ . Ibi . iii . piſcariæ de . vi . ſoł . 7 xv . ac̃ ꝑti .
Silua ꞏ iii . porc̃ . De hac tra ten Iuo de Roƀto . iii . v træ
7 ibi hꞇ . i . uiłłm .
T.R.E. uałb . iiii . lib . 7 poſt ꞏ xl . ſoł . Modo ꞏ c . ſoł .
BENESTEDE . ten Oiſmelin de com _IN BENESTEDE HVND_ .
Tres libi hões tenueꝝ . T.R.E. Ꞇc̃ 7 m̃ ꝑ . iiii . hiđ ſe defđ . Ꞇra . ē
. ii . car̄ . In dñio ſunt . ii . car̄ . 7 ii . uiłłi . cū . vi . cot . cū dim car̄
Ibi . viii . ac̃ ꝑti . 7 ſilua ꞏ de vi . porc̃ .
T.R.E. uałb . iii . lib . 7 poſt ꞏ xl . ſoł . Modo ꞏ iii . lib .
Wiłłs ten de com _WALBVRGETONE_ . Tres libi hões tenueꝝ
T.R.E. Ꞇc̃ 7 m̃ ſe defđ ꝑ . xi . hiđ . Ꞇra . ē . vi . car̄ . In dñio . iii . car̄ .
7 xix . uiłłi 7 xiii . cot cū . v . car̄ . Ibi æccła . 7 vi . ſerui . 7 xiiii .
ac̃ ꝑti . 7 ſilua ꞏ de . iiii . porc̃ .
T.R.E. uałb . x . lib . 7 poſt ꞏ vi . lib . Modo ꞏ xii . lib .

76 In the same manor St. Martin's of Sees holds 11 hides from
the Earl in alms. It answered for as much before 1066 and now.
Earl Godwin held it. Land for 9 ploughs. In lordship 2 ploughs;
   26 villagers and 24 cottagers with 7 ploughs.
   A church; meadow, 12 acres; woodland, 20 pigs.
Value before 1066 £20; later and now £15.

77 In LITTLEHAMPTON William holds 1 hide from the Earl.
Countess Goda held it. It answered for 1 hide Land for 1 plough.
It is there, in lordship, with
   2 cottagers.
   Meadow, 1 acre.
The value is and always was 10s.

  In BURY Hundred
78 Robert holds BIGNOR from the Earl, and Ralph from him. 3 free
men held it before 1066. Then and now it answered for 4 hides.
Land for 3 ploughs. In lordship 2 ploughs;
   9 villagers and 5 cottagers with 2 ploughs.
   A church; 2 mills at 28s; 1 millstone quarry at 4s.
    2 slaves; meadow, 2 acres; woodland at 3 pigs.
Value before 1066 £3; later 40s; now £4.

79 Robert holds HARDHAM from the Earl. Godwin, a free man,
[held it] before 1066. Then and now it answered for 5 hides.
Land for 4 ploughs. In lordship 2;
   10 villagers and 4 cottagers with 3 ploughs.
   3 fisheries at 6s; meadow, 15 acres; woodland, 3 pigs.
   Of this land Ivo holds 3 virgates of land from Robert. He has
    1 villager.
Value before 1066 £4; later 40s; now 100s.

  In BINSTED Hundred
80 Osmelin holds BINSTED from the Earl. 3 free men held it
before 1066. Then and now it answered for 4 hides.
Land for 2 ploughs. In lordship 2 ploughs;
   2 villagers with 6 cottagers with ½ plough.
   Meadow, 8 acres; woodland at 6 pigs.
Value before 1066 £3; later 40s; now £3.

81 William holds WALBERTON from the Earl. 3 free men held it
before 1066. Then and now it answered for 11 hides and 2 virgates.
Land for 6 ploughs. In lordship 3 ploughs;
   19 villagers and 13 cottagers with 5 ploughs.
   A church; 6 slaves; meadow, 14 acres; woodland at 4 pigs.
Value before 1066 £10; later £6; now £12.

Ɖe hac tra ten Rolland . i . hiđ unā v̄ miñ . 7 hanc h̄t ipſe
cōm in ſuo parco . 7 ibi . ii . uiłłi cū . iiii . coť h̄nt . i . car̄.
7 Acarđ pƀr ten . ii . v̄ in p̄bẹnda . ꝛ ibi h̄t . i . uiłłm.
Toṭū hoc uał . xx . ſoliđ.

BERNEHĀ ten Wiłłs de cōm . Alnod un̄ lib h̄o
tenuit . T . R . E . T̄c 7 m̄ ſe defđ ꝑ . iiii . hiđ . Tra . ē . iiii . ĉar.
In dñio . ē una . 7 xii . uiłłi 7 xii . coť cū . iiii . car̄.
Ibi æccła . 7 xx . aĉ p̄ti . 7 ſilua . de . iii . porĉ . 7 uñ moliñ.
T . R . E . 7 poſt . 7 m̄ . uał . iiii . liƀ.
MIDDELTONE ten Wiłłs de cōm . Quinq̣ libi h̄oēs
tenuer̄ . T . R . E . T̄c 7 m̄ ſe defđ ꝑ . v . hiđ 7 ii . uirgis.
Tra . ē . iii . car̄ . Ibi æccła . 7 ii . uiłłi cū dim̄ car̄.
De tra huj m̄ ten . iii . francig . iiii . hiđ 7 v . uirg . de Wiłło.
7 ibi in dñio . i . car̄ . 7 . x . uiłłi 7 iiii . coť . cū . i . car̄ 7 dim̄.
Toṭū m̄ T . R . E . uał . iiii . liƀ.
Ernald ten de cōm STOCHES . Vlnod . i . liƀ h̄o tenuit
T . R . E . T̄c 7 m̄ ſe defđ ꝑ . iiii . hiđ . Tra . ē . ii . car̄ . In dñio . ē
una car̄ . 7 x . uiłłi 7 iiii . coť cū . ii . car̄ . Ibi æccła 7 xx . iiii.
aĉ p̄ti . T . R . E . 7 poſt . 7 m̄ . iiii . liƀ.
TORTINTON ten Ernucion de cōm . Leuuin . i . liƀ h̄o tenuit
T . R . E . T̄c ſe defđ ꝑ . iiii . hiđ . m̄ ꝑ . iii . hiđ . qa cōm h̄t unā
in parco ſuo . Tra . ē . ii . car̄ . 7 ibi ſunt in dñio . 7 vi . uiłłi
7 ii . coť . Ibi . xxx . aĉ p̄ti . 7 ſilua . de . vi . porĉ.
T . R . E . uałƀ . lx . ſoł . 7 poſt . xxx . ſoł . Modo . xl . ſoł.

Roland holds 1 hide less 1 virgate of this land; the Earl
has it himself in his park.
   2 villagers with 4 cottagers have 1 plough.
   Acard the priest holds 2 virgates in prebend. He has
      1 villager.
Value of all this 20s.

82 William holds BARNHAM from the Earl. Alnoth, a free man,
      held it before 1066. Then and now it answered for 4 hides.
      Land for 4 ploughs. In lordship 1;
         12 villagers and 12 cottagers with 4 ploughs.
         A church; meadow, 20 acres; woodland at 3 pigs; 1 mill.
      Value before 1066, later and now £4.

25 b

83 William holds MIDDLETON from the Earl. 5 free men held it
      before 1066. Then and now it answered for 5 hides and 2 virgates.
      Land for 3 ploughs.
         A church; 2 villagers with ½ plough.
         3 Frenchmen hold 4 hides and 5 virgates of this manor's
         land from William. In lordship 1 plough;
            10 villagers and 4 cottagers with 1½ ploughs.
      Value of the whole manor before 1066 £4.

84 Arnold holds (SOUTH) STOKE from the Earl. Wulfnoth, a free man,
      held it before 1066. Then and now it answered for 4 hides.
      Land for 2 ploughs. In lordship 1 plough;
         10 villagers and 4 cottagers with 2 ploughs.
         A church; meadow, 24 acres.
      [Value] before 1066, later and now £4.

85 Ernucion holds TORTINGTON from the Earl. Leofwin, a free man,
      held it before 1066. Then it answered for 4 hides; now for 3 hides,
      because the Earl has 1 in his park. Land for 2 ploughs.
      They are there, in lordship;
         6 villagers and 2 cottagers.
         Meadow, 30 acres; woodland at 6 pigs.
      Value before 1066, 60s; later 30s; now 40s.

BILESHAM . ten̄ Hugo de com̄ . Goduin̄ . I . lib̄ hō tenuit

T.R.E. Tc̄ 7 m̄ se defd̄ p̄ . IIII . hid̄ . Tra . ē. III . car̄ . In dn̄io

eſt una . 7 XIIII . uiłłi cū . II . car̄ . 7 VIII . āc p̄ti.

T.R.E. uałb̄ . IIII . lib̄ . 7 poſt . XL . ſoł . Modo . L . ſoł.

Iſdē Hugo ten̄ de com̄ . III . hid̄ . 7 Warin̄ de eo . Tres

libi hōes tenuer̄ . T.R.E. Tc̄ 7 m̄ se defd̄ p̄ . III . hid̄.

Tra . ē . II . car̄ . In dn̄io . ē una car̄ . 7 V . uiłłi 7 V . cot

cū . I . car̄ . Ibi . III . āc p̄ti . T.R.E. 7 m̄ . XXX . ſoł . Qdo recep̄.

Iſd̄ Hugo ten̄ de com̄ *ESLINDONE* . Azor ⨏ XX . ſoł.

qdā lib̄ hō tenuit T.R.E. Tc̄ 7 m̄ se defd̄ p̄ . VIII . hid̄.

Tra . ē . VIII . car̄ . In dn̄io . ē una car̄ 7 dim . 7 XXIII . uiłłi

7 XII . cot . cū . VII . car̄ . Ibi æccła

T.R.E. uałb̄ . XX . lib̄ . 7 poſt 7 m̄ . XVI . lib̄.

Iſdē Hugo ten̄ de com̄ . VIII . hid̄.

Nouē libi hōes tenuer̄ . T.R.E. Tc̄ se defd̄ . p̄ VIII . hid̄.

Modo . una v̄ min . quā com̄ hī | 7 n̄ geld Tra . ē . IIII . car̄.

7 XVI . uiłłi cū . V . car̄ . Ibi . VIII . āc p̄ti.

T.R.E. 7 poſt . 7 m̄ . uał . III . lib̄.

Morin̄ ten̄ de com̄ *BORHĀ* . Vn̄ lib̄ hō tenuit . T.R.E.

Tc̄ 7 m̄ se defd̄ p̄ . I . v̄ . | Ibi duæ virgæ Ibi ſunt . V . bou arant cū . I . cot.

T.R.E. 7 m̄ . uał . XX . ſoł . Qdo recep̄ . X . ſolid.

In eod̄ *HVND* ten̄ Wiłłs de com̄ . III . hid̄ . 7 p̄ tanto

se defd̄ . Duo libi hōes tenuer̄ . T.R.E. Tra . ē . III . car̄.

In dn̄io . ē una 7 dim . 7 V . uiłłi 7 V . cot . 7 ii . ſerui cū . II . car̄.

T.R.E. 7 m̄ . uał . IIII . lib̄ . Qdo recep̄ . III . lib̄.

Azo ten̄ de com̄ *OFFHĀ* . Aluuin̄ lib̄ hō tenuit . T.R.E.

Tc̄ 7 m̄ se defd̄ p̄ . IIII . hid̄ . Tra . ē . II . car̄ . In dn̄io . ē una.

7 VIII . uiłłi 7 V . cot cū . II . car̄ . Ibi . V . ſerui . 7 XLVIII.

āc p̄ti . 7 piſcaria de . II . ſoł . Silua . de . III . porc.

Totū T.R.E. uałb̄ . VII . lib̄ . 7 poſt . VI . lib̄ . Modo . IIII . lib̄.

Ibi hī com̄ . II . molin̄ . Paſtura 7 exitū ſiluæ . Vał . IIII . lib̄.

⨏ 7 X . ſoł.

86 Hugh holds BILSHAM from the Earl. Godwin, a free man, held
it before 1066. Then and now it answered for 4 hides.
Land for 3 ploughs. In lordship 1;
    14 villagers with 2 ploughs.
    Meadow, 8 acres.
Value before 1066 £4; later 40s; now 50s.

87 Hugh also holds 3 hides from the Earl, and Warin from him. 3 free
men held it before 1066. Then and now it answered for 3 hides.
Land for 2 ploughs. In lordship 1 plough;
    5 villagers and 5 cottagers with 1 plough.
    Meadow, 3 acres.
[Value] before 1066 and now 30s; when acquired 20s.

88 Hugh also holds SLINDON from the Earl. Azor, a free man,
held it before 1066. Then and now it answered for 8 hides.
Land for 8 ploughs. In lordship 1½ ploughs;
    23 villagers and 12 cottagers with 7 ploughs. A church.
Value before 1066 £20; later and now £16.

89 Hugh also holds a further 8 hides from the Earl. 9 free men
held it before 1066. Then it answered for 8 hides; now
less 1 virgate, which the Earl has. It does not pay tax.
Land for 4 ploughs.
    16 villagers with 5 ploughs.
    Meadow, 8 acres.
Value before 1066, later and now £3.

90 Morin holds BORHAM from the Earl. A free man held it before 1066.
Then and now it answered for 1 virgate. 2 virgates there; 5
ploughing oxen, with
    1 cottager.
Value before 1066 and now 20s; when acquired 10s.

91 In the same Hundred William holds 3 hides from the Earl.
It answers for as much. Two free men held it before 1066.
Land for 3 ploughs. In lordship 1½;
    5 villagers, 5 cottagers and 2 slaves with 2 ploughs.
Value before 1066 and now £4; when acquired £3.

92 Azor holds OFFHAM from the Earl. Alwin, a free man, held it
before 1066. Then and now it answered for 4 hides.
Land for 2 ploughs. In lordship 1;
    8 villagers and 5 cottagers with 2 ploughs.
    5 slaves; meadow, 48 acres; a fishery at 2s; woodland at 3 pigs.
Total value before 1066 £7; later £6; now £4.
    The Earl has 2 mills, the pasture and the income from the woodland.
Value £4 10s.

G̅ATE ten S̅ Martin de Sais in elemoſina de com̅.

Herald tenuit. Ibi . iii . hidæ . Sed tc̅ 7 m̅ ꝑ. ii . hid̅ . Tra . e̅

iiii . car̅ . Iñ dn̅io ſunt . ii . car̅ . 7 . xviii . uilli 7 x . cot.

cu̅ . ii . car̅ . Ibi æccl̅a . 7 iiii . ac̅ p̅ti . Silua . v . porc̅ .

T . R . E . 7 m̅ . ual . iiii . lib̅ . Q̲do recep̅: iii . lib̅ .

In iſto HV̅ND̅ BENESTEDE . ten Warin de com̅

dimid hid̅ . Azor uñ lib̅ ho̅ tenuit 7 nu̅q̲ geldauit .

Tra . e̅ . i . car̅ . 7 ibi . e̅ cu̅ . ii . uillis . Val 7 ualuit . xxx . ſol .

G̅ondran ten de com̅ ibid̅ . i . hid̅ . 7 ꝓ tanto ſe defd̅ ſep̅ .

Herulf tenuit de Goduino . Tra . e̅ . i . car̅ . 7 ibi . e̅ in dn̅io .

cu̅ uno uillo 7 iiii . cot . 7 ii . ac̅ p̅ti . 7 ſilua . iii . porc̅ . Sep̅ . xx . ſol .

In ipſo HV̅ND̅ ten Acard de com̅ . ii . hid̅ 7 dim . ꝑ . ii . hid̅

dimid̅ v min̄ ſe defd̅ tc̅ 7 m̅ . Tra . e̅ . ii . car̅ . In dn̅io e̅ una car̅ .

7 vi . uilli 7 vi . cot cu̅ . i . car̅ . Ibi æccl̅a . 7 ſilua . vi . porc̅ .

Anſgot tenuit de Goduino . Tc̅ 7 m̅ xl . ſol . Cu̅ recep̅: xx . ſol .

Ibid̅ ten Pagen de com̅ una̅ v 7 ꝓ tanto ſep̅ ſe defd̅ .

Anſgot tenuit de Goduino . Ibi . e̅ uñ cot . Sep̅ . xxx . den .

In eod̅ HV̅ND̅ ten Wills de com̅ dim hid̅ 7 ii . v . 7 ꝓ tanto .

ſe defd̅ ſep̅ . Duo Angli tenuer̅ de Goduino . Tra . e̅ . i . car̅ .

Ibi ſunt . iiii . uilli 7 i . cot cu̅ dim car̅ . Val 7 ualuit . x . ſol .

In eod̅ HV̅ND̅ ten Hugo de com̅ . v . uirg̅ 7 dimid̅ . 7 pro

tanto ſe defd̅ ſep̅ . Azor lib̅ ho̅ tenuit T . R . E . Tra . e̅ . ii .

car̅ . Ibi . e̅ uñ uills 7 i . cot . Tc̅ 7 poſt 7 m̅ . ual . viii . ſol .

In ipſo HV̅ND̅ ten Rolland de com̅ . i . hid̅ . 7 ꝓ tanto

ſe defd̅ ſep̅ . Goduin lib̅ ho̅ tenuit . Tra . e̅ . ii . car̅ . In dn̅io

e̅ una car̅ . 7 ii . uilli 7 iiii . cot cu̅ . i . car̅ . Val 7 ualuit . xx . ſol .

11

93 St. Martin's of Sees holds (EASTER)GATE from the Earl in alms.   25 c
Earl Harold held it. 3 hides there, but then and now it answered
for 2 hides. Land for 4 ploughs. In lordship 2 ploughs;
    18 villagers and 10 cottagers with 2 ploughs.
    A church; meadow, 4 acres; woodland, 5 pigs.
Value before 1066 and now £4; when acquired £3.

94 In this Hundred of BINSTED Warin holds ½ hide from the Earl.
Azor, a free man, held it. It never paid tax. Land for 1 plough.
It is there, with
    2 villagers.
The value is and was 30s.

95 Guntram holds 1 hide there from the Earl. It always answered for
as much. Herewulf held it from Earl Godwin. Land for 1 plough.
It is there, in lordship, with
    1 villager and 4 cottagers.
    Meadow, 2 acres; woodland, 3 pigs.
[Value] always 20s.

96 In this Hundred Acard holds 2½ hides from the Earl. Then and now it
answered for 2 hides less ½ virgate. Land for 2 ploughs.
In lordship 1 plough;
    6 villagers and 6 cottagers with 1 plough.
    A church; woodland, 6 pigs.
Ansgot held it from Earl Godwin.
[Value] then and now 40s; when acquired 20s.

97 Payne holds 1 virgate there from the Earl. It always answered
for as much. Ansgot held it from Earl Godwin.
    1 cottager.
[Value] always 30d.

98 In the same Hundred William holds ½ hide and 2 virgates from the
Earl. It always answered for as much. Two Englishmen held
it from Earl Godwin. Land for 1 plough.
    4 villagers and 1 cottager with ½ plough.
The value is and was 10s.

99 In the same Hundred Hugh holds 5½ virgates from the Earl. It always
answered for as much. Azor, a free man, held it before 1066.
Land for 2 ploughs.
    1 villager and 1 cottager.
Value then, later and now 8s.

100 In this Hundred Roland holds 1 hide from the Earl.
It always answered for as much. Godwin, a free man, held it.
Land for 2 ploughs. In lordship 1 plough;
    2 villagers and 4 cottagers with 1 plough.
The value is and was 20s.

In eođ *HVND* ten̄ Wineman de com̄ unā v̄ . 7 p̄ tanto ſe

defđ ſep̄ . Turchil tenuit . lib̄ hō fuit . Val̄ 7 ualuit . v . ſol̄ .

Wil̄s ten̄ de com̄ *BOSGRAVE* . *IN BOSGRAVE HVND*.

Duo lib̄i hōes tenuer̄ . T . R . E . Tc̄ 7 m̄ ſe defđ p̄ . vi . hiđ .

Tra . ē . iiii . car̄ . De hac tra ten̄ Hunfrid . iii . hiđ 7 unā v̄ .

Nigell . i . hiđ 7 unā v̄ . Wil̄s dim̄ hiđ . Clerici æcctæ . i . hiđ .

In dn̄io . ſt̄ . ii . car̄ 7 un uil̄s 7 xii . cot cū una car̄ .

Tot̄ T . R . E . ual̄b̄ xl . ſol̄ . 7 poſt̄ . ſimilit̄ . 7 m̄ ſimilit̄ .

Iſdē Wil̄s ten̄ de com̄ *ANTONE* . 7 Nigell de eo .

Aluuard lib̄ hō tenuit . Tc̄ 7 m̄ ſe defđ p̄ . vii . hiđ . 7 viii .

uil̄i 7 xi . cot cū . iii . car̄ . ſunt ibi . Tra . ē . iiii . car̄.

In dn̄io ſunt . ii . car̄ . 7 iii . ac̄ p̄ti .

T . R . E . ual̄b̄ . lx . ſol̄ . 7 poſt̄ . xl . ſol̄ . Modo . l . ſoliđ .

Iſdē Wil̄s ten̄ *HELNACHE* de com̄ . Aluuard tenuit

T . R . E . 7 Tc̄ 7 m̄ ſe defđ p̄ . ix . hiđ . Tra . ē . v . car̄ . In dn̄io

ſunt . ii . car̄ . 7 xvii . uil̄i 7 xii . cot . cū . ii . car̄ . Ibi . viii .

ac̄ p̄ti . 7 ſilua . ix . porc̄ . In Ciceſtre . iii . burḡſes de . v . ſol̄ .

T . R . E . 7 poſt̄ . ualuit . iiii . lib̄ . Modo . c . ſol̄ .

Iſdē Wil̄s ten̄ de com̄ *HENTONE* . Duo lib̄i hōes tenuer̄

de Goduino . Tc̄ 7 m̄ ſe defđ p̄ . ix . hiđ . Tra . ē

Ibi ht̄ Wil̄s . i . molin̄ de . v . ſol̄ . 7 xii . cot . 7 ſilua . vi . porc̄ .

7 in Ciceſtre . i . hagā .

De hac tra ten̄ Wil̄s . i . hiđ . Reſtold . i . hiđ . Ricard . iii . uirḡ .

Godefrid . i . uirḡ . In dn̄io . i . car̄ . 7 iiii . cot . 7 una æccta .

Tot̄ T . R . E . ualeb̄ . lx . ſol̄ . 7 poſt̄ . xl . ſol̄ . m̄ . lx . ſoliđ .

Iſdē Wil̄s ten̄ de com̄ . iii . hiđ . 7 p̄ tanto ſe defđ in eođ

HVND . Duo lib̄i hōes tenuer̄ . T . R . E . Tra . ē . i . car̄ .

De hac tra ten̄ Ricard . ii . hiđ . Turgiſus . i . hiđ .

In dn̄io . i . car̄ . cū . ix . cot . 7 i . molin̄ de . iii . ſol̄ . 7 ii . hagæ .

de ix . denar̄ . T . R . E . ual̄b̄ . xx . ſol̄ . 7 poſt̄ . xv . ſol̄ . Modo . x . ſol̄ .

01 In the same Hundred Winman holds 1 virgate from the Earl. It always
answered for as much. Thorkell held it; he was a free man.
The value is and was 5s.

In BOX Hundred

02 William holds BOXGROVE from the Earl. Two free men held
it before 1066. Then and now it answered for 6 hides.
Land for 4 ploughs. Humphrey holds 3 hides and 1 virgate
of this land; Nigel 1 hide and 1 virgate; William ½ hide;
the clergy of the church 1 hide. In lordship 2 ploughs;
    1 villager and 12 cottagers with 1 plough.
Total value before 1066, 40s; later the same; now the same.

03 William also holds (EAST) HAMPNETT from the Earl and Nigel from him.
Alfward, a free man, held it. Then and now it answered for 7 hides.
    8 villagers and 11 cottagers with 3 ploughs.
Land for 4 ploughs. In lordship 2 ploughs.
Meadow, 3 acres.
Value before 1066, 60s; later 40s; now 50s.

04 William also holds HALNAKER from the Earl. Alfward held it
before 1066. Then and now it answered for 9 hides.
Land for 5 ploughs. In lordship 2 ploughs;
    17 villagers and 12 cottagers with 2 ploughs.
    Meadow, 8 acres; woodland, 9 pigs; 3 burgesses in Chichester at 5s.
Value before 1066 and later £4; now 100s.

05 William also holds (WEST)HAMPNETT from the Earl. 2 free men held
it from Earl Godwin. Then and now it answered for 9 hides.
Land for .... William has
    1 mill at 5s.
    12 cottagers.
    Woodland, 6 pigs; 1 site in Chichester.
William holds 1 hide of this land; Restald 1 hide; Richard
    3 virgates; Godfrey 1 virgate. In lordship 1 plough;
    4 cottagers; 1 church.
Total value before 1066, 60s; later 40s; now 60s.

06 William also holds 3 hides from the Earl. It answers for as much   25 d
in the same Hundred. 2 free men held it before 1066.
Land for 1 plough. Richard holds 2 hides of this land;
Thorgils 1 hide. In lordship 1 plough, with
    9 cottagers.
    1 mill at 3s; 2 sites at 9d.
Value before 1066, 20s; later 15s; now 10s.

Iſdē Wilts ten̄ de com̄ STRATONE .Quattuor libi hōēs te
nuer̄ . T.R.E. Tc̄ 7 m̄ ſe defd̄ ꝑ . x . hid̄ . Tra . ē . vi . car̄ . Ibi ſuɴ
vi . uiłłi 7 xvi . cot cū . ii . car̄ . In Ciceſtre . iii . hagæ de . ii . ſolid̄ .
T.R.E. uałb̄ . vi . lib̄ . 7 poſt . 7 modo ꞉ xl . ſoł .

Auguſtin ten̄ de com̄ STRATONE . Goduin un̄ lib̄ hō tenuit .
T.R.E. Tc̄ 7 m̄ ſe defd̄ ꝑ . iii . hid̄ . Tra . ē . i . car̄ . 7 ibi . ē in dn̄io .
cū . ii . uiłłis 7 ii . cot . 7 una haga . de . iii . den̄ . 7 ii . ſerui . 7 i . ac̄ p̄ti .
T.R.E. uałb̄ . xx . ſoł . 7 poſt ꞉ x . ſoł . Modo ꞉ xxx . ſoł .

In eod̄ m̄ ten̄ Arnald de com̄ . ii . hid̄ . 7 ꝑ tanto ſe defd̄ . Goduin
lib̄ hō tenuit . T.R.E. Tra . ē . i . car̄ . 7 ibi . ē in dn̄io cū . ii . cot .
7 ii . ſeruis ꞉ 7 una haga de . viii . denar̄ .
T.R.E. uałb̄ . iii . lib̄ . 7 poſt 7 m̄ ꞉ xx . ſolid̄ .

Mersitone ten̄ Oiſmelin de com̄ . Gort tenuit de rege . E.
Tc̄ ſe defd̄ ꝑ . viii . hid̄ m̄ ꝑ . vi . hid̄ . Tra . ē . iii . car̄ . In dn̄io ſuɴ
ii . car̄ . 7 x . uiłłi cū . vi . cot . hn̄t . iii . car̄ . 7 iii . molini de . vii . ſoł .
7 duæ hagæ de . ii . ſoł . 7 x . ac̄ p̄ti .
T.R.E. uałb̄ . v . lib̄ . 7 poſt ꞉ iiii . lib̄ . Modo ꞉ vr . lib̄ .

Rochintone ten̄ abbatia de Troard in elemoſin̄a de com̄ .
Duo libi hōēs tenuer̄ . T.R.E. Tc̄ ſe defd̄ ꝑ viii . hid̄ m̄ ꝑ . ii . hid̄ .
Tra . ē . iii . car̄ . In dn̄io ſunt . ii . car̄ . 7 vi . uiłłi 7 xv . cot cū . i . car̄ .
Ibi . v . ſerui . 7 ii . molini . de . xii . ſolid̄ . 7 vi . denar̄ . 7 piſcaria
de . vi . denar̄ . 7 ii . hagæ de xviii . denar̄ .
T.R.E. uałb̄ . v . lib̄ . 7 poſt ꞉ iiii . lib̄ . Modo ꞉ vi . lib̄ .

Ernald ten̄ de com̄ WALTHAM . Goduin . un̄ lib̄ hō tenuit .
Tc̄ ſe defd̄ ꝑ . vi . hid̄ . m̄ ꝑ . iiii . Ernald hc̄ . ii . hid̄ . 7 . ibi . ii . cot ſunt .
7 un ſeruus . 7 abbatia de Troard hc̄ . ii . hid̄ . 7 ibi ſunt . iii . cot .
7 una haga de . xvi . den̄ 7 de herbagio . ii . ſolid̄ .
7 com̄ hc̄ . ii . hid̄ in parco ſuo . Tra . ē una car̄ .
Tot̄ T.R.E. uałb̄ . xl . ſoł . 7 poſt ꞉ xx . ſolid̄ .
Qd̄ Ernald ꞉ uał . x . ſoł . Pars abbatiæ ꞉ xxxv . ſoł .

07 William also holds STRETTINGTON from the Earl. 4 free men
held it before 1066. Then and now it answered for 10 hides.
Land for 6 ploughs.
    6 villagers and 16 cottagers with 2 ploughs.
    3 sites in Chichester at 2s.
Value before 1066 £6; later and now 40s.

08 Augustine holds STRETTINGTON from the Earl. Godwin, a free man,
held it before 1066. Then and now it answered for 3 hides.
Land for 1 plough. It is there, in lordship, with
    2 villagers and 2 cottagers.
    1 site at 3d; 2 slaves; meadow, 1 acre.
Value before 1066, 20s; later 10s; now 30s.

09 In the same manor Arnold holds 2 hides from the Earl.
It answers for as much. Godwin, a free man, held it before 1066.
Land for 1 plough. It is there, in lordship, with
    2 cottagers and 2 slaves.
    1 site at 8d.
Value before 1066 £3; later and now 20s.

10 Osmelin holds MERSTON from the Earl. Gyrth held it from King
Edward. Then it answered for 8 hides; now for 6 hides.
Land for 3 ploughs. In lordship 2 ploughs.
    10 villagers with 6 cottagers have 3 ploughs.
    3 mills at 7s; 2 sites at 2s; meadow, 10 acres.
Value before 1066 £5; later £4; now £6.

11 Troarn Abbey holds RUNCTON from the Earl in alms. 2 free
men held it before 1066. Then it answered for 8 hides;
now for 2 hides. Land for 3 ploughs. In lordship 2 ploughs;
    6 villagers and 15 cottagers with 1 plough.
    5 slaves; 2 mills at 12s 6d; a fishery at 6d; 2 sites at 18d.
Value before 1066 £5; later £4; now £6.

12 Arnold holds (UP) WALTHAM from the Earl. Godwin, a free man,
held it. Then it answered for 6 hides; now for 4. Arnold has 2 hides.
    2 cottagers and 1 slave.
Troarn Abbey has 2 hides.
    3 cottagers.
    1 site at 16d; from grazing 2s.
    The Earl has 2 hides in his park. Land for 1 plough.
Total value before 1066, 40s; later 20s; value of what Arnold
holds, 10s; the Abbey's part, 35s.

Goisfrid ten de com̃ WALTHÃ. Duo liɓi hões tenueř. T.R.E.

Tc̃ ſe defđ ꝑ. iiii. hiđ. m̃ ꝑ. iiiᵇ. q̃a com̃ h̃t unã in ſuo parco.

Tra. ē. iiii. cař. In dñio. ē una. cũ. v. cot̃. 7 ſilua de. x. porc̃.

7 una haga de. vii. denař. herbag. ii. ſot

T.R.E. xxx. ſot. 7 poſt. x. ſot. Modo. xx. ſoliđ.

In ipſo HVND ten Witts de com̃ unã hiđ. Aluuard un lib̃ hõ tenuit.

7 ꝑ una hida ſe defđ in HELNECHE. tc̃ 7 m̃. Tc̃. xv. ſot. 7 poſt. v. m̃. x. ſot.

In ipſo HVND ten Siuuard de com̃ unã hiđ. 7 ꝑ tanto ſe defđ

ſēꝑ. Siret tenuit. lib̃ hõ fuit. Tra. ē. i. cař. Tc̃ 7 m̃. xx. ſot.

In ipſo HVND ten Rainald de com̃ dimiđ hiđ. 7 ꝑ tanto ſe

defđ. Helghin tenuit. T.R.E. Tc̃. iii. ſot. 7 poſt. ii. ſot. Modo. xii. den.

TERRA WILLELMI DE WARENE.

.XII. *BVRGV DE LEWES* T.R.E. reddebat vi. libras

7 iiii. ſot 7 iii. obolos. de gablo 7 de theloneo. Ibi rex. E.

habebat. cxxvii. burgenſes in dñio. Eoꝛ c̃ſuetudo erat.

Si rex ad mare cuſtodiendũ ſine ſe mittere ſuos uoluiſſet꞉

de om̃ibꝫ hõïbꝫ cujcunq̃ tra fuiſſet colligebaꝗ. xx. ſoliđ.

7 hos habebant qui in nauibꝫ arma cuſtodiebant.

Qui in burgo uendit equũ꞉ dat ꝓpoſito nũmũ. 7 qui emit꞉ aliũ.

De boue꞉ obolũ. De homine꞉ iiii. denař. quocũqꝫ loco emat

infra rapũ. ⌐Sanguine fundeꝭ꞉ emdat ꝑ. vii. ſot 7 iiii. den.

Adulteriũ uel raptũ faciens꞉ viii. ſot 7 iiii. den. emdat homo.

7 femina tntđ. Rex h̃t hõem adulterũ. Archieꝑs feminã.

⌐De fugitiuo ſi recupat fuerit꞉ viii. ſot 7 iiii. denař.

⌐Cũ moneta renouat꞉ dat. xx. ſot unquiſqꝫ monetari.

⌐De his om̃ibꝫ ſunt. ii. partes regis. 7 tcia comitis.

Modo ꝑ om̃a reddit burg̃ ſicut tc̃. 7 xxxviii. ſot de ſuꝑ plus.

De Rapo de Peueneſel. xxxix. manſuræ hoſpitate.

7 xx. inhoſpitatæ. ex quibꝫ rex h̃t xxvi. ſot 7 vi. denarios.

7 de his h̃t Witts de Warene medietate.

13 Geoffrey holds (UP) WALTHAM from the Earl. 2 free men held it
    before 1066. Then it answered for 4 hides; now for 3, because
    the Earl has 1 in his park. Land for 4 ploughs. In lordship 1, with
      5 cottagers.
    Woodland at 10 pigs; 1 site at 7d; grazing 2s.
    [Value] before 1066, 30s; later 10s; now 20s.

14 In this Hundred William holds 1 hide from the Earl. Alfward, a free
    man, held it. It answered for 1 hide, in HALNAKER, then and now.
    [Value] then 15s; later 5s; now 10s.

15 In this Hundred Siward holds 1 hide from the Earl. It always
    answered for as much. Sired held it; he was a free man.
    Land for 1 plough.
    [Value] then and now 20s.

16 In this Hundred Reginald holds ½ hide from the Earl. It answers
    for as much. Helgi held it before 1066.
    [Value] then 3s; later 2s; now 12d.

12   LAND OF WILLIAM OF WARENNE   26 a
(Lewes Rape)

1 The Borough of LEWES
    before 1066 paid £6 4s and 3 halfpence from tribute and toll.
    King Edward had 127 burgesses in lordship. Their custom was,
    if the King wished to send his men in his absence to guard the sea,
    they collected 20s from all men whosesoever the land was, and
    those who had charge of arms in the ships had these (shillings).
    Whoever sells a horse in the Borough gives a penny to the reeve;
    the buyer gives another; for an ox ½d; for a man 4d, wherever
    he buys within the Rape.
    Whoever sheds blood is fined 7s 4d. A man who commits
    adultery or rape is fined 8s 4d, and a woman as much.
    The King has the adulterous man, the Archbishop the woman.
    For a fugitive, 8s 4d if he is recovered.
    When the money is renewed, each moneyer gives 20s.
    Of all this, two parts were the King's; the third was the Earl's.
    In all, the Borough pays now as it did then, and 38s in addition.
    In the Rape of Pevensey 39 inhabited dwellings and 20 uninhabited,
    from which the King has 26s 6d; William of Warenne has
    half of them.

T.R.E.ualeb̄ totū   XXVI . lib̄ . Rex medietatē 7 com̄ aliā hab̄.

Modo ual XXXIIII . lib̄ . 7 de noua moneta . c . sol̄ 7 XII.

de his om̄ib₂ hr̄ Wilts medietatē . 7 rex alterā.

In Rapo de Peuenesel hr̄ Wilts de Warene . XII . mansuras.

VII . hospitatas . 7 v . non . jn Lestun M̄ comitis moritoñ.

IN SONEBERGE HVND̄.

WILLELM⁹ de Warene teñ in dñio *NIWORDE*.

    Eddid regina tenuit . T.R.E.se defd̄ ₰ LXXVII . hid̄

7 dim̄ . Q̇do Wilts recep̄:´ nisi . LVIII . hid̄ . q̇a aliæ fuer̄

intra rap̄ comit morit . He . LVIII . hidæ defd̄ se m̄ ₰ . XXXVI.

hid̄ . Tra . ē . LII . car̄ . In dñio sunt . v . car̄ . 7 c . uilti . III.ᵉˢ

min⁹ 7 XXXII . bord̄ hñt . XXXIIII . car̄ . Ibi æccla . 7 VI . serui.

7 II . molini de XXIII . sol̄ . 7 cc . 7 VIII . ac̄ p̄ti . Silua . XXX . porc̄.

In burgo de Lewes . XXVI . burgses . de XIII . solid̄ . De pastura

xv . sol̄ 7 VIII . deñ . 7 XVI . millenar alleciū.

De hac tra teñ monachi S̃ pancratij . VI . hid̄ 7 dim̄ . 7 ibi hñt

in dñio . II . car̄ . 7 x . uittos cū . III . car̄ . Non geldant hæ hidæ.

De ead̄ tra hr̄ Hugo . II . hid̄ . 7 Tosard̄ . I . hid̄ 7 dim̄ . In dñio hñt

II . car̄ . cū . IIII . bord̄ . Has tras tenuer̄ uilti.

Totū M̄ T.R.E.ualeb̄ . L . lib̄ . 7 post . xx . lib̄ . Modo dñium

Wilti:´ xxxv . lib̄ . Monacho₂:´ III . lib̄ . Hominū:´ LXXV . solid̄.

IN HOMESTREV HVND̄.

Ipse Wilts teñ in dñio *RAMELLE* . Herald cõm⁹ tenuit . T.R.E.

se defd̄ ₰ . LXX 7 IX . hid̄ . Wilts recep̄:´ LXIIII . hid̄ . q̇a alie

in rapo comitis 7 Witti de Braiose . Hæ . LXIIII . hidæ defd̄ se

m̄ ₰ . XXX.III . hid̄ . Tra . ē . xxxvi . car̄ . In dñio sunt . vi . car̄.

7 cvii . uilti 7 xxv . bord̄ cū xxxiiii . car̄ . Ibi . xi . salinæ

de . xxvi . solid̄ . 7 cxl . ac̄ p̄ti . 7 silua:´ xxiii . porc̄ . In M̄ . ē æccla

26 a

Total value before 1066 £26. The King had one half, and the
Earl the other; value now £34, and 112s from the
new mint; William has half of all this, and the King the other half.

2 In the Rape of Pevensey William of Warenne has 12 dwellings, 7
inhabited and 5 not, in Laughton, the Count of Mortain's manor.

In SWANBOROUGH Hundred
3 William of Warenne holds IFORD in lordship. Queen Edith
held it. Before 1066 it answered for 77½ hides. When William
acquired it there were only 58 hides because the others were
in the Count of Mortain's Rape. These 58 hides now answer for 36
hides. Land for 52 ploughs. In lordship 5 ploughs.
   100 villagers, less 3, and 32 smallholders have 34 ploughs.
   A church; 6 slaves; 2 mills at 23s; meadow, 208 acres;
      woodland, 30 pigs; 26 burgesses in the Borough of Lewes
      at 13s; from pasture 15s 8d; 16 thousands of herrings.
The monks of St. Pancras (of Lewes) hold 6½ hides of this land.
They have 2 ploughs in lordship, and
   10 villagers with 3 ploughs.
These hides do not pay tax.
Hugh has 2 hides of this land; Tosard 1½ hides. They have 2 ploughs
in lordship, with
   4 smallholders.
The villagers held these lands.
Value of the whole manor before 1066 £50; later £20; now, William's
lordship £35, the monks' £3; the men's 75s.

In HOLMESTROW Hundred
4 William holds RODMELL himself, in lordship. Earl Harold held it.
Before 1066 it answered for 79 hides. William acquired 64 hides,
because the others were in the Earl's Rape and the Rape of William of
Braose. These 64 hides now answer for 33 hides. Land for 36 ploughs.
In lordship 6 ploughs;
   107 villagers and 25 smallholders with 34 ploughs.
   11 salt-houses at 26s; meadow, 140 acres; woodland, 23 pigs.
There is a church in the manor.

In *LEWES.* XLIIII . hagæ . de xxii . folid . 7 iiii . miliá alleciũ.

De hac tra ten Norman . ii . hid de Witto . 7 ibi . i . car in dñio . cũ . ii . bord 7 uno feruo . Hanc tra qui tenebat.' non poterat recede cũ ea.

Tot Ḿ . T . R . E . ualeb . LX . lib . 7 poft.' xx . lib . Modo.' xxxvii . lib.

IN PRESTETVNE HVND.

Ipfe Witts ten *PICEHĀ* in dñio . Herald tenuit . T . R . E.

Tc̄ fe defd ꝑ LX . hid . 7 m̄ ꝑ . XL . Tra . ē qt xx . car.

In dñio . VIII . car . 7 CXLX.III . uitti 7 XL.V . bord cũ qt xx 7 II . car . Ibi æccta 7 VI . ferui . 7 x . berquarij.

Ibi qt xx 7 IIII . ac pti . 7 filuá.' c . porc.

In Lewes.' xxvi . hagæ . de . xiii . folid.

De hac tra ten Ricoard VII . hid . 7 miles ej . i . hid 7 dim.

In dñio hn̄t . ii . car . cũ . ii . bord.

T . R . E . ualeb tot . c . lib . 7 poft.' L . lib . m̄.' qt xx . lib.

IN SOANBERGE HVND.

Ipfe Witts ten in dñio *DICELINGES* . Rex . E . tenuit . Nunq geldau.

T . R . E . fe defd ꝑ . XLVI . hid . Qdo recep.' nifi . XL.II . hidæ aliæ fuer in rapo comit morit . 7 VI . filuæ quæ ptineba ad cap Manerij . Modo fe defd ꝑ . xxxiii . hid . Tra . ē . LX . car.

In dñio . VIII . car . 7 c.VIII . uitti 7 XL . bord hn̄t qt xx . car 7 unã . Ibi æccta 7 un̄ molin de . xxx . den . 7 cxxx . ac pti . Silua . qt xx . porc . In Lewes.' xi . mafuras . de . xii . fot.

De hac tra ten Gisleb̄t . i . hid 7 dim . Hugo . ii . hid.

Aluuard . iii . hid . Warin . iii . hid . Ricard . i . hidã.

In dñio hn̄t . VII . car 7 dim . cũ . xxix . bord . 7 iii . uitti 7 x . ferui . cũ . iii . car . In Lewes . VI . burg̃fes de . XLIII . den.

12

In Lewes 44 sites at 22s; 4,000 herrings.
Norman holds 2 hides of this land from William. 1 plough
in lordship with
    2 smallholders and 1 slave.
The holder of this land could not withdraw with it.
Value of the whole manor before 1066 £60; later £20; now £37.

In PRESTON Hundred

5 William holds PATCHAM himself, in lordship. Earl Harold held it
before 1066. Then it answered for 60 hides; now for 40.
Land for 80 ploughs. In lordship 8 ploughs;
    163 villagers and 45 smallholders with 82 ploughs.
    A church; 6 slaves; 10 shepherds; meadow, 84 acres;
        woodland, 100 pigs; 26 sites in Lewes at 13s.
Richard holds 7 hides of this land; and a man-at-arms of his 1½ hides.
In lordship they have 2 ploughs, with
    2 smallholders.
Total value before 1066 £100; later £50; now £80.

In SWANBOROUGH [STREAT] Hundred

6 William holds DITCHLING himself in lordship. King Edward held it.
It never paid tax. Before 1066 it answered for 46 hides; when
acquired only 42 hides; the others were in the Count of Mortain's
Rape, and 6 woods which belonged to the head of the manor.
Now it answers for 33 hides. Land for 60 ploughs.
In lordship 8 ploughs.
    108 villagers and 40 smallholders have 81 ploughs.
    A church; 1 mill at 30d; meadow, 130 acres; woodland, 80 pigs;
        11 dwellings in Lewes at 12s.
Gilbert holds 1½ hides of this land; Hugh 2 hides; Alfward 3 hides;
Warin 3 hides; Richard 1 hide. In lordship they have 7½ ploughs, with
    29 smallholders, 3 villagers and 10 slaves with 3 ploughs.
    6 burgesses in Lewes at 43d.

Totū ⊕.T.R.E. ualeḃ q̃t̄ xx . liḃ . 7 lxvi . denar̄ . 7 poſt:
xxv . liḃ . Modo dñiū Wiłłi: lx . liḃ . Hominū ū:
xii . liḃ . 7 x . foliđ.   *In Falemere Hvnd.*
Sc̄s Pancrati͆ ten de Wiłło *Falemere* . Abbatia
de Wiltunia tenuit . T.R.E. 7 in die ej̄ fuit faifita.
T.R.E. fe defđ p̱ . xx̃ . una hida . 7 modo p̱ . xviii . hiđ.
aliæ funt in rapo com moritoñ . 7 ñ geldant . Tra: xv . car̄.
In dñio . ii . car̄ . 7 xxxv . uiłłi 7 vii . borđ cū . xiii . car̄.
Ibi æccła . 7 uñ feruus . Ibi . iiii . āc p̃ti . 7 filua de . xx . porc̄.
T.R.E. 7 poſt . 7 modo: xx̃ . liḃ.

                    In Homestrev Hvnd.
Godefrid teñ de Wiłło *Herbertinges* . Alnođ
tenuit T.R.E. 7 potuit ire quo uoluit . Tc̄ fe defđ p̱ . x . hiđ.
7 dimiđ . Modo p̱ . vi . hiđ . fed dimiđ hida . ē in rapo
comit morit . Tra . ē . iiii . car̄ . In dñio funt . ii . car̄.
7 xiiii . uiłłi 7 vi . borđ cū . ii . car̄ . Ibi . xvii . āc p̃ti.
7 filua de . xxx . porc̄ . In Lewes . iiii . hagæ de . xx . deñ
T.R.E. uałeḃ xl . foł . 7 poſt: l . foł . Modo: lx . fol.
Nigellus teñ de com *Laneswice*.
Goduin tenuit . 7 de eo . vii . aloarij . T.R.E. fe defđ
p̱ vi . hiđ 7 dimiđ . M p̱ . v . hiđ . Tra . ē . iiii . car̄.

26 c
In dñio . ē una car̄ . 7 xi . uiłłi 7 vi . borđ cū . ii . car̄ . Ibi
ii . ferui . 7 xvii . āc p̃ti . In Lewes . ii . hagæ . de . x . foł.
T.R.E. uałḃ . xxx . foliđ . 7 poſt: xl . foł . Modo: lx . foł.
Hugo teñ de Wiłło *Rotingedene* . *In Welesmere Hd*
Haminc tenuit de Goduino . Tc̄ 7 m̃ fe defđ p̱ . ii . hiđ.
7 jacuit in *Ferle* q̃ ten com moritoñ in fuo rapo . Tra . ē
ii . car̄ . Ibi funt in dñio cū . x . borđ.
T.R.E. uałḃ . xl . foł . 7 poſt: xx . foł . Modo: lx . foliđ.

Value of the whole manor before 1066 £80 and 66d; later £25;
now, William's lordship £60; his men's £12 10s.

In FALMER Hundred

7 St. Pancras holds FALMER from William. Wilton Abbey held it
before 1066 and was in possession on King Edward's (death) day.
Before 1066 it answered for 21 hides; now for 18 hides; the others
are in the Count of Mortain's Rape and do not pay tax.
Land for 15 ploughs. In lordship 2 ploughs;
   35 villagers and 7 smallholders with 13 ploughs.
   A church; 1 slave. Meadow, 4 acres; woodland at 20 pigs.
[Value] before 1066, later and now £20.

In HOLMESTROW Hundred

8 Godfrey holds HARPINGDEN from William. Alnoth held it before
1066; he could go where he would. Then it answered for 10½ hides;
now for 6 hides, but ½ hide is in the Count of Mortain's Rape.
Land for 4 ploughs. In lordship 2 ploughs;
   14 villagers and 6 smallholders with 2 ploughs.
   Meadow, 17 acres; woodland at 30 pigs; 4 sites in Lewes at 20d.
Value before 1066, 40s; later 50s; now 60s.

9 Nigel holds 'ORLESWICK' from the Earl. Earl Godwin held it and 7
freeholders from him. Before 1066 it answered for 6½ hides;
now for 5 hides. Land for 4 ploughs. In lordship 1 plough;   26 c
   11 villagers and 6 smallholders with 2 ploughs. 2 slaves.
   Meadow, 17 acres; 2 sites in Lewes at 10s.
Value before 1066, 30s; later 40s; now 60s.

In WHALESBOURNE Hundred

10 Hugh holds ROTTINGDEAN from William. Heming held it from
Earl Godwin. Then and now it answered for 2 hides. It lay in (the
lands of) (Frog) Firle, which the Count of Mortain holds in his Rape.
Land for 2 ploughs. They are there, in lordship, with
   10 smallholders.
Value before 1066, 40s; later 20s; now, 60s.

Godefrid ten de Wilło *HOVINGEDENE*. Alnod tenuit

de rege.E.7 potuit ire quo uoluit.Tc se defd p.v.hid.

In ead uilla tenuit Eddeua.iiii.hid de rege in paragio.

Qdo Godefrid recep: tc inuen in uno M. Sed de his.viii.

hid hт com moriton hidā 7 dim in suo rapo.Qd ten

Godefrid gtdat p.vi.hid modo.Tra.e.iiii.car.In dnio

sunt.ii.car.7 v.uilti 7 v.bord.cū una car.Ibi eccłola.

7 iiii.serui.In Lewes.x.hage de.v.sol.

Cū his hid ten Godefrid.ii.hidas de qda M Wilti dni sui.

quæ nunq geldauer.7 ibi nihil habet.

Tot T.R.E.uatb.vi.lib.7 post.iiii.lib.Modo: vii.lib.

In ead uilla ten Bricmær de Wilło.ii.hid.Ipse tenuit

de Azor.T.R.E.7 tc 7 m p.ii.hid se defd.Ibi hт.i.car

cū.ii.bord.Val 7 ualuit sep.xx.solid.

Radulf ten de Wilło *BRISTELMESTVNE*.Brictric

tenuit de dono Goduini.T.R.E 7 m se defd p.v.hid

7 dimid.Tra.e.iii.car.In dnio.e dim car.7 xviii.uilti

7 ix.bord.cū.iii.car.7 uno seruo.De gabło.iiii.mil alleciū.

T.R.E.uatb viii.lib 7 xii.sol.7 post: c.sol.Modo: xii.lib.

In ead uilla ten Widard de Wilło vi.hid 7 unā v.7 p tanto

se defd.Tres aloarij tenuer de rege.E.7 potuer ire qlibet.

Vn ex eis habuit Aulā.7 uilti tenuer partes alioʒ duoʒ.

Tra.e.v.car.7 est in uno M.In dnio.i.car 7 dim.7 xiiii.

uilti 7 xxi.bord cū.iii.car.7 dimid.Ibi.vii.ac pti.7 silua

.iiii.porc.In Lewes.iiii.hagæ.

T.R.E.uatb.x.lib.7 post: viii.lib.Modo: xii.lib.

Ibidē ten Wilts de Wateuile *BRISTELMETVNE* de Wilło.

Vluuard tenuit de rege.E.Tc 7 m se defd p.v.hid 7 dim.

Tra.e.iiii.car.In dnio est.i.car.7 xiii.uilti 7 xi.bord

cū una car.Ibi æccła.

T.R.E.uatb.x.lib.7 post: viii.lib.Modo: xii.lib.

11 Godfrey holds OVINGDEAN from William. Alnoth held it from
King Edward; he could go where he would. Then it answered
for 5 hides. In the same village Edeva held 3 hides from the
King, jointly. When Godfrey acquired them he found them in
one manor, but of these 8 hides the Count of Mortain has 1½ hides
in his Rape. What Godfrey holds pays tax for 6 hides now.
Land for 4 ploughs. In lordship 2 ploughs;
    5 villagers and 5 smallholders with 1 plough.
    A small church; 4 slaves. 10 sites in Lewes at 5s.
With these hides Godfrey holds 2 hides of a manor of William's,
his lord, which never paid tax; he has nothing there.
Total value before 1066 £6; later £4; now £7.

12 In the same village Brictmer holds 2 hides from William.
He held it himself from Azor before 1066. Then and now it answered
for 2 hides. He has 1 plough, with
    2 smallholders.
The value is and always was 20s.

13 Ralph holds BRIGHTON from William. Brictric held it by gift of Earl
Godwin. Before 1066 and now it answered for 5½ hides.
Land for 3 ploughs. In lordship ½ plough;
    18 villagers and 9 smallholders with 3 ploughs and 1 slave.
    From tribute 4,000 herrings.
Value before 1066 £8 12s; later 100s; now £12.

14 In the same village Widard holds 6 hides and 1 virgate from William.
It answers for as much. 3 freeholders held it from King Edward;
they could go wherever they would. One of them had a hall; the
villagers held the parts of the other two. Land for 5 ploughs; it is
in one manor. In lordship 1½ ploughs;
    14 villagers and 21 smallholders with 3½ ploughs.
    Meadow, 7 acres; woodland, 3 pigs; 4 sites in Lewes.
Value before 1066 £10; later £8; now £12.

15 William of Watteville also holds BRIGHTON from William.
Wulfward held it from King Edward. Then and now it answered
for 5½ hides. Land for 4 ploughs. In lordship 1 plough;
    13 villagers and 11 smallholders with 1 plough.
    A church.
Value before 1066 £10; later £8; now £12.

Goze ten de Witto *BVRGEMERE* . Vitti tenuer̄ q̄ jac̄
in Falemere T.R.E. Tc̄ 7 m̄ se defd̄ ꝑ . iiii . hid . Tra . ē
ii . car̄ . In dn̄io . ē una . cū uno uitto 7 ii . bord̄ . 7 ii . ſeru̅ .
Ibi æcctola . 7 ſilua de . iiii . porc̄ .
T.R.E. uatb̄ xx . ſot . 7 poſt 7 m̄ . xxx . ſolid̄ .
Euſtachi ten de Witto . i . hidā *IN FALEMERE HVND* .
Vn̄ uitts de Falemere tenuit eā . ꝑ una hida ſe defd̄ .
Vat . vi . ſolid̄ .
Walteri ten de Witto *BEVEDENE* . Azor tenuit
de rege . Tc̄ 7 m̄ ſe defd̄ ꝑ . iiii . hid . Vna v̄ c̄ inſuꝑ

26 d

quæ n̄ geldat . q̄a eſt foris rap . Tra . ē . iii . car̄ . In dn̄io ſunt : ii . car̄ .
7 ii . uitti 7 iii . bord̄ . cū una car̄ . In Lewes : ii . hagæ de . xviii . den̄ .
T . R . E . uatb̄ . c . ſot . 7 poſt . iiii . lib̄ . Modo . vi . lib̄ . Hanc tr̄a tenuer̄
uitti de Chemele .   *IN SVANEBERGE HVND* .
Eldeid ten de Witto *WINTREBVRNE* . una hida . ē 7 ꝑ tanto ſe
defd̄ . Eddeua tenuit de rege . E . Tra . ē dim̄ car̄ : 7 ibi . ē in dn̄io .
cū . vi . bord̄ . 7 una ac̄ ꝑti 7 dim . In Lewes . iii . hage . 7 tcia pars
uni̅ hage de xviii . den̄ . T . R . E . 7 poſt . uatb̄ . x . ſot . Modo . xx . ſolid̄ .
Godefrid ten de Witto   *IN DIMID HVND DE ELDRETVNE* .
ELDRETVNE . Jacuit in Beddinges Man . R . E . 7 m̄ ten Witts
de braioſe in ſuo rapo . Godefrid ten . vii . hid 7 dim v̄ . Tra . ē
vii . car̄ . Non geldau . Vitti tenuer̄ . T . R . E . Ibi ſunt . xl . i . uitts
7 x . bord̄ cū . vii . car̄ . T . R . E . 7 poſt uatb̄ . iiii . lib̄ . Modo . vi . lib̄ .
In ead̄ uilla ten iſd̄ Godefrid de Witto . ix . hid . 7 ꝑ tanto
ſe defd̄ . Wigot tenuit de rege . E . 7 jacuer̄ in Bradeuuatre
q̄ ten Witts de braioſe in ſuo rapo . Tra . ē . iiii . car̄ . In dn̄io
eſt una car̄ . 7 x . uitti 7 xii . bord̄ cū . ii . car̄ .   ſuna halla .
T . R . E . 7 poſt . uatb̄ . iiii . lib̄ . Modo . c . ſolid̄ . In his duab̄ tris . niſi

26 c, d

[In FALMER Hundred]

16 Gozo holds BALMER from William. Before 1066 the villagers who lay in Falmer held it. Then and now it answered for 4 hides. Land for 2 ploughs. In lordship 1, with
  1 villager, 2 smallholders and 2 slaves.
  A small church; woodland at 4 pigs.
Value before 1066, 20s; later and now 30s.

In FALMER Hundred

17 Eustace holds 1 hide from William. One villager of Falmer held it. It answered for 1 hide.
Value 6s.

18 Walter holds BEVENDEAN from William. Azor held it from the King. Then and now it answered for 4 hides. In addition there is 1 virgate which does not pay tax because it is outside the Rape.   26 d
Land for 3 ploughs. In lordship 2 ploughs;
  2 villagers and 3 smallholders with 1 plough.
  2 sites in Lewes at 18d.
Value before 1066, 100s; later £4; now £6.
  The villagers of Keymer held this land.

In SWANBOROUGH Hundred

19 Aldith holds WINTERBOURNE from William. 1 hide. It answers for as much. Edeva held it from King Edward. Land for ½ plough. It is there, in lordship, with
  6 smallholders.
  Meadow, 1½ acres; 3 sites and the third part of 1 site
    in Lewes at 18d.
Value before 1066 and later 10s; now 20s.

In the Half-Hundred of ALDRINGTON

20 Godfrey holds ALDRINGTON from William. It lay in (the lands of) Beeding, King Edward's manor. Now William of Braose holds it in his Rape. Godfrey holds 7 hides and ½ virgate. Land for 7 ploughs. It did not pay tax. The villagers held it before 1066.
  41 villagers and 10 smallholders with 7 ploughs.
Value before 1066 and later £4; now £6.

21 In the same village Godfrey also holds 9 hides from William. It answers for as much. Wigot held it from King Edward. It lay in (the lands of) Broadwater which William of Braose holds in his Rape. Land for 4 ploughs. In lordship 1 plough;
  10 villagers and 12 smallholders with 2 ploughs.
Value before 1066 and later £4; now 100s.
  In these two lands there is only one hall.

Nigellus ten de Wilło *ESMEREWIC* . Azor tenuit
de rege . E . Tc 7 m̃ se defď p una hida 7 dim̃ . Tra . ē . iiii . car.
In dñio sunt . ii . car . 7 iiii . uilłi 7 vi . borď cū . ii . car.
T.R.E. uałb . xl . soł . 7 post . xxx . soł . Modo . iiii . lib.

Wilłs de Wateuile ten de Wilło *HANGETONE* . Azor
tenuit de rege . E . Tc se defď p . xiiii . hiď . 7 una v̄ . Modo
p . viii . hiď 7 dim̃ . Tra . ē . viii . car . In dñio sunt . ii . car.
7 xxxi . uilłs 7 xiii . borď cū . v . car.
H̃ tra jacuit ad Chingestone c̃ō Wilłi de Braiose.
T.R.E. 7 m̃ . ual . x . lib . Q̃do recep . viii . lib.

Osward ten de Wilło *PORTESLAGE* dim̃ hiď . Ipse
tenuit T.R.E. 7 ñ geldauit . Iste potuit ire cū tra quo uo
luit . Ibi . ē un̊ uilłs . Val . vi . soliď.

Albtus ten dim̃ hiď in *PORTESLAMHE* . Non geldau.
Ibi . ē un̊ uilłs cū dim̃ car . Val 7 ualuit . vi . soliď.

IN PONINGES HVND.

Leuenot ten de Wilło *PAVEORNE* . Ipse tenuit de
rege . E . 7 potuit ire q̃libet . Tc se defď p . iiii . hiď . modo
p una hida 7 dim̃ . q̃a aliæ sunt in rapo Wilłi de braiose.
Tra . ē . i . car . 7 ibi . ē in dñio . cū . ii . borď.
In Leuues . iii . hagæ de . xviii . denar . Val 7 ualuit . xxx . soł.

Osuuard ten de Wilło *BERCHINGES* . Ipse tenuit . T.R.E.
7 potuit ire quo uoluit . Tc 7 m̃ se defď p . iii . hiď . Tra . ē
ii . car 7 dimiď . In dñio . ē una . 7 ii . uilłi 7 iiii . borď cū una
car . 7 dimiď molin̄ de . xl . den̄ . 7 vii . ãc p̃ti . Silua . ii . porc.
In Leuues una haga 7 dim̃ de . ix . den̄ . Val 7 ualuit . xl . soł.

In ead̃ uilla ten Tezelin de Wilło . ii . hiď . 7 p tanto se
defď . In Trailgi jacuer̃ q̃ ten Wilłs de braiose . Bellinc
tenuit de Goduino . In dñio . ē una car . 7 iii . uilłi 7 ii . borď
cū dimiď car . Dimiď molin̄ de xiii . soliď 7 iiii . denar.
7 iii . ãc p̃ti . Silua . ii . porc . In Leuues dim̃ haga de . ii . den̄

22   Nigel holds BENFIELD from William. Azor held it from King
Edward. Then and now it answered for 1½ hides. Land for 4
ploughs. In lordship 2 ploughs;
    4 villagers and 6 smallholders with 2 ploughs.
Value before 1066, 40s; later 30s; now £4.

23   William of Watteville holds HANGLETON from William. Azor
held it from King Edward. Then it answered for 14 hides
and 1 virgate; now for 8½ hides. Land for 8 ploughs.
In lordship 2 ploughs;
    31 villagers and 13 smallholders with 5 ploughs.
This land lay in (the lands of) Kingston, a manor of William of Braose.
Value before 1066 and now £10; when acquired £8.

24   Osward holds ½ hide [in] PORTSLADE from William. He held it
before 1066. It did not pay tax. He could go where he would
with the land.
    1 villager.
Value 6s.

25   Albert holds ½ hide in PORTSLADE. It did not pay tax.
    1 villager with ½ plough.
The value is and was 6s.

In POYNINGS Hundred

26   Leofnoth holds PAWTHORNE from William. He held it from
King Edward; he could go wherever [he would]. Then it answered
for 4 hides; now for 1½ hides because the others are in the Rape
of William of Braose. Land for 1 plough. It is there in lordship, with
    2 smallholders.
    3 sites in Lewes at 18d.
The value is and was 30s.

27   Osward holds PERCHING from William. He held it before 1066;
he could go where he would. Then and now it answered for 3 hides.
Land for 2½ ploughs. In lordship 1;
    2 villagers and 4 smallholders with 1 plough.
    ½ mill at 40d; meadow, 7 acres; woodland, 2 pigs;
      1½ sites in Lewes at 9d.
The value is and was 40s.

28   In the same village Tesselin holds 2 hides from William. It answers
for as much. It lay in (the lands of) Truleigh, which William of Braose
holds. Belling held it from Earl Godwin. In lordship 1 plough;
    3 villagers and 2 smallholders with ½ plough.
    ½ mill at 13s 4d; meadow, 3 acres; woodland, 2 pigs;
      ½ site in Lewes at 2d.

Iſdē Tezelinꝰ ten de Wiłło *FOCHINGES* . In Sepelei

jacuit q̓ ten Wiłłs de braioſe Herald tenuit T.R.E .T̄c 7 m̊ ſe

defđ ꝓ.iii.hiđ 7 una v̓.Viłłi.vi.ibi ſunt cū.ii.car̓.

He duæ tre Tezelini inſimul ſunt.Val 7 ualuer̄ ſēp.l.ſoł.

Wiłłs fili ꝰRainaldi ten de Wiłło *PONINGES* .Cola̱ tenuit

de Goduino.q̓a dedit ei.T,R.E.7 m̊ ꝓ.viii.hiđ.ſeđ nunꝗ g̓dauit.

Tra̓.ē.xiii.car.In dn̄io ſunt.ii.car.7 xxv.uiłłi 7 viii.borđ cū xv.

car̄.Ibi æccła.7 ii.ſerui.7 ii.molini de.xii.ſoliđ.7 l.ac̄ p̄ti.Silua꞉

de.xl.porc̄.T.R.E.̓ ualb̄ xii.lib̄.7 poſt 7 m̊.̓ x.lib̄.

Iſđ Wiłłs ten de Wiłło *PINHEDENE* .Leufel tenuit de rege.E.

T̄c 7 m̊ ſe defđ ꝓ.x.hiđ.̓Tra̓.ē xi.car̄.In dn̄io.ē una car̄.7 xv.uiłłi

7 viii.borđ cū.viii.car̄.Ibi ſilua de.ii.porc̄.In Leuues.ii.hage

de.ii.ſoliđ.7 una ac̄ p̄ti.T.R.E.7 m̊.̓ ual.c.ſoliđ Cū recep̄.̓ vi.lib̄.

Iſđ Wiłłs ten de Wiłło *PINWEDENE* .Oſuuarđ tenuit de rege.E.

7 potuit ire quo uoluit.T̄c 7 m̊ ſe defđ ꝓ.ix.hiđ.Tra̓.ē x.car̄.

In dn̄io.ē una.7 xv.uiłłi 7 vi.borđ cū.vi.car̄.In Leuues.ii.hagæ

de.ii.ſoł.T.R.E.7 poſt꞉̓ ualuit.vi.lib̄.Modo꞉̓ c.ſoliđ.

De eađ tra̓ ten Rogeri 7 Walter ꝰde Wiłło.ii.car̄.cū.iiii.borđ.

Val.xxx.ſoliđ.

Radulf ꝰten de Wiłło *SALESCOME* .Goduin ꝰtenuit de Goduino.com̄

In Boſehā jacebat.T̄c 7 m̊ ſe defđ ꝓ.xvii.hiđ.Tra̓.ē.x.car̄.

In dn̄io ſunt.ii.car̄.7 xxiiii.uiłłi 7 iiii.borđ cū.vii.car̄.

Ibi.xiii.ac̄ p̄ti.De ſale꞉̓ xv.denar̄.In Leuues.i.haga.

Silua fuit de.v.porc̄.quæ m̊ eſt in rapo Wiłłi de braioſe.

De hac tra̓ ten Radulf.iiii.hiđ.7 ibi h̄t in dn̄io.i.car̄.7 iii.es

uiłłos 7 ii.borđ cū dim̄ car̄.

Totū T.R.E.ualb̄.xv.lib̄.7 poſt꞉̓ x.lib̄.Modo꞉̓ xi.lib̄.

Iſdē Radulf ꝰten de Wiłło *NIVEMBRE* .Ælfech tenuit de rege.E.

7 potuit ire quo uoluit.T̄c 7 m̊ ſe defđ ꝓ x.hiđ.Tra̓.ē.vii.car̄.

In dn̄io ſunt.ii.car̄.7 xiiii.uiłłi 7 vii.borđ cū.v.car̄.Ibi un̄

9 Tesselin also holds FULKING from William. It lay in (the lands of)
Shipley, which William of Braose holds. Harold held it before
1066. Then and now it answered for 3 hides and 1 virgate.
   6 villagers with 2 ploughs.
These two lands of Tesselin are together.
The value is and always was 50s.

0 William son of Reginald holds POYNINGS from William. Cola held
it from Earl Godwin because he gave it to him. Before 1066 and now
[it answered for] 8 hides but it never paid tax. Land for 13 ploughs.
In lordship 2 ploughs;
   25 villagers and 8 smallholders with 15 ploughs.
   A church; 2 slaves; 2 mills at 12s; meadow, 50 acres;
      woodland at 40 pigs.
Value before 1066 £12; later and now £10.

1 William also holds PANGDEAN from William. Leofhelm
held it from King Edward. Then and now it answered for 10 hides.
Land for 11 ploughs. In lordship 1 plough;
   15 villagers and 8 smallholders with 8 ploughs.
   Woodland at 2 pigs; 2 sites in Lewes at 2s; meadow, 1 acre.
Value before 1066 and now 100s; when acquired £6.

2 William also holds PANGDEAN from William. Osward
held it from King Edward; he could go where he would.
Then and now it answered for 9 hides. Land for 10 ploughs.
In lordship 1;
   15 villagers and 6 smallholders with 6 ploughs.
   2 sites in Lewes at 2s.
Value before 1066 and later £6; now 100s.
   Of this land Roger and Walter hold from William 2 carucates, with
     4 smallholders.
Value 30s.

3 Ralph holds SADDLESCOMBE from William. Godwin the priest
held it from Earl Godwin. It lay in Bosham (lands). Then and now it
answered for 17 hides. Land for 10 ploughs. In lordship 2 ploughs;
   24 villagers and 4 smallholders with 7 ploughs.
   Meadow, 13 acres; from salt, 15d; 1 site in Lewes; there was
     woodland at 5 pigs, which is now in the Rape of William of Braose.
   Ralph holds 4 hides of this land. He has in lordship 1 plough and
     3 villagers and 2 smallholders with ½ plough.
Total value before 1066 £15; later £10; now £11.

4 Ralph also holds NEWTIMBER from William. Alfheah held it from
King Edward; he could go where he would. Then and now it
answered for 10 hides. Land for 7 ploughs. In lordship 2 ploughs;
   14 villagers and 7 smallholders with 5 ploughs.

moliñ de.xx.denar. 7 ii.ac̄ p̃ti. 7 ſilua.iii.porc̄.

T.R.E.7 poſt. ualb.vii.lib.modo. viii.lib.

Wilts de Wateuile ten̄ PCINGES. Azor tenuit de rege.E.

7 ii.hões de Azor. p.v.hiđ 7 dimiđ ſe defđ tc̄ 7 modo.Tc̄ fuer̄

ii.Hallæ.m̄ in uno M̄.Tra.ē.v.car̄ 7 dimiđ.In dñio.ē una.

7 iiii.uitti 7 iii.borđ cū una car̄.Ibi.ii.ſerui.7 iii.ac̄ p̃ti.

Silua.iii.porc̄.de paſtura.vi.denar̄.

T.R.E.ualb.lx.ſot. 7 poſt. xl.ſot.Modo. l.ſolid.

Rotbtus de Witto ten̄ HERST. IN BOTINGELLE HVND.

Goduin com̄ ꝯ tenuit.Tc̄ ſe defđ p xl 7 una hida.m̄ p nichilo.q̄a

nunꝗ geldauit.Qdo recep̄. n̄ niſi xviii.hiđ 7 dimidia.

In rapo comit moriton.ſunt.iii.hidæ 7 dimiđ.In rapo Witti

de braioſe.ſunt.xix.hide.Tra.ē.xxv.car̄.

In dñio ſunt.ii.car̄. 7 xxxv.uitti 7 viii.borđ cū xxi.car̄ 7 dim̄.

Ibi æccta 7 viii.ſerui.7 iii.molini de.ix.ſot.7 q̄t xx.ac̄ p̃ti.

Silua de.l.porc̄.

De hac tra ten̄ Witts.iii.hiđ.Giſlebt̄.iii.hiđ 7 dim̄.Vitti tenuer̄.

Tot T.R.E.ualb xxxvi.lib. 7 poſt. ix.lib.Modo.xii.lib jnt totū.

Vxor Witti de Wateuile ten̄ de Witto CLAITVNE.Azor

tenuit de rege.E.Tc̄ 7 m̄ ſe defđ p.vii.hiđ.Tra.ē.xii.car̄.

27 b

In dñio ſunt.ii.car̄. 7 xxvi.uitti 7 v.borđ cū.xiiii.car̄.

Ibi æccta.7 xxiii.ac̄ p̃ti.Silua de.xv.porc̄.In Leuues.

ix.hagæ de.iiii.ſolid 7 vii.den̄.T.R.E.ualb x.lib. 7 poſt

7 modo. viii.lib.

De ipſa femina ten̄ Aluuin ꝯ Wichā. ipſe de Azor tenuit.

Tc̄ 7 m̄ ſe defđ p.iii.hiđ.In dñio.ē una car̄. 7 iii.uitti

cū.i.car̄. 7 in Leuues.iii.partes uni ꝯ hagæ de.xv.den̄.

Witts de Wateuile ten̄ de Witto CHEMERE.Azor

tenuit de rege.E.Tc̄ 7 m̄ ſe defđ p xiiii.hiđ.Tra.ē

xxv.car̄.In dñio ſunt.ii.car̄. 7 xxxvi.uitti 7 xi.borđ

1 mill at 20d; meadow, 2 acres; woodland, 3 pigs.
Value before 1066 and later £7; now £8.

35 William of Watteville holds PERCHING. Azor held it from
King Edward, and 2 men from Azor. Then and now it answered
for 5½ hides. Then there were 2 halls; now it is in 1 manor.
Land for 5½ ploughs. In lordship 1;
    4 villagers and 3 smallholders with 1 plough.
    2 slaves; meadow, 3 acres; woodland, 3 pigs; from pasture 6d.
Value before 1066, 60s; later 40s; now 50s.

In BUTTINGHILL Hundred
36 Robert holds HURSTPIERPOINT from William. Earl Godwin held it.
Then it answered for 41 hides; now for nothing, because it never
paid tax. When acquired there was nothing but 18½ hides.
In the Count of Mortain's Rape are 3½ hides; in the Rape of
William of Braose, 19 hides. Land for 25 ploughs. In lordship 2 ploughs;
    35 villagers and 8 smallholders with 21½ ploughs.
    A church; 8 slaves; 3 mills at 9s; meadow, 80 acres;
      woodland at 50 pigs.
    William holds 3 hides of this land; Gilbert 3½ hides.
    The villagers held it.
Total value before 1066 £36; later £9; now £12 in all.

37 William of Watteville's wife holds CLAYTON from William.
Azor held it from King Edward. Then and now it answered
for 7 hides. Land for 12 ploughs. In lordship 2 ploughs;   27 b
    26 villagers and 5 smallholders with 14 ploughs.
    A church; meadow, 23 acres; woodland at 15 pigs;
      9 sites in Lewes at 4s 7d.
Value before 1066 £10; later and now £8.

38 Alwin holds WICKHAM from this woman. He held it himself from Azor.
Then and now it answered for 3 hides. In lordship 1 plough;
    3 villagers with 1 plough.
    3 parts of 1 site in Lewes at 15d.
[Value...]

39 William of Watteville holds KEYMER from William. Azor held
it from King Edward. Then and now it answered for 14 hides.
Land for 25 ploughs. In lordship 2 ploughs;

cū. xvii . car . Ibi æccła 7 iii . ſerui . 7 xl . ac pti . 7 ii.

molini de. xii . ſolid . In Leuues . vii . hagæ de. xxvi . den.

T.R.E. 7 poſt: ualb. xiiii . lib . Modo: xii . lib.

Radulf ten de Witło ESTRAT . IN ESTRAT HVND.

Leuuin tenuit de rege .E. Tc ſe defd p. ix . hid . m p. viii . hid.

Tra . e . xvi . car . In dnio ſunt . iii . car . 7 xx . uitti 7 xii.

bord . cū . viii . car . Ibi . vi . ac pti . De ſilua: xvi . porc.

In Leuues . iii . hagæ . de . xviii . denar.

De hac tra ten q̃dā Radulf . i . hid . 7 ibi ht . i . car cū . i . uitło.

Ibi . ii . æccleſiolæ . T.R.E. 7 poſt 7 modo: ual . c . ſol.

Rotbt ten de Witło | In WESMESTVN . xii . hidas.

comitiſſa
Gueda tenuit . 7 ſub ea teneb uillani . Ñ fuit ibi halla.

neq̃ geldauit ut dicunt . Tra . e . ix . car . In dnio . e una

car . 7 iiii . uitti 7 xii . bord . cū . ii . car . Ibi . iii . ac pti.

7 ſilua de . x . porc.

De hac tra ten un miles . iii . hid 7 iii . v . 7 ibi ht in dnio

una car . 7 ii . uitti 7 v . bord . In Leuues . i . haga nichil redd.

T.R.E. ualb. vii . lib . 7 poſt: c . ſol . Modo . vi . lib.

Hugo fili Rannulfi ten de Witło PLVNTVNE . pbr Goduin

coin.
tenuit de Goduino Tc ſe defd p. xxxii . hid . Modo p. xxx.

Tra . e . xxiiii . car . In dnio ſunt . iii . car . 7 li . uitts

7 vi . bord cū . xxii . car . Ibi æccła . 7 viii . ſerui . 7 ii.

molini de . xx . ſolid . Silua: de xx . porc . De gablo . xvii.

porc . ptū . In Leuues . ix . hagæ . de . iiii . ſol 7 v . den.

T.R.E. 7 m . ualb . xxv . lib . Cū recep: xv . lib.

Rotbt ten de Witło CHILDELTVNE . Fredri te

nuit de rege . E . 7 potuit ire quo uoluit . Tc ſe defd

7 una uirga.
p. vii . hid . Modo p. v . hid | aliæ ſunt in rapo comit

moriton . Tra . e . vi . car . In dnio . e una car . 7 iii . uitti

cū una car . In Leuues . i . haga de . xii . den.

36 villagers and 11 smallholders with 17 ploughs.
A church; 3 slaves; meadow, 40 acres; 2 mills at 12s;
7 sites in Lewes at 26d.
Value before 1066 and later £14; now £12.

In STREAT Hundred

40 Ralph holds STREAT from William. Leofwin held it from
King Edward. Then it answered for 9 hides; now for 8 hides.
Land for 16 ploughs. In lordship 3 ploughs;
20 villagers and 12 smallholders with 8 ploughs.
Meadow, 6 acres; from woodland 16 pigs; 3 sites in Lewes at 18d.
One Ralph holds 1 hide of this land. He has 1 plough, with
1 villager. 2 small churches.
Value before 1066, later and now 100s.

41 Robert holds 12 hides in WESTMESTON from William. Countess
Gytha held it. The villagers held it under her. There was no
hall there nor did it pay tax, as they state. Land for 9 ploughs.
In lordship 1 plough;
4 villagers and 12 smallholders with 2 ploughs.
Meadow, 3 acres; woodland at 10 pigs.
A man-at-arms holds 3 hides and 3 virgates of this land.
He has 1 plough in lordship.
2 villagers and 5 smallholders.
1 site in Lewes which pays nothing.
Value before 1066 £7; later 100s; now £6.

42 Hugh son of Ranulf holds PLUMPTON from William. Godwin
the priest held it from Earl Godwin. Then it answered for 32
hides; now for 30. Land for 24 ploughs. In lordship 3 ploughs;
51 villagers and 6 smallholders with 22 ploughs.
A church; 8 slaves; 2 mills at 20s; woodland at 20 pigs;
from tribute 17 pigs; meadow
9 sites in Lewes at 4s 5d.
Value before 1066 and now £25; when acquired £15.

43 Robert holds (EAST) CHILTINGTON from William. Frederic
held it from King Edward; he could go where he would.
Then it answered for 7 hides; now for 5 hides and 1 virgate.
The others are in the Count of Mortain's Rape. Land for 6 ploughs.
In lordship 1 plough;
3 villagers with 1 plough.
1 site in Lewes at 12d.

De hac tra ten q̃dã miles . ii . hiđ 7 dim . 7 ibi hr̃ in

dñio . i . car̃ . 7 vi . uiłłi 7 ii . borđ cũ . i . car̃ 7 dim molin

de xv . denar̃ . 7 una haga 7 dim de . viii . den.

T . R . E . uałb . iiii . lib . 7 poſt: Modo: c . ſoliđ.

Godefrid ten de Wiłło *CHILDETVNE* . Godricus

tenuit de rege . E . Tc̃ ſe defđ ꝓ . ii . hiđ . Modo ꝓ una

hida 7 dim . q̃a dimiđ . ẽ in rapo comit moriton̄.

Tra . ẽ . ii . car̃ . In dñio . ẽ una car̃ . 7 v . uiłłi 7 iii . borđ.

cũ . i . car̃ . Ibi . ii . ãc p̃ti . Silua . de xii . porc̃ . In Leuues . i . burg

£ de . vi . den.

T . R . E . 7 poſt: uałb . xvi . ſoł . Modo . xx . ſoliđ.

Nigellus ten̄ de Wiłło . i . hidã in *ODINTVNE*.

Godric⁹ tenuit de rege . E . Non deđ geldũ . Nullus ibi

manet . uał xii⌊ᶠᵒᵗ.

Hugo ten̄ de Wiłło *VENNINGORE* . Quattuor aloarij

tenuer̃ de rege . E . 7 potuer̃ ire quo uołuer̃ cũ ſuis tr̃is.

Tc̃ ſe defđ ꝓ . iii . hiđ 7 dim . Modo . ẽ dim in rapo comit

moriton̄ . Tra . ẽ . iii . car̃ . In dñio ſunt . iii . car̃ . 7 vi . uiłłi

7 v . borđ cũ . iii . car̃.   Tres hagæ de xxi.

denar̃ . T . R . E . uałb xl . ſoł . 7 poſt: xxx . ſoł . Modo: lx . ſoł.

Iſdẽ Hugo ten̄ de Wiłło . iii . uirg in Bedinges q̃ ten̄

Wiłłs de braioſe . Viłłi tenuer̃ . T . R . E . Nunꝗ geldau.

In dñio . ẽ una car̃ . 7 xv . uiłłi 7 iii . borđ cũ . v . car̃.

Tra . ẽ . v . car̃ . Ibi . iii . ãc p̃ti . Silua de . x . porc̃.

T . R . E . 7 poſt . uałb . xv . ſoliđ . Modo: xxx . ſoliđ .   *IN BERCHÃ*

Wiłłs de Wateuile ten̄ de Wiłło *BERCHAM* .   *HVND.*

Azor tenuit de Goduino . Tc̃ ſe defđ ꝓ xiii . hiđ.

Modo ꝓ . x . hiđ 7 dim . Aliæ ſunt in rapo comit morit.

Nunꝗ geldauer̃ ut dicunt . Tra . ẽ . xx . car̃ . In dñio

ſunt . ii . car̃ . 7 xxiiii . uiłłi 7 ii . borđ cũ . ix . car̃ . Ibi æccła

A man-at-arms holds 2½ hides of this land. He has 1
plough in lordship;
    6 villagers and 2 smallholders with 1 plough.
    ½ mill at 15d; 1½ sites at 8d.
Value before 1066 and later £4; now 100s.

44 Godfrey holds (EAST) CHILTINGTON from William. Godric held
it from King Edward. Then it answered for 2 hides; now for 1½
hides because ½ is in the Count of Mortain's Rape.
Land for 2 ploughs. In lordship 1 plough;
    5 villagers and 3 smallholders with 1 plough.
    Meadow, 2 acres; woodland at 12 pigs; 1 burgess
      in Lewes at 6d.
Value before 1066 and later 16s; now 20s.   27 c

45 Nigel holds 1 hide in WOOTTON from William.
Godric held it from King Edward. It did not give tax.
No one lives there.
Value 12s.

46 Hugh holds WARNINGORE from William. Four freeholders held
it from King Edward; they could go where they would with
their lands. Then it answered for 3½ hides; now ½ is in
the Count of Mortain's Rape. Land for 3 ploughs.
In lordship 3 ploughs;
    6 villagers and 5 smallholders with 3 ploughs.
    3 sites at 21d.
Value before 1066, 40s; later 30s; now 60s.

47 Hugh also holds 3 virgates from William in BEEDING which
William of Braose holds. The villagers held it before 1066.
It never paid tax. In lordship 1 plough;
    15 villagers and 3 smallholders with 5 ploughs.
    Land for 5 ploughs.
    Meadow, 3 acres; woodland at 10 pigs.
Value before 1066 and later 15s; now 30s.

 .In BARCOMBE Hundred
48 William of Watteville holds BARCOMBE from William. Azor
held it from Earl Godwin. Then it answered for 13 hides;
now for 10½ hides. The others are in the Count of Mortain's
Rape. They never paid tax, as they state. Land for 20 ploughs.
In lordship 2 ploughs;
    24 villagers and 2 smallholders with 9 ploughs.

7 III . molini 7 dim̄ de . xx . ſolid̄ . In Leuues . xvIII . hagæ
de . vIII . ſolid̄ 7 vII . den̄.

T.R̄.E. ualb̄ . xII . lib̄ . 7 poſt.ꞌ vI . lib̄ . Modo.ꞌ vIII . lib̄.

Radulf⁹ ten̄ de Witło *Hame* . Vlueua tenuit
de rege . E . Tc̄ ſe deſd̄ ꝑ xxv . hid̄ . modo ſunt . xIIII.
q̄a aliæ ſunt in rapo comit̄ morit̄ . ſcilicet . vII . hidæ.
7 in rapo Rogerij com̄ . IIII . hidæ dim̄ v min⁹.

Modo qd̄ Radulf⁹ ht̄ geldat ꝑ xIII . hid̄ . Tra . ē xIII.
car̄ . In dn̄io ſunt . II . hidæ . 7 xvI . uiłłi 7 xIIII . bord̄
cū . x . car̄ . Ibi æccła . 7 cc . ac̄ p̄ti . Silua . de . x . porc̄.
De herbagio . xIII . ſoł.

De ead̄ tra ten̄ Hugo . I . hid̄ꝑ Radulf⁹ dim̄ hid̄.

Totū T.R̄.E. ualb̄ . xx . lib̄ . 7 poſt.ꞌ x . lib̄ . Modo.ꞌ x . lib̄.

Radulf⁹ iſd̄e ten̄ de Witło *Alintvne*.

Vluuard⁹ tenuit de rege . E . Tc̄ 7 m̄ ſe deſd̄ ꝑ . vI . hid̄.
Tra . ē . vI . car̄ . Ibi ſunt . vIII . uiłłi 7 III . bord̄ cū
II . car̄ 7 dim̄ . In Leuues . I . haga de . vI . denar̄.
De hac tra ten̄ Warner⁹ . I . hid̄ā . Oſmund⁹ . I . hid̄ā.

Totū T.R̄.E. ualb̄ . IIII . lib̄ 7 II . ſoł . 7 poſt . lxII . ſoł . Modo.ꞌ
In ead̄ uiłła ten̄ Hugo de Witło . II . hidas.   ⌐ l . ſolid̄.
Eddeua tenuit T.R̄.E. 7 quo uoluit ire potuit . Tc̄ 7 m̄
ſe deſd̄ ꝑ . II . hid̄ . Tra . ē . I . car̄ . In dn̄io . ē dim̄ car̄ . 7 III.
uiłłi 7 II . bord̄ cū . I . car̄ . In Leuues.ꞌ IIII . hagæ . de . IIII . ſoł.
Vał 7 ualuit . xx . ſolid̄.

Ibid̄e ten̄ Nigellus dimid̄ v . 7 ꝑ tanto geldat . Ibi
q̄dā uiłłs ht̄ dim̄ vcar̄ .   Vał 7 ualuit . x . ſoł.

Gozelin⁹ ten̄ de Witło . I . hid̄ā *In Falemere hvnd̄*.

in *Molstan* . Azor tenuit de rege . E . ad̄ maneriū
de Hoingeſdene . Non geldau̇ . In dn̄io . ē una car̄.
Vał 7 ualuit . xx . ſolid̄.

A church. 3½ mills at 20s; 18 sites in Lewes at 8s 7d.
Value before 1066 £12; later £6; now £8.

49 Ralph holds HAMSEY from William. Wulfeva held it from
King Edward. Then it answered for 25 hides; now there
are 14 because the others are in the Count of Mortain's
Rape, namely 7 hides; and in Earl Roger's Rape 4 hides less ½
virgate. Now what Ralph has pays tax for 13 hides.
Land for 13 ploughs. In lordship 2 hides;
   16 villagers and 14 smallholders with 10 ploughs.
   A church; meadow 200 acres; woodland at 10 pigs;
     from grazing 13s.
Hugh holds 1 hide of this land; Ralph ½ hide.
Total value before 1066 £20; later £10; now £10.

50 Ralph also holds ALLINGTON from William. Wulfward held
it from King Edward. Then and now it answered for 6 hides.
Land for 6 ploughs.
   8 villagers and 3 smallholders with 2½ ploughs.
   1 site in Lewes at 6d.
Warner holds 1 hide of this land; Osmund 1 hide.
Total value before 1066 £4 2s; later 62s; now 50s.

51 In the same village Hugh holds 2 hides from William. Edeva
held it before 1066; she could go where she would. Then and
now it answered for 2 hides. Land for 1 plough. In lordship
½ plough;
   3 villagers and 2 smallholders with 1 plough.
   4 sites in Lewes at 4s.
The value is and was 20s.

52 Nigel also holds ½ virgate there. It pays tax for as much.
   A villager has ½ plough.
The value is and was 10s.

In FALMER Hundred
53 Jocelyn holds 1 hide from William in MOULSTONE. Azor
held it from King Edward at the manor of Ovingdean. It
did not pay tax. In lordship 1 plough.
The value is and was 20s.

Scolland ten̄ de Witto   In Wingehā hvnd.

Benefelle . Turgod tenuit de Cola . 7 Cola de rege . E.

Tc̄ ſe deſđ ꝓ . ii ᷝ hiđ . m̄ ꝓ nichilo . Tra . ē . iii . car̄.

In dn̄io . ii . car̄ . 7 v . uilti cū . viii . borđ hn̄t . ii . car̄.

T.R.E. uatb lx . ſot . 7 poſt . ſimilit̄ . Modo ፦ vi . liƀ.

Alfred ten̄ de Witto . i . hidā in Benefelle . 7 unā v . 7 pro

tanto ſe deſđ . T.R.E. Modo ꝓ nichilo . Leuuin̄ tenuit in

paragio . Tra . ē . i . car̄ . 7 ibi . ē in dn̄io . 7 iiii . uilti cū dim car̄.

Ibi . iiii . ac̄ p̄ti . 7 ſilua de . iii . porc̄.

T.R.E. 7 poſt . uatb . x . ſot . Modo ፦ xl . ſot . In Soaneberg hđ.

Witts fili Reinaldi ten̄ de Witto Acescome . Cola tenuit.

T.R.E. Tc̄ 7 m̄ ſe deſđ ꝓ . ii . hiđ . In dn̄io . ē una car̄ . 7 v . uilti cū

.iii . car̄ . Ipſi uilti ſt̄ in rapo comit morit̄ . ſ; ſep̄ fuer̄ ext̄ rapū.

T.R.E. 7 poſt . 7 m̄ ፦ uat .xxvi . ſot.

.XIII.   Terra Willi De Braiose In Bvrbece hvnđ.

Willelm De Braiose ten̄ Beddinges . Rex . E.

tenuit in firmā ſuā . Tc̄ deſđ ſe ꝓ . xxxii . hiđ . Non̄

geldauit . De his hiđ h̄t Witts de Warene . x . hiđ in ſuo rapo.

Alias ten̄ Witts de braioſe . Tra . ē . xxviii . car̄ . In dn̄io . iiii . car̄ ſt̄፦

7 lxii . uilti 7 xlviii . borđ cū . xxiiii . car̄ . Ibi . ii . æcclæ ፦ 7 vi . ac̄

p̄ti . Silua ፦ lxx . porc̄ . 7 xx . porc̄ de gablo . 7 ii . ſext mellis.

T.R.E. reddeƀ un̄ diē de firma . 7 uatb q̄t xx . 7 xv . liƀ . 7 v . ſot 7 vi . den.

7 poſt ፦ ualuit . l . liƀ . Modo ፦ xl . liƀ . H̄ tota tra redđ Herdigelt.

Ipſe Witts ten̄ . viii . hiđ . quæ jacuer̄ in Redmelle . q̄ ten̄ Witts

de Warene in ſuo rapo . 7 deſđ ſe ꝓ v . hiđ 7 dim . Ibi ſunt . x . uilti

hn̄tes . v . car̄ 7 dimid . 7 iiii . ac̄ p̄ti . T.R.E. 7 poſt . 7 m̄ ፦ uat .viii . liƀ.

Iſđē Witts ten̄ . vii . hiđ quæ jacuer̄ in Berts q̄ h̄t Witts in ſuo

rapo . Bereuuiche fuit . M̄ deſđ ſe ꝓ una hidā 7 dim . In dn̄io ſuṇ

.ii . car̄ . 7 iii . uilti 7 vi . borđ cū . ii . car̄ 7 dim.

T.R.E. uatb . vi . liƀ . 7 poſt ፦ lv . ſoliđ . Modo ፦ iiii . liƀ.

In WYNDHAM Hundred

54 Scolland holds 'BENEFELD' from William. Thorgot held it
from Cola and Cola from King Edward. Then it answered for 2 hides;
now for nothing. Land for 3 ploughs. In lordship 2 ploughs.
      5 villagers with 8 smallholders have 2 ploughs.
Value before 1066, 60s; later the same; now £6.

55 Alfred holds 1 hide and 1 virgate in 'BENEFELD' from William.
It answered for as much before 1066; now for nothing.
Leofwin held it jointly. Land for 1 plough. It is there,
in lordship;
      4 villagers with ½ plough.
      Meadow, 4 acres; woodland at 3 pigs.
Value before 1066 and later 10s; now 40s.

In SWANBOROUGH Hundred

56 William son of Reginald holds ASHCOMBE from William. Cola
held it before 1066. Then and now it answered for 2 hides.
In lordship 1 plough;
      5 villagers with 3 ploughs.
      The villagers themselves are in the Count of Mortain's
      Rape, but they were always outside the Rape.
Value before 1066, later and now 26s.

13   **LAND OF WILLIAM OF BRAOSE**   28 a
(Bramber Rape)

In BURBEACH Hundred

1 William of Braose holds BEEDING.   King Edward held it in
his revenue. Then it answered for 32 hides. It did not pay tax.
Of these hides William of Warenne has 10 in his Rape; William of
Braose holds the others. Land for 28 ploughs. In lordship 4 ploughs;
      62 villagers and 48 smallholders with 24 ploughs.
      2 churches; meadow, 6 acres; woodland, 70 pigs;
      20 pigs from tribute; 2 sesters of honey.
Before 1066 it paid one day's revenue; value £95 5s 6d;
value later £50; now £40. The whole of this land pays hearth-tax.

2 William holds 8 hides himself which lay in the (lands of) Rodmell,
which William of Warenne holds in his Rape. It answers for 5½ hides.
      10 villagers who have 5½ ploughs.
      Meadow, 4 acres.
Value before 1066, later and now £8.

3 William also holds 7 hides which lay in (the lands of) Berth which
William (of Warenne) has in his Rape. It was an outlier.
Now it answers for 1½ hides. In lordship 2 ploughs;
      3 villagers and 6 smallholders with 2½ ploughs.
Value before 1066 £6; later 55s; now £4.

Ipſe Wilts ten ⁊ ERINGEHA̅ . Fredri tenuit de rege . E . 7 potuit
ire quo uoluit . Tc̅ ſe defd̅ ꝑ . v . hid̅ . 7 m̅ ꝑ dim̅ hida . Ibi . ii̅ . uilli
7 . v . bord̅ nil hn̅tes . T.R.E. 7 m̅ ⫽ ual . xl . ſol . Cu̅ recep̅ ⫽ xx . ſol .
Ipſe Wilts ten ⁊ SORESHA̅ . Azor tenuit de rege . E . Tc̅ ſe
defd̅ ꝑ . xii . hid̅ . modo ꝑ . v . hid̅ 7 dimid̅ uirga . Tra . e̅ xv . car̅ .
In dn̅io ſunt . iii . car̅ . 7 xxvi . uilli 7 xlix . bord̅ cu̅ . xii . car̅ .
Ibi æccla . 7 vi . ac̅ p̅ti . 7 ſilua de . xl . porc̅ .
T.R.E. ual b . xxv . lib̅ . 7 poſt ⫽ xvi . lib̅ . Modo ⫽ xxxv . lib̅ . 7 tam̅
fuit ad firma̅ ꝑ . l . lib̅ . ſed̅ n̅ potuit pati .
Wilts| Miles de Wilto ten ⁊ TRAILGI . Bedling de Goduino . T.R.E. com̅
Tc̅ ſe defd̅ ꝑ . iiii . hid̅ . m̅ ꝑ nichilo . Tra . e̅ . ii . car̅ 7 dim̅ . In dn̅io . i .
car̅ . 7 iii . uilli 7 vi . bord̅ cu̅ dim̅ car̅ . 7 ii . molini de . lxv . denar̅ .
De hac tra ten Anſfrid dim̅ hid̅ . 7 ibi ht̅ dim̅ car̅ .
Totu̅ co̅ T.R.E. ual b . iiii . lib̅ . 7 poſt . lx . ſol . Modo ⫽ lxx . ſol .
Ipſe Wilts ten in dn̅io TOTINTVNE . In Fintune jacuit . Bereuuicha .
Hairaud tenuit . T.R.E : Tc̅ ſe defd̅ ꝑ . vi . hid̅ . m̅ ꝑ una hida . Tra . e̅
v . car̅ . In dn̅io . e̅ una . 7 iii . uilli 7 vii . bord̅ cu̅ . ii . car̅ . 7 iiii . ac̅ p̅ti .
De hac tra ten Wilts q̅da̅ . ii . hid̅ . 7 ibi ht̅ . iii . uillos cu̅ . i . car̅ 7 dim̅ .
Totu̅ T.R.E. 7 poſt . 7 m̅ ⫽ ual vi . lib̅ . IN STANINGES HVND .
Ipſe Wilts ten ⁊ HANINGEDVNE . Norman tenuit de rege . E .
Tc̅ ſe defd̅ ꝑ . xii . hid̅ . m̅ ꝑ . vi . hid̅ . Tra . e̅ . v . car̅ . In dn̅io . e̅ una .
7 xv . uilli 7 xxxiiii . bord̅ cu̅ . iiii . car̅ . Ibi æccla . Silua . x . porc̅ .
T.R.E. 7 poſt ⫽ ual b . xii . lib̅ . Modo ⫽ xxv . lib̅ .
Ipſe Wilts ten ⁊ WASINGETVNE . Guerd tenuit . T.R.E. Tc̅ ſe com̅
defd̅ ꝑ . lix . hid̅ . Modo n̅ dat geldu̅ . In una ex hid̅ ⫽ ſedet his
caſtellu̅ BREBRE . Tra . e̅ . xxx.iiii . car̅ . In dn̅io ſunt . v . car̅ .
7 cxx . uilli 7 xxv . bord̅ cu̅ . xxxiiii . car̅ . Ibi . v . ſalinæ de
cx . ambris ſalis . aut . ix . ſol 7 ii . den̅ . 7 iiii . ac̅ p̅ti . De paſnag
ſiluæ ⫽ lx . porc̅ . Ibi . vi . ſerui .

4 William holds ERRINGHAM himself. Frederic held if from
  King Edward; he could go where he would. Then it answered
  for 5 hides; now for ½ hide.
    2 villagers and 5 smallholders who have nothing.
  Value before 1066 and now 40s; when acquired 20s.

5 William holds SHOREHAM himself. Azor held it from King Edward.
  Then it answered for 12 hides; now for 5 hides and ½ virgate.
  Land for 15 ploughs. In lordship 3 ploughs;
    26 villagers and 49 smallholders with 12 ploughs.
    A church; meadow, 6 acres; woodland at 40 pigs.
  Value before 1066 £25; later £16; now £35. However
  it was at a revenue at £50, but it could not bear it.

6 William, a man-at-arms, holds TRULEIGH from William. Belling
  [held] it from Earl Godwin before 1066. Then it answered
  for 4 hides; now for nothing. Land for 2½ ploughs.
  In lordship 1 plough;
    3 villagers and 6 smallholders *with ½ plough.*
    2 mills at 65d.
    Ansfrid holds ½ hide of this land. He has ½ plough.
  Value of the whole manor before 1066 £4; later 60s; now 70s.

  William himself holds
7 TOTTINGTON, in lordship. It lay in (the lands of) Findon.
  An outlier. Harold held it before 1066. Then it answered
  for 6 hides; now for 1 hide. Land for 5 ploughs. In lordship 1;
    3 villagers and 7 smallholders with 2 ploughs.
    Meadow, 4 acres.
  One William holds 2 hides of this land. He has
    3 villagers with 1½ ploughs.
  Total value before 1066, later and now £6.

  In STEYNING Hundred
8 ANNINGTON. Norman held it from King Edward. Then it answered
  for 12 hides; now for 6 hides. Land for 5 ploughs. In lordship 1;
    15 villagers and 34 smallholders with 4 ploughs.
    A church; woodland, 10 pigs.
  Value before 1066 and later £12; now £25.

9 WASHINGTON. Earl Gyrth held it before 1066. Then it answered
  for 59 hides; now it does not give tax. Bramber Castle is situated
  in one of these hides. Land for 34 ploughs. In lordship 5 ploughs;
    120 villagers and 25 smallholders with 34 ploughs.
    5 salt-houses at 110 ambers of salt or 9s 2d; meadow, 4 acres.
    from woodland pasturage 60 pigs; 6 slaves.

De hac t̄ra ten̄ Giſleḃt̄ dim̄ hiđ .Radulꝰ. ı .hiđ .Witſ .ɪɪɪ. virg.

Leuuin̄ dim̄ hiđ q́ potuit recede̅ cū t̄ra ſua. 7 deđ geld dn̄o ſuo.

7 dn̄s ſuus nichil dedit. Hi hn̄t .ɪɪɪɪ. uiłłos 7 ıı . borđ. cū. ıı. car

7 dimiđ. 7 vɪɪ. ac̄s p̄ti. 7 ſilua de .x. porc̄.

28 b

Totū m̄ T.R.E. uałḃ. ʟ . liḃ. 7 poſt.ʹ ʟ .liḃ .Modo

dn̄ium Witłi.ʹ ʟ .liḃ. 7 v .ſoł. Militū.ʹ ʟ . ſoł 7 xɪɪ .den̄

Tam̄ hoc m̄ fuit ad firmā.ʹ ad .c .liḃ.

Ipſe Witſ ten̄ *STANINGES* .Rex .E. tenuit ad ſuā

firmā. Tc̄ ſe defđ p̄ .xvɪɪɪ. hiđ 7 ɪɪɪ. uirḡ. Nunq geldau.

De his hiđ h̄t Witſ .xɪɪ .hiđ . aliæ ſunt in Rapo Rogerij.

in Garinges . In hiđ q̊s h̄t Witſ.ʹ Tra .e̅ .xxɪ. car̄. In dn̄io

ſunt .ɪɪ. car̄. 7 xʟv. uiłłi 7 xxxɪɪɪ. borđ. cū .xvɪɪɪ. car̄.

Ibi un̄ molin̄ ſine cenſu. 7 ɪɪɪ. ſalinæ de xxx. den̄. 7 v.ac̄ p̄ti.

Silua.ʹ xx. porc̄ de paſnag.

T.R.E. uałḃ.xxvɪɪɪ. liḃ. 7 poſt.ʹxx. liḃ.Modo.ʹxxv. liḃ.

Ipſe Witſ ten̄ *FINDVNE* .Herald tenuit T.R.E. Tc̄ ſe

defđ p̄ .xxx. hiđ 7 dim̄. De his ſunt .x. hidæ in rapo Rogerij.

Aliæ n̄ geldaueꝛ niſi .ɪɪɪ. hidæ. Tra .e̅ .xvɪɪ. car̄. In dn̄io

ſunt .ɪɪɪ. car̄. 7 xxvɪɪ. uiłłi 7 xvɪɪ. borđ cū xvɪɪ. car̄. Ibi æccła

7 vɪ. ſerui. 7 Silua .xx. porc̄.

De hac t̄ra ten̄ qđā Witſ .v. hiđ. 7 ibi .ɪɪ. car̄ in dn̄io. 7 ɪɪ. uiłłi

7 vɪ. borđ.cū uɪɪa car̄.

Totū.T.R.E.uałḃ.xxvɪɪɪ.liḃ.7 poſt.ʹxx. liḃ.Modo.ʹxxvɪɪɪ.liḃ 7 x.ſoł.

Ipſe Witſ ten̄ *SEMLINTVN*. Vluuard tenuit de rege.E.

Tc̄ ſe defđ p̄ .ɪx. hiđ . m̄ p̄ .ɪɪɪɪ. hiđ .De hac t̄ra ſunt .ɪɪɪ. uirg

in rapo de Arundel. Tra .e̅ .vɪɪ. car̄. In dn̄io ſunt .ɪɪɪ. car̄.

7 xx. uiłłi. 7 xɪɪɪɪ.borđ. cū .vɪ. car̄. Ibi .ı. molin̄ de .vɪ. ſoliđ.

7 vɪ. ac̄ p̄ti. Silua.ʹ xxx. porc̄.

T.R.E.ʹuałḃ.ıx. liḃ. 7 poſt. 7 modo.ʹvɪɪɪ. liḃ.

Gilbert holds ½ hide of this land, Ralph 1 hide, William 3 virgates, Leofwin ½ hide; he could withdraw with his land. He gave tax to his lord and his lord gave nothing. These have
    4 villagers and 2 smallholders with 2½ ploughs.
    Meadow, 7 acres; woodland at 10 pigs.
Value of the whole manor before 1066 £50; later £50; now   28 b
William's lordship £50 5s, his men-at-arms' 50s and 12d.
However this manor was at a revenue at £100.

10 STEYNING. King Edward held it at a revenue. Then it answered for 18 hides and 3 virgates. It never paid tax. Of these hides William has 12 hides; the others are in Earl Roger's Rape, in Goring. On the hides which William has, land for 21 ploughs.
In lordship 2 ploughs;
    45 villagers and 33 smallholders with 18 ploughs.
    1 mill without dues; 3 salt-houses at 30d; meadow, 5 acres;
       woodland, 20 pigs from pasturage.
Value before 1066 £28; later £20; now £25.

11 FINDON. Harold held it before 1066. Then it answered for 30½ hides. Of these, 10 hides are in Earl Roger's Rape. The others did not pay tax, except for 3 hides. Land for 17 ploughs.
In lordship 3 ploughs;
    27 villagers and 17 smallholders with 17 ploughs.
    A church; 6 slaves; woodland, 20 pigs.
One William holds 5 hides of this land. In lordship 2 ploughs;
    2 villagers and 6 smallholders with 1 plough.
Total value before 1066 £28; later £20; now £28 10s.

12 SULLINGTON. Wulfward held it from King Edward. Then it answered for 9 hides; now for 4 hides. 3 virgates of this land are in Arundel Rape. Land for 7 ploughs. In lordship 3 ploughs;
    20 villagers and 14 smallholders with 6 ploughs.
    1 mill at 6s; meadow, 6 acres; woodland, 30 pigs.
Value before 1066 £9; later and now £8.

Radulf⁹ ten de Witto *WISTANESTVN*. Azor tenuit
de Goduino. Tc se defd ꝓ xii . hid . Modo ꝓ nichilo . Tra e
viii . car . In dnio funt . ii . car . 7 x . uitti 7 xxiiii . bord
cu . v . car . Ibi æccta 7 v . serui . 7 vii . ac pti . Silua: xxx.
porc . T.R.E. 7 m: uat . xii . lib . Qdo recep: iiii . lib.

Witts fili⁹ mahne . ten de Witto *WAPINGETORNE*
Carle tenuit de rege.E. Tc se defd ꝓ . vi . hid . Modo
ꝓ . ii . hid . Tra . e . vi . car . In dnio . e una car . 7 vii . uitti
7 xv . bord cu . iiii . car . Ibi . vii . ac pti . Silua . de . v . denar .
De fale: xx . den . 7 i . fext mellis.

T.R.E: uatb . c . fot . 7 poft: xx . fot . Modo: iiii . lib.

Giflebt⁹ ten de Witto *CLOPEHA* . Aluuin⁹ tenuit de rege.E.
7 jacuit in Lolinminftre q̃ ten Rogeri⁹ in suo rapo . Tc se
defd . ꝓ viii . hid . fed . ii . hidæ funt in rapo Rogerij comit .
Qd Giflebt ten: geldau ꝓ . iii . hid . Tra . e . iiii . car .
In dnio funt . ii . car . 7 v . uitti 7 viii . bord cu . ii . car .
T.R.E. uatb . viii . lib . 7 poft . iiii . lib . Modo: vi . lib.

Ifde Giflebt ten de Witto tra . iii . car . H jacuit in
Garinges q̃ eft in rapo Rog comit . Foris rap eft 7 extra
numer hidar . Nunq geldau . Ibi funt . vi . uitti 7 v . bord
cu . iii . car .   T.R.E. 7 poft 7 m: uat xxx . folid.

Ricard⁹ ten de Witto *CENGELTVNE* . Effocher tenuit
de Goduino . Tc se defd ꝓ . iiii . hid . modo ꝓ nichilo . Tra . e
ii . car . In dnio . e una car . cu . v . bord .

T.R.E. uatb . iiii . lib . 7 poft: xl . fot . Modo . lx . folid.

Tetbert⁹ ten una hida In Cengeltunæ de Witto

p.r. hida geldau
M ꝓ nichilo.

Vuerun tenuit de Goduino . Nichil ibi . e . Vat . xi . fot.

Witts fili⁹ Norman ten *CVMBE* de Witto . Guert
tenuit T.R.E. Tc se defd ꝓ . x . hid . m ꝓ . v . hid . Tra
eft . viii . car . In dnio funt . ii . 7 xxvii . uitti 7 iiii .

13 Ralph holds WISTON from William. Azor held it from Earl Godwin.
Then it answered for 12 hides; now for nothing. Land for 8 ploughs.
In lordship 2 ploughs;
10 villagers and 24 smallholders with 5 ploughs.
A church; 5 slaves; meadow, 7 acres; woodland, 30 pigs.
Value before 1066 and now £12; when acquired £4.

14 William son of Mann holds WAPPINGTHORNE from William. Karl
held it from King Edward. Then it answered for 6 hides;
now for 2 hides. Land for 6 ploughs. In lordship 1 plough;
7 villagers and 15 smallholders with 4 ploughs.
Meadow, 7 acres; woodland at 5d; from salt 20d; 1 sester
of honey.
Value before 1066, 100s; later 20s; now £4.

15 Gilbert holds CLAPHAM from William. Alwin held it from King
Edward. It lay in (the lands of) Lyminster, which Earl Roger holds in
his Rape. Then it answered for 8 hides, but 2 hides are in Earl
Roger's Rape. What Gilbert holds paid tax for 3 hides.
Land for 4 ploughs. In lordship 2 ploughs;
5 villagers and 8 smallholders with 2 ploughs.
Value before 1066 £8; later £4; now £6.

16 Gilbert also holds land for 3 ploughs from William. It lay in
(the lands of) Goring, which is in Earl Roger's Rape. It is outside
the Rape, and not in the numeration of hides. It never paid tax.
6 villagers and 5 smallholders with 3 ploughs.
Value before 1066, later and now 30s.

17 Richard holds CHANCTON from William. Essocher held it from
Earl Godwin. Then it answered for 4 hides; now for nothing.
Land for 2 ploughs. In lordship 1 plough, with
5 smallholders.
Value before 1066 £4; later 40s; now 60s.

18 Theodbert holds 1 hide in CHANCTON from William. It paid   28 c
tax for 1 hide; now for nothing. Werun held it from Earl Godwin.
Nothing there.
Value 11s.

19 William son of Norman holds COOMBES from William. Gyrth held it
before 1066. Then it answered for 10 hides; now for 5 hides.
Land for 8 ploughs. In lordship 2;

borđ cũ . x . car̄ . Ibi æccła 7 ıı . ſerui . 7 de ſalinis .
.ʟ . ſoł . 7 v . denar̄ . Silua . de . ıııı . porc .

T . R . E . uałb xıı . lib . 7 poſt . x . lib . Modo . xııı . lib .
Iſđē Witts ten̄ de Witto APLESHAM . Leuuin⁹
tenuit de Goduino . Tc̄ ſe deſđ ꝑ . vıı . hiđ 7 dimiđ .
Modo ꝑ nichilo . Tra . ē . v . car̄ . In dn̄io ſunt . ııı . car̄ .
7 vıı . uiłti 7 vıı . borđ cũ . ıı . car̄ . Ibi un̄ ſeru̅ . 7 un̄
molin̄ de . vı . ſoł . 7 v . ac̄ p̄ti . 7 ſilua de . v . porc .

T . R . E . 7 poſt 7 m̄ . uał . vı . lib .

Duo milit̄ ten̄ de hac tra . ı . hiđ 7 dim̄ . 7 ibi . ē . ı . borđ
7 ıı . ſaline de . v . ſolid̄ . Vał . xxııı . ſoł 7 ıııı . den̄ .
Iſđē Witts ten̄ de Witto jn oſintune . ıı . hiđ . Non
geldaue‾ . Goduin̄⁹ tenuit . Ibi . ē una car̄ in dn̄io .
Nichil plus . Vał 7 ualuit . xxvı . ſolid̄ .

Witts filius Rannulfi ten̄ de Witto IN HĀFELT HĐ .
ODEMANSCOTE . Guda comitiſſa tenuit .
Tc̄ ſe deſđ ꝑ ııı . hiđ 7 dim̄ . Modo ꝑ . ıı . hiđ . Tra . ē
.ıx . car̄ . In dn̄io . ē una car̄ . 7 xvı . uiłti 7 ıııı . borđ
cũ . vııı . car̄ . Ibi æccła . 7 v . ac̄ p̄ti . Silua . xııı . porc .
De hac tra ten̄ q̄đa miles . ı . hiđ . 7 ibi h̄t . ı . car̄ cũ
uno uiłło . T . R . E . 7 poſt . 7 m̄ . uał . ııı . lib 7 x . ſolid̄ .

Radulf⁹ ten̄ de Witto WANTELEI . Bricmar tenuit
de Azor . 7 azor de Heraldo . Tc̄ ſe deſđ ꝑ . ıııı . hiđ
7 dim̄ . Modo ꝑ nichilo . Tra . ē . ıı . car̄ . In dn̄io . ē una .
7 ıı . uiłti . 7 ıı . borđ cũ dim̄ car̄ . Ibi . ıı . ſerui . 7 un̄
molin̄ de . xx . denar̄ . 7 x . ac̄ p̄ti . ꟼ HVND .
T . R . E . 7 poſt . uałb . xʟ . ſoł . Modo . xxıı . ſoł . WINDEHĀ
Iſđē Radulf⁹ ten̄ de Witto in Ovelei dimiđ hiđ .
Aluuin̄ tenuit de Azor 7 tc̄ deſđ ſe ꝑ dim̄ hida .
Modo ꝑ nichilo . Nichil ibi niſi . x . ac̄ p̄ti . Vał . v . ſoł .

27 villagers and 4 smallholders with 10 ploughs.
A church; 2 slaves; from the salt-houses 50s 5d; woodland at 4 pigs.
Value before 1066 £12; later £10; now £13.

20 William also holds APPLESHAM from William. Leofwin held it from
Earl Godwin. Then it answered for 7½ hides; now for nothing.
Land for 5 ploughs. In lordship 3 ploughs;
7 villagers and 7 smallholders with 2 ploughs.
1 slave; 1 mill at 6s; meadow, 5 acres; woodland at 5 pigs.
Value before 1066, later and now £6.
2 men-at-arms hold 1½ hides of this land.
1 smallholder; 2 salt-houses at 5s.
Value 23s 4d.

21 William also holds 2 hides in OFFINGTON from William. It did
not pay tax. Godwin held it. In lordship 1 plough. Nothing more.
The value is and was 26s.

In HENFIELD Hundred
22 William son of Ranulf holds WOODMANCOTE from William.
Countess Gytha held it. Then it answered for 3½ hides; now
for 2 hides. Land for 9 ploughs. In lordship 1 plough;
16 villagers and 4 smallholders with 8 ploughs.
A church; meadow, 5 acres; woodland, 13 pigs.
A man-at-arms holds 1 hide of this land. He has 1 plough, with
1 villager.
Value before 1066, later and now £3 10s.

23 Ralph holds WANTLEY from William. Brictmer held it from Azor,
and Azor from Harold. Then it answered for 4½ hides; now
for nothing. Land for 2 ploughs. In lordship 1;
2 villagers and 2 smallholders with ½ plough.
2 slaves; 1 mill at 20d; meadow, 10 acres.
Value before 1066 and later 40s; now 22s.

In WYNDHAM Hundred
24 Ralph also holds ½ hide in WOOLFLY from William. Alwin held it
from Azor. Then it answered for ½ hide; now for nothing.
Nothing there except meadow, 10 acres.
Value 5s.

Isdē Radulf⁹ ten⁷ de Wiłło SALMONESBERIE.

Azor tenuit de Heraldo . Tc̄ se defđ ꝑ . 11 . hiđ.

Modo ꝑ nichilo . Tⁱ̄ra . ē . 11 . car̄ . In dn̄io est una car̄.

7 un uiłłs 7 111 . borđ cū . 1 . car̄ . Ibi æcclesiola 7 1111 . serui.

T.R.E. 7 post . 7 modo: uał . xx1111 . soliđ.

Wiłłs fili⁹ Rannulsi ten⁷ de Wiłło dimiđ hiđ jn Morleia.

Aluuarđ tenuit de Azor . 7 defđ se ꝑ dim hiđ . tc̄ 7 m̄.

Ibi . ē dim car̄ . cū . 11 . borđ . T.R.E. 7 post: uałb . x . soł M̄ . v . soł.

Isđ Wiłłs ten⁷ de Wiłło SACHEHA . Brictuin te

nuit de Azor . Tc̄ se defđ ꝑ . 11 . hiđ m̄ ꝑ nichilo . Tⁱ̄ra

est . 11 . car̄⁷ . Ibi m̄ nisi . 11 . aalia 7 1⁹ . uiłłs 7 11 . borđ.

Silua de . x . den⁷ . T.R.E. 7 post . uałb . x . soł . M̄ . v . soł.

Radulf⁹ ten⁷ de Wiłło IN ELDRITVNE HVND⁷.

CHINGESTVNE . Azor tenuit de Heraldo . Tc̄ se defđ

ꝑ . xx1 . hida . Ex his sunt . v1 . hidæ in rapo Wiłłi de Warene.

Qđ Radulf⁹ ten̄: geldau⁷ ꝑ . v1 . hiđ . Tⁱ̄ra . ē . v111 . car̄⁷.

In dn̄io sunt . 11 . car̄⁷ . 7 x11 . uiłłi 7 xx . borđ . cū . x . car̄ . Ibi

æccła . 7 v1 . salinæ de . xx . soliđ . 7 x . ambræ salis.

De hac⁷ tⁱ̄ra ten⁷ . 111 . milites . 1111 . hiđ 7 dimiđ . 7 ibi hn̄t

.11 . car̄ . 7 11 . uiłłos 7 v1 . borđ.

Totū m̄ T.R.E. uałb . xv . lib . Modo pars Radulfi . x1 . lib

7 v11 . soł 7 v1 . denar̄ . Qđ milites ten̄: uał . c . soliđ.

In ead⁷ uilla ten⁷ Wiłłs fili⁹ Rannulsi de Wiłło . v11 . hiđ

una v⁷ min⁹ . Gunnild tenuit de heraldo . 7 ꝑ tanto se defđ.

Tⁱ̄ra . ē . 111 . car̄ . In dn̄io sunt . 11 . car̄ . 7 1111 . uiłłi 7 v111 . borđ

cū . 1 . car̄ . Ibi æccła 7 un⁹ seruus . 7 111 . salinæ de . xx11 . den⁷.

De pastura . xv1 . soł . 7 1111 . ac̊ p̄ti.

T.R.E. 7 m̄: uałb v11 . lib . Qđo recep: 111 . lib . IN BREDFORD

ᒑHVND⁷.

Rotbt⁷ ten⁷ de Wiłło BRADEWATRE . Wigot tenuit de

rege . E . Tc̄ se defđ ꝑ xx1x . hiđ . Ex his sunt . 1x . hidæ in

25 Ralph also holds SHERMANBURY from William. Azor held it
from Harold. Then it answered for 2 hides; now for nothing.
Land for 2 ploughs. In lordship 1 plough;
   1 villager and 3 smallholders with 1 plough.
   A small church; 4 slaves.
Value before 1066, later and now 24s.

26 William son of Ranulf holds ½ hide in MORLEY from William. Alfward
held it from Azor. Then and now it answered for ½ hide.
½ plough, with
   2 smallholders.
Value before 1066 and later 10s; now 5s.

27 William also holds SAKEHAM from William. Brictwin held it
from Azor. Then it answered for 2 hides; now for nothing.
Land for 2 ploughs. Now nothing there except 2 cattle and
   1 villager and 2 smallholders.
   Woodland at 10d.
Value before 1066 and later 10s; now 5s.

In ALDRINGTON Hundred
28 Ralph holds KINGSTON from William. Azor held it from Harold.
Then it answered for 21 hides; of these, 6 hides are in William
of Warenne's Rape. What Ralph holds paid tax for 6 hides.   **28 d**
Land for 8 ploughs. In lordship 2 ploughs;
   12 villagers and 20 smallholders with 10 ploughs.
   A church; 6 salt-houses at 20s and 10 ambers of salt.
   3 men-at-arms hold 4½ hides of this land. They have 2 ploughs and
      2 villagers and 6 smallholders.
Value of the whole manor before 1066 £15; now Ralph's part
£11 7s 6d; what the men-at-arms hold 100s.

29 In the same village William son of Ranulf holds 7 hides
less 1 virgate from William. Gunhild held it from Harold.
It answers for as much. Land for 3 ploughs. In lordship 2 ploughs;
   4 villagers and 8 smallholders with 1 plough.
   A church; 1 slave; 3 salt-houses at 22d; from pasturage 16s;
      meadow, 4 acres.
Value before 1066 and now £7; when acquired £3.

In BRIGHTFORD Hundred
30 Robert holds BROADWATER from William. Wigot held it from King
Edward. Then it answered for 29 hides. Of these, 9 hides are

rapo Wilłi de Warene . 7 Wilłs de braiose hŧ . ıı . hiđ in dñio.

Qđ Rotͬ tenͬ geldaũ ꝓ . vı . hiđ . Tra . ē . vıı . car . In dñio

funt . ıı . car . 7 xxx . uiłłi 7 ıııı . borđ cū . x . car . Ibi æccła

7 ııı . ſerui . 7 uñ moliñ de . vıı . ſoliđ . 7 ʟx . ađ ꝑti . Silua . xx.

porc.   De hac tra tenͬ uñ miles . ı . hidā.

Totū T.R.E. ualͭ 7 poſt. xv . lib . Modo. xıııı . lib.

Radulf tenͬ de Wiłło HENE . Leuret tenuit de Goduino

Tē 7 m̄ ſe defđ ꝓ . ıı . hiđ 7 dim . In dñio . ē una car . 7 ııı . uiłłi

7 ıı . borđ cū . ı . car . 7 uñ ſeru . 7 ııı . ađ ꝑti . Val 7 ualuit . xʟ . ſoł.

In eađ uilla tenͬ Aluuarđ de Wiłło . ıı . hiđ 7 dim . Ipſemet

tenuit de rege . E . Tē 7 m̄ ſe defđ ꝓ . ıı . hiđ 7 dim.

In dñio . ē una car 7 ııı . uiłłi 7 v . borđ cū . ı . car . Val . xʟ . ſol 7 ualuit.

Rotͬ tenͬ de Wiłło DERENTVNE . Vluuarđ tenuit de

Heraldo . Tē ſe defđ ꝓ . ıııı . hiđ . m̄ ꝓ una hida . Tra . ē . ıı . car.

Ibi funt . ıı . uiłłi 7 v . borđ cū dim car . 7 ıııı . ađ ꝑti . Silua

ıııı . porc . De hac tra tenͬ uñ francig . ı . hiđ 7 dim . 7 ibi . ıı . borđ.

T.R.E. 7 poſt. ualͭ . xʟ . ſoł . Modo. ʟx . ſoliđ.

Iſđē Rotͬ tenͬ ibidē de Wiłło DERENTVNE . Eduuarđ te

nuit de rege . E . Tē ſe defđ ꝓ . vııı . hiđ . Modo ꝓ . ıı . hiđ.

7 una v . Tra . ē . vı . car . In dñio eſt . ı . car . 7 ıx . uiłłi 7 ıx.

borđ cū . vıı . car . Ibi æccła . 7 ıııı . ſerui . 7 vııı . ađ ꝑti . Silua.

.x . porc.   T.R.E. 7 poſt. 7 m̄. ual . c . ſoł.

Iſđē Rotͬ tenͬ de Wiłło ORDINGES . Septē alodarij

tenueͬ de Goduino . Tē ſe defđ ꝓ . xı . hiđ . Modo hŧ Rotͬ

ıx . hiđ 7 geldaueͬ ꝓ ıı . hiđ . Tra . ē . ııı . car . In dñio funt

ıı . car . 7 vı . uiłłi 7 ıx . borđ cū . ı . car . Ibi uñ ſeruus . 7 vıı.

ađ ꝑti.   T.R.E. 7 poſt. 7 modo. ual . c . ſoliđ.

Rotͬ tenͬ de Wiłło MORDINGES . Ibi una hida 7 dim

Leuuiñ tenuit de rege . 7 ꝓ dim hida gelđ.

Ibi uñ uiłłs . 7 v . borđ . 7 dim ađ ꝑti . Val 7 ualuit xıı . ſoł

in William of Warenne's Rape and William of Braose has 2 hides
in lordship. What Robert holds paid tax for 6 hides.
Land for 7 ploughs. In lordship 2 ploughs;
   30 villagers and 4 smallholders with 10 ploughs.
   A church; 3 slaves; 1 mill at 7s; meadow, 60 acres;
   woodland, 20 pigs.
   A man-at-arms holds 1 hide of this land.
Total value before 1066 and later £15; now £14.

31 Ralph holds HEENE from William. Leofred held it from Earl Godwin.
   Then and now it answered for 2½ hides. In lordship 1 plough;
      3 villagers and 2 smallholders with 1 plough; 1 slave.
      Meadow, 3 acres.
   The value is and was 40s.

32 In the same village Alfward holds 2½ hides from William. He held
   it himself from King Edward. Then and now it answered for 2½ hides.
   In lordship 1 plough;
      3 villagers and 5 smallholders with 1 plough.
   The value is and was 40s.

33 Robert holds DURRINGTON from William. Wulfward held it from
   Earl Harold. Then it answered for 4 hides; now for 1 hide.
   Land for 2 ploughs.
      2 villagers and 5 smallholders with ½ plough.
      Meadow, 4 acres; woodland, 4 pigs.
      A Frenchman holds 1½ hides of this land; 2 smallholders there.
   Value before 1066 and later 40s; now 60s.

34 Robert also holds DURRINGTON there from William. Edward held it
   from King Edward. Then it answered for 8 hides; now for 2 hides
   and 1 virgate. Land for 6 ploughs. In lordship 1 plough;
      9 villagers and 9 smallholders with 7 ploughs.
      A church; 4 slaves; meadow, 8 acres; woodland, 10 pigs.
   Value before 1066, later and now 100s.

35 Robert also holds WORTHING from William. 7 freeholders held it from
   Earl Godwin. Then it answered for 11 hides; now Robert has 9 hides.
   They paid tax for 2 hides. Land for 3 ploughs. In lordship 2 ploughs;
      6 villagers and 9 smallholders with 1 plough.
      1 slave; meadow, 7 acres.
   Value before 1066, later and now 100s.

36 Robert holds WORTHING from William. 1½ hides. Leofwin held it
   from the King. It paid tax for ½ hide.
      1 villager and 5 smallholders.
      Meadow, ½ acre.
   The value is and was 12s.

In ead uilla teñ Radulf⁹dim̄ hidā . Jacuit in Stultinges.

Tofti tenuit de Leuuino . 7 p̄ tanto fe defđ . tc̄ 7 m̄.

Ibi funt . IIII . boū . 7 I . borđ . 7 una ac̄ p̄ti . Val . v . fol 7 ualuit.

Radulf⁹ teñ de Wilło SVLTINGES . Leuuiñ⁹ tenuit

de rege . E . Tc̄ fe defđ p̄ . XVII . hiđ . De his funt . II . hidæ

in rapo Rogcerij . In Garinges . 7 alibi funt . III . hidæ 7 dimiđ

29 a

quas teñ alij hōes . Radulf⁹ hꝰ in fua manu . XI . hiđ

7 dimiđ . Modo gelđ p̄ . II . hiđ 7 III . uirg . Tra . ē . v . car.

in d̄ funt . II . car . 7 XIX . uilłi 7 XVI . borđ ; cū IX . car.

Ibi æccta 7 v . ferui . 7 uñ meliñ de . III . fol . 7 VIII . falinæ

de . XIII . fol . 7 XXX . ac̄ p̄ti.

De hac tra teñ uñ miles . I . hidā , 7 hꝰ in dñio . I . car . 7 II.

uilłos 7 IIII . borđ . 7 falinā de . II . foliđ . 7 II . ac̄s p̄ti.

Totū T.R.E. 7 poft ualuit . VIII . liƀ . Modo : VII . liƀ 7 VIII . fol.

De eod m̄ teñ alt Rodulf⁹ de Wilło . II . hiđ . fed funt fup

numerū hidař fupioꝛ . Leuuiñ⁹ tenuit de rege . E . 7 tc̄ fe

defđb p̄ . II . hiđ . m̄ p una 7 dim . Ibi funt . IIII . uilłi 7 uñ

borđ cū dim car . 7 II . ac̄ p̄ti . Tra . ē . I . car.

T.R.E. 7 poft . ualuit . L . fol . Modo : LXX . foliđ.

De ipfo m̄ teñ Robt⁹ de Wilło . I . hiđ fup numer̄ hidař

fupioꝛ . Leuuiñ⁹ tenuit . 7 tc̄ fe defđ p̄ . I . hida . m̄ p una v.

Ibi . ē uñ uilłs 7 uñ borđ 7 IIII . ac̄ p̄ti . Val . VIII . fol 7 ualuit.

Radulf⁹ teñ de Wilło COCHELIA . Grene tenuit de

Heraldo . Tc̄ fe defđ p̄ . II . hiđ 7 una v . Modo p nichilo

In dñio . ē . I . car . cū . v . borđ . 7 VIII . ac̄ p̄ti . Val . L.v . fol . 7 fēp

Iſđ Radulf⁹ teñ de Wilło DENTVNE . Auti tenuit

de Goduino . Tc̄ fe defđ p̄ . v . hiđ . m̄ p una hida . 7 III . uirg.

Tra . ē . II . car . De hac tra teñ Wilłs . II . hiđ 7 unā v . Robt⁹

unā hiđ 7 unā v̄ . 7 alt miles . I . hiđ 7 dim . In dñio nichil . ē.

fed tanť . II . uilłi 7 III . borđ . 7 x . ac̄ p̄ti.

Totū . T.R.E. 7 poft . 7 m̄ . LXXII . foliđ.

28 d, 29 a

37 In the same village Ralph holds ½ hide. It lay in (the lands of)
Sompting. Tosti held it from Leofwin. Then and now it answered
for as much, ½ hide.
    4 oxen and 1 smallholder.
    Meadow, 1 acre.
The value is and was 5s.

38 Ralph holds SOMPTING from William. Leofwin held it from King Edward.
Then it answered for 17 hides. Of these 2 hides are in Earl Roger's
Rape, in Goring. 3½ hides elsewhere, which other men hold.   29 a
Ralph has 11½ hides in his own hands. Now it pays tax for 2 hides
and 3 virgates. Land for 5 ploughs. In lordship 2 ploughs;
    19 villagers and 16 smallholders with 9 ploughs.
    A church; 5 slaves; 1 mill at 3s; 8 salt-houses at 13s;
        meadow, 30 acres.
    A man-at-arms holds 1 hide of this land. He has 1 plough in lordship and
    2 villagers and 4 smallholders.
        A salt-house at 2s; meadow, 2 acres
Total value before 1066 and later £8; now £7 8s.

39 Another Ralph holds 2 hides of this manor from William but they
are additional to the numeration of the above hides. Leofwin held it from
King Edward. Then it answered for 2 hides; now for 1½.
    4 villagers and 1 smallholder with ½ plough.
    Meadow, 2 acres. Land for 1 plough.
Value before 1066 and later 50s; now 70s.

40 Robert holds 1 hide of this manor from William, additional to the
numeration of the above hides. Leofwin held it.
Then it answered for 1 hide; now for ½ virgate.
    1 villager and 1 smallholder.
    Meadow, 4 acres.
The value is and was 8s.

41 Ralph holds COKEHAM from William. Green held it from Earl Harold.
Then it answered for 2 hides and 1 virgate; now for nothing.
In lordship 1 plough, with
    5 smallholders.
    Meadow, 8 acres.
The value is and always was 55s.

42 Ralph also holds DANKTON from William. Auti held it from Earl Godwin.
Then it answered for 5 hides; now for 1 hide and 3 virgates.
Land for 2 ploughs. William holds 2 hides and 1 virgate of this land;
Robert 1 hide and 1 virgate; another man-at-arms 1½ hides.
Nothing in lordship, but only
    2 villagers and 3 smallholders.
        Meadow, 10 acres.
Total value before 1066, later and now 72s.

Rōbt̃ ten de Willo *LANCINGES*. Leuuin tenuit de rege . E.

Tc̃ ſe defd̃ p̄ . xvi . hid̃ 7 una v̄ . De his hr̄ ipſe Rotbt

xii . hid̃ 7 unā v̄ . 7 geldaueř p̄ . v . hid̃ 7 una v̄ 7 dimid̃.

Tra . ē . v . cař . In dñio ſunt . ii . cař 7 dim̄ . 7 xiii . uilli 7 vii.

bord̃ cū . ii . cař . Ibi . i . moliñ de . viii . ſol . 7 vii . ſaline

de . xx . ſol 7 iii . den.

De hac tra ten . ii . milit̃ . ii . hid̃ 7 dim̄ . 7 dimid̃ v̄ . 7 ibi hñt

in dñio . ii . cař . 7 xi . ſalinæ de xii . ſol 7 vi . den.

Tot̃ . T.R.E. ualb̃ ix . lib̃ . 7 poſt: vii . lib̃ . Modo . xiiii . lib̃ 7 x . ſol.

In ead̃ uilla ten Radulf . iii . uirg 7 dim̄ . 7 ſunt de . xvi . hid̃

ſupd̃ictis . 7 p̄ una v̄ geldaueř . Ibi . ē un uills 7 ii . bord̃ . Val . v . ſol.

De ipſo ꝏ ten alt̃ Radulf . iii . hid̃ 7 una v̄ . 7 ſunt ſimilit̃

de ſupioribʒ xvi . hid̃ . H̄ tra Radulfi geldau p̄ . iii . uirg

7 m̄ facit . In dñio . ē una cař . 7 ii . uilti . 7 ii . bord̃ cū dim̄ cař.

Ibi . v . ſalinæ de . xii . ſol 7 vi . den̄ . Val 7 ualuit . l . ſol.

ꝼEt iteř ten Radulf unā v̄ quæ jacuit in Lancinges . 7 geld̃

dedit . Vn uilts ten 7 tenuit . Val 7 ualuit . v . ſolid̃.

Radulf fili Tedrici ten de Willo *COCHEHA* . Briſmar

tenuit de Azor . Tc̃ 7 m̄ ſe defd̃ p̄ una hid̃ 7 dim̄ . In dñio . ē

dim̄ cař . 7 i . uilt 7 iii . bord̃ . cū dim̄ cař . Salina de . xl . den̄.

7 ii . ac̄ p̃ti . Silua . i . porc̄ . Val . xx . ſol 7 ualuit.

Wills fili Bonardi ten de Willo unā Bereuuicū quæ ja

cuit in *HERST* ꝏ qd̃ ten Wills de Warene . Vocat̃ *Howe*.

Goduin tenuit . Tc̃ ſe defd̃ p̄ . vi . hid̃ . Modo p̄ . ii . hid̃

una v̄ min̄ . Tra . ē . vi . cař . In dñio ſunt . ii . cař . 7 xiiii . uilli

29 b

7 viii . bord̃ cū . iiii . cař . Ibi . vi . ſaliñe de . vii . ſol

7 vi . denar.

De hac tra ten un̄ miles . i . hid̃ . 7 ibi hr̄ dim̄ cař.

Totū T.R.E. 7 poſt . ualb̃ . iiii . lib̃ . Modo: vi . lib̃

Rotbt̃ ten de Willo *ESSINGETVNE*. *IN ISEWERIT HD.*

Duo alodiarij tenueř de Goduino . Tc̃ ſe defd̃

43 Robert holds LANCING from William. Leofwin held it from King Edward.
Then it answered for 16 hides and 1 virgate; of these Robert has 12 hides
and 1 virgate himself. They paid tax for 5 hides and 1½ virgates.
Land for 5 ploughs. In lordship 2½ ploughs;
   13 villagers and 7 smallholders with 2 ploughs.
   1 mill at 8s; 7 salt-houses at 20s 3d.
   2 men-at-arms hold 2½ hides and ½ virgate of this land.
      They have 2 ploughs in lordship, and 11 salt-houses at 12s 6d.
Total value before 1066 £9; later £7; now £14 10s.

44 In the same village Ralph holds 3½ virgates. They are of the said 16 hides.
They paid tax for 1 virgate.
   1 villager and 2 smallholders.
Value 5s.
   Another Ralph holds 3 hides and 1 virgate of this manor. They are
likewise of the above 16 hides. This land of Ralph's paid tax
for 3 virgates and it does so now. In lordship 1 plough;
   2 villagers and 2 smallholders with ½ plough.
   5 salt-houses at 12s 6d.
The value is and was 50s.
   And again Ralph holds 1 virgate which lay (in the lands of) Lancing
and paid tax. 1 villager holds and held it.
The value is and was 5s.

45 Ralph son of Theodoric holds COKEHAM from William. Brictmer
held it from Azor. Then and now it answered for 1½ hides.
In lordship ½ plough;
   1 villager and 3 smallholders with ½ plough.
   A salt-house at 40d; meadow, 2 acres; woodland, 1 pig.
The value is and was 20s.

46 William son of Bonnard holds an outlier from William which lay in
(the lands of) Hurstpierpoint manor, which William of Warenne holds.
It is called HOE. Earl Godwin held it. Then it answered for 6 hides;
now for 2 hides less 1 virgate. Land for 6 ploughs. In lordship 2 ploughs;
   14 villagers and 8 smallholders with 4 ploughs.   29 b
   6 salt-houses at 7s 6d.
   A man-at-arms holds 1 hide of this land. He has ½ plough.
Total value before 1066 and later £4; now £6.

In EASEWRITHE Hundred
47 Robert holds ASHINGTON from William. 2 freeholders held it from
Earl Godwin. Then it answered for 2½ hides; now for nothing.

ꝑ . ii . hiđ 7 dim̅ . M̅ ꝑ nichilo . In Wafingetune jac̅.

Tra . ē . iii . car̅ . In dn̅io . ē una . 7 vi . uilli 7 ii . borđ

cū . i . car̅ 7 dim̅ . Val̅ 7 ualuit fēp . xxx . fol̅.

Radulf ten de Wilto . iii . hiđ in Cilletune qđ . ē

in rapo Rogerij . Non geldau . Tra . ē . vi . car̅ . In

dn̅io . ē dim̅ car̅ ; 7 xviii . uilli 7 vi . borđ cū . iii . car̅;

7 dimiđ . Ibi . vi . ac̅ p̅ti . 7 filua . xxx . porc̅.

T.R.E. 7 poft . 7 m̅ ual . lx . fol̅.

Morin ten de Wilto *TACEHĀ* . Brixi tenuit de

rege . E. Tc̅ fe defđ ꝑ . xx . hiđ 7 iii . uirg̅ . Modo ꝑ . v . hiđ;

Tra . ē . xiiii . car̅ . In dn̅io funt . ii . car̅ . 7 xxx . uilli 7 xii.

borđ cū . viii . car̅ . Ibi æccła 7 un̅ molin̅ de . iii . fol̅.

7 xvi . ac̅ p̅ti . Silua . lx . porc̅.

De hac tra ten un miles . i . hiđ . Ibi hr̅ . v . boues cū . i . borđ;

Totū T.R.E. 7 m̅ . ual . xiiii . lib̅ . Q̅do recep̅ . x . lib̅.

Ifđē Morin ten de Wilto *MOHĀ* . Ofuuard tenuit

de rege . E. Tc̅ fe defđ ꝑ . iii . hiđ . m̅ ꝑ nichilo . Tra . ē

ii . car̅ . Ibi funt . v . uilli 7 vi . borđ cū . ii . car̅ . Silua;

v . porc̅ . T.R.E. ual̅ . l . fol̅ . 7 poft; xxx . fol̅ . Modo; lxx . fol̅.

Ifđē Morin ten de Wilto . i . hidā . quæ jacuit in

Wafingetune . Eduuin tenuit de Goduino . Tc̅ ꝑ . i . hida

fe defđ . m̅ ꝑ nichilo . Ibi . ē un̅ uilt 7 i . molin̅ de . xv . den̅.

Aluiet ten de Wilto tra ad unā car̅ . ⌐ Val̅ . x . fot 7 fēp;

de dn̅io Wilti fine numero hidæ . Ibi . ē una car̅ . 7 un̅

molin̅ de . iii . fol̅ . In Storgetune jacuit . in paftura.

Modo nouit . ē hofpitata . Val̅ . x . folid̅.

Wilts fili Bonardi ten de Wilto *IN GRENESTEDE H̅D̅.*

ETVNE . Turgod tenuit de Goduino . Tc̅ fe defđ

ꝑ . iii . hiđ 7 dim̅ . M̅ ꝑ una hida . In Garnecapo jacuit

qđ . ē in rapo Rogerij . Tra . ē . ii . car̅ . In dn̅io . ē una.

It lay (in the lands of) Washington. Land for 3 ploughs. In lordship 1;
6 villagers and 2 smallholders with 1½ ploughs.
The value is and always was 30s.

48 Ralph holds 3 hides from William in (WEST) CHILTINGTON which is in
Earl Roger's Rape. It did not pay tax. Land for 6 ploughs.
In lordship ½ plough;
18 villagers and 6 smallholders with 3½ ploughs.
Meadow, 6 acres; woodland, 30 pigs.
Value before 1066, later and now 60s.

49 Morin holds THAKEHAM from William. Brictsi held it from
King Edward. Then it answered for 20 hides and 3 virgates;
now for 5 hides. Land for 14 ploughs. In lordship 2 ploughs;
30 villagers and 12 smallholders with 8 ploughs.
A church; 1 mill at 3s; meadow, 16 acres; woodland, 60 pigs.
A man-at-arms holds 1 hide of this land. He has 5 oxen, with
1 smallholder.
Total value before 1066 and now £14; when acquired £10.

50 Morin also holds MUNTHAM from William. Osward held it from
King Edward. Then it answered for 3 hides; now for nothing.
Land for 2 ploughs.
5 villagers and 6 smallholders with 2 ploughs.
Woodland, 5 pigs.
Value before 1066, 50s; later 30s; now 70s.

51 Morin also holds 1 hide from William which lay in (the lands of)
Washington. Edwin held it from Earl Godwin. Then it answered
for 1 hide; now for nothing.
1 villager.
1 mill at 15d.
The value is and always was 10s.

52 Alfgeat holds from William land for 1 plough, from William's lordship,
without numeration in hides. 1 plough.
1 mill at 3s.
It lay in Storrington (lands), in pasturage; now it is newly settled.
Value 10s.

In (WEST) GRINSTEAD Hundred

53 William son of Bonnard holds EATONS from William. Thorgot held it
from Earl Godwin. Then it answered for 3½ hides; now for 1 hide.
It lay (in the lands of) Warningcamp, which is in Earl Roger's Rape.
Land for 2 ploughs. In lordship 1;

7 v. uitt 7 iii. borđ cū. i. car̄. 7 vi. ac pti. Silua. de. v. den.

T.R.E. uatb. xx. fot. 7 poſt.' xv. fot. Modo.' xl. fot.

Witts fili⁹ Rannulfi ten de Witto *IN TIFELD HVND.*

IFELT. Aluui tenuit de rege. E. Tc 7 m̄ ſe defđ p una

hida. In dn̄io nichil. e. 7 v. uitti 7 iiii. borđ cū. i. car̄.

7 vi. ac pti. 7 Silua. vi. porc. Vat. xx. fot. 7 ualuit.

Iſdē Witts ten dim hidā. q̄ jacuit in *SOREHA.* qđ ten Witts.

de braioſe. H̄ hida. e q̄eta de geldo. Ibi. e un uitts cū dim car̄.

Robt⁹ ten de Witto *IN STANINGES HVND.* Vat. vi. ſoliđ.

BONGETVNE. Leuuin tenuit de rege. E. Tc ſe defđ

p. iiii. hiđ 7 dim. Modo p nichilo. Tra. e. v. car̄. In dn̄io

eſt una car̄. 7 xix. uitti 7 vii. borđ. cū. v. car̄. Ibi. ii. ac

pti. Silua.' x. porc. 7 i. molin de. ii. fot. T.R.E. 7 poſt.' xxx. fot. M̄.' xl. fot.

Iſdē Robt h̄t paruā paſturā cū. ii. borđ q̄ redđ. v. fot.

Hoc. e in Langemare qđ ten Rogeri ^{com} in ſuo rapo.

.XIIII. TERRA ODON 7 ELDRED *IN ESBORNE HVND.*

Odo ten de rege *WELBEDLINGE.* Fulcui

tenuit de rege. E. alodiū. Tc 7 m̄ ſe defđ

p. vi. hiđ. Tra. e vii. car̄. In dn̄io eſt una car̄.

7 xiiii. uitti 7 v. borđ. cū. vi. car̄. Ibi. v. ſerui.

7 un molin de. x. ſoliđ. 7 xxiii. ac pti. Silua.'

de. xxx. porc. Ibi æccta.

T.R.E. 7 m̄. uat. vi. lib. Q̆do recep.' iiii. lib.

Aldred ten de rege *EPINGES.*

Oualet tenuit de rege. E. Tc 7 m̄ ſe defđ

p. iiii. hiđ. Tra. e. iii. car̄. In dn̄io. e una car̄.

7 viii. uitti 7 ii. borđ cū. ii. car̄. Ibi. v. ſerui.

7 un molin de. iii. ſoliđ 7 ^{or} iiii. denar̄. 7 iii. ac pti.

Silua de xx. porc. 7 quadraria de. ix. fot.

7 iiii. denar̄. Vna haga de. xx^{ti}. den. de Circet

xl. denar̄. T.R.E. 7 m̄.' iiii. lib. Cū recep.' iii. lib.

5 villagers and 3 smallholders with 1 plough.
Meadow, 6 acres; woodland at 5d.
Value before 1066, 20s; later 15s; now 40s.

In IFIELD Hundred
54 William son of Ranulf holds IFIELD from William. Alfwy held it
from King Edward. Then and now it answered for 1 hide.
In lordship nothing.
5 villagers and 4 smallholders with 1 plough.
Meadow, 6 acres; woodland, 6 pigs.
The value is and was 20s.

55 William also holds ½ hide which lay in (the lands of) Shoreham,
which William of Braose holds. This hide is exempt from tax.
1 villager with ½ plough.
Value 6s.

In STEYNING Hundred
56 Robert holds BUNCTON from William. Leofwin held it from
King Edward. Then it answered for 4½ hides; now for nothing.
Land for 5 ploughs. In lordship 1 plough;
19 villagers and 7 smallholders with 5 ploughs.
Meadow, 2 acres; woodland, 10 pigs; 1 mill at 2s.
[Value] before 1066 and later 30s; now 40s.

57 Robert also has a small pasture, with 2 smallholders who pay 5s.
It is in Angmering, which Earl Roger holds in his Rape.

14   **LAND OF ODO AND ALDRED**   29 c

In EASEBOURNE Hundred
1 Odo holds WOOLBEDING from the King. Fulk held it from
King Edward, freehold. Then and now it answered for 6 hides.
Land for 7 ploughs. In lordship 1 plough;
14 villagers and 5 smallholders with 6 ploughs.
5 slaves; 1 mill at 10s; meadow, 23 acres;
woodland at 30 pigs. A church.
Value before 1066 and now £6; when acquired £4.

2 Aldred holds IPING from the King. Oualet held it from
King Edward. Then and now it answered for 4 hides.
Land for 3 ploughs. In lordship 1 plough;
8 villagers and 2 smallholders with 2 ploughs.
5 slaves; 1 mill at 3s 4d; meadow, 3 acres; woodland at 20 pigs;
a quarry at 9s 4d; 1 site at 20d; from church dues 40d.
[Value] before 1066 and now £4; when acquired £3.

Blank column   29 d

E 1
Surrey
19   LAND OF RICHARD SON OF COUNT GILBERT   34

In REIGATE Hundred...   34

13   Siward holds WORTH from Richard. Oswald held it from King
      Edward. It answered for ½ hide, then and now.
         1 villager with ½ plough.
      Value before 1066, 30s; later 2s; now 20s.

The Latin text of this entry is printed in the Surrey volume.

NOTES

ABBREVIATIONS used in the notes.

BCS..Birch *Cartularium Saxonicum.*   DB..Domesday Book.   DM..*Domesday Monachorum*
of Canterbury , ed. D.C.Douglas 1944.   Ellis..*General Introduction to Domesday Book,*
folio edition, DB 4, i - cvii; quarto edition, 1833 (reprint 1971).   Ely..*Liber Eliensis* ed.
E.O. Blake 1962.   EPNS..English Place-Name Society Survey*.   Exon..*Liber
Exoniensis* DB 3.   Heming..*Chartularium Ecclesiae Wigorniensis* ed. T. Hearne 1723.
JEPN..Journal of the English Place-Name Society.   KCD..Kemble *Codex Diplomaticus.*
LEEK..*Laws of the Earliest English Kings* ed. F.L. Attenborough 1922 (reprint 1963).
Liebermann..*Gesetze der Angelsachsen* 1903-1916.   LKE..*Laws of the Kings of
England* ed. A.J. Robertson 1925.   MS..Manuscript.   OEB..G. Tengvik *Old English
Bynames* Uppsala 1937.†   PNDB..O. von Feilitzen *Pre-Conquest Personal Names of
Domesday Book* Uppsala 1938.†   Robertson..*Anglo-Saxon Charters* ed. A.J. Robertson,
Cambridge 1939.   SAC..Sussex Archaeological Collections.   VCH..Victoria County
History, vol. 1.*

*refers to the County volume, unless otherwise stated. †'Nomina Germanica,' volumes 3 and 4.

The manuscript is written on leaves, or folios, of parchment (sheep-skin), measuring about 15
inches by 11 (38 by 28 cm), on both sides. On each side, or page, are two columns, making
four to each folio. The folios were numbered in the 17th century, and the four columns of
each are here lettered a,b,c,d. The manuscript emphasises words and usually distinguishes
chapters and sections by the use of red ink. Underlining indicates deletion.

SUSSEX. In red, across the top of the page, spread above both columns.
Sudssexe on p.22 ab, *Sudsexe* on all other pages.

The Rapes

Sussex was divided into six north-south divisions, called Rapes. In Kent, somewhat similar
divisions, there of great antiquity, were called Lathes. Sussex and Kent, Essex and East
Anglia had been separate kingdoms from the 5th century to the 8th, and at times underkings
had ruled portions of the territories of the Kings of Sussex and Kent. These former kingdoms
are not, and never have been, Shires, the word applied to the divisions of Wessex and Mercia.
The heartland of the South Saxon kingdom was in the Lewes-Pevensey area, where almost all the
fifth century cemeteries are concentrated.

The Rapes were named from fortified centres, and by 1086, probably by 1067, each had
been placed under a magnate, a relative or a trusted friend of the King, each of whom held all
the lay land in the Rape, except for two holdings (ch.14). Earl Roger (ch. 11) held Chichester
and Arundel Rapes, William of Braose (ch. 13) held Bramber, William of Warenne (ch.12), Lewes
the Count of Mortain (ch.10) Pevensey, and the Count of Eu (ch.9) Hastings, which included
Rye, sited in 1086 at the 'New Borough' (5,1 and note). DB identifies the Rapes either by
their centres or, more frequently, by their lords. Each Rape also had its own Sheriff.

The origin of the Rapes is not known. They were not a Norman innovation, since DB sometimes refers to them as existing before 1066 (e.g. 9,122; 9,125; 10,96; 12,56). Some such district divisions evidently existed by the early 10th century, though they may not have been called Rapes, and the names and boundaries were not always the same. Many fortresses were built throughout England, south of the Trent, during the Danish wars, with districts assigned to their support, and in the midlands many of them became the centres of the later Shires. In the south, the 'Burghal Hidage' (BCS 1335; Robertson p. 246) assigns a stated number of hides, each probably located in a single district, to each Borough. The number of hides allocated to the Sussex Boroughs, together with an approximate and provisional count of hides reported by DB in 1066, is as follows:

DB Hides, before 1066				Burghal Hidage Hides	
Hastings	200			324	(H)Eorepeburnan
Pevensey	690			500	Hastings
		890		824	
Lewes	690				
Bramber	550				
		1240		1200	Lewes
			2130	2024	
Arundel	470			720	Burpham
Chichester	775			1500	Chichester
			1245	2220	
			3375	4244	

The Burghal Hidage lists Boroughs in geographical order; Burpham was the predecessor of Arundel, and *Heorepeburnan* should be the predecessor of Rye (5,1 note). Pevensey and Steyning were not included. It looks as though Steyning lands served Lewes, and Pevensey served Hastings, while the eastern portion of the later Hastings Rape was attached to the Rye area. In East Sussex the figures closely correspond; but in West Sussex the DB hides are only a little over half the number of those reported in the Burghal hidage. The districts however seem to correspond.

The Rapes, or similar predecessors, may have been created for the purpose of maintaining early 10th century Boroughs; or they may have been earlier divisions, utilised, and perhaps rearranged, for that purpose. The DB boundary between Lewes and Pevensey Rapes cuts through the middle of Lewes, putting a third, or perhaps a half its houses in Pevensey Rape; and even if these were later suburban houses, the boundary lay very near the original fortifications, whereas all the other Rape Boroughs are central to their areas. Lewes, unlike other Boroughs, is not recorded before the early 10th century, and was therefore probably then new. It is therefore likely that this boundary is earlier than the Borough, older than the 10th century.

If one boundary existed so early, there may have been other earlier divisions. But they were probably not identical with those of DB, since some of the 1066 Rape boundaries cut through the middle of Hundreds, and Hundred boundaries cut through villages. Such bounds were probably relatively recent. The names, borders and numbers of the internal divisions of Sussex were repeatedy adjusted, and DB reports them at one particular time. The northern border between Pevensey and Lewes Rapes changed after 1086 (see note on Outliers); Arundel and Bramber replaced Burpham and Steyning as Rape centres. The number and names of Hundreds also changed. There were 59 in 1086, though one, Wittering (3,8 note) was probably then recent, and was short-lived, while Steyning, Totnore and some others may have been amalgamations of older units into double and triple Hundreds. By the end of the 18th century, amalgamation and subdivision had increased the total to 63. In the 7th century, Sussex had been estimated at approximately 70 hundreds of hides (see Appendix), and the DB figure suggests that the estimate may not have been far from reality. There is no evidence to show when they were first grouped into larger divisions, or when such divisions were first called Rapes.

Though the origin and original purpose of the Rapes is not known, their function after 1066 is clear. With its own lord and Sheriff, each was an administrative and fiscal unit. The Survey took unusual trouble to determine which manors and which outliers were in which Rape, and to record recent transfers. The organisation of the whole county, apart from royal and ecclesiastical lands, in territorial blocks, each with a fortress near the sea and each with a single authority, was exceptional King William's victory had shown that Sussex was vulnerable to invasion. He reshaped the remnant of an earlier coastal defence system to ensure that no other invader could repeat his own success. The steps that he took to rationalise the government and taxation of Sussex are the main cause of the complexities which make the DB Survey of the county peculiarly difficult to interpret.

The Outliers

Many manors in many counties had outlying dependencies. In Sussex, though the word *(berewicae)* is used only occasionally, outliers were many, often distant, in the Downs and coastlands as well as in the wooded interior. But in Sussex they are differently recorded. In most of the south and midlands, it was sufficient to note that a place 'lay in (the lands of)' this or that manor; in the north, the name of the 'head of the manor' was commonly followed by a list of named dependencies, with marginal initials to distinguish the M(anor) from the B*(erewica)* or S(*oca*). Normally the manor kept its dependencies undisturbed, but Sussex records the transfer of large numbers of outliers to the Rapes in which they were situated, occasionally with an indication of the date of transfer. Osbern, brother of Earl William of Hereford, had been one of King Edward's secretaries, and had held from him Bosham Church (6,1), in Chichester Rape, with 112 hides. By 1086 he had become Bishop of Exeter, but previously, when he 'acquired' Bosham Church (from King William's confirmation, hardly later than 1067), he had to surrender 47 hides, situated in Lewes Rape, to William of Warenne lord of Lewes. The 65 hides which he retained were presumably in Chichester Rape, since very many entries in West Sussex report that the number of hides had been reduced since 1066 because the othe hides lay in another Rape.

In West Sussex most outliers were large, not many to each manor. They are rarely named, and mentioned only when they were transferred. DB does not report how many of the hides were in the head of the manor, or how many were elsewhere in the same Rape. Sometimes the outliers had the same name as their manor, and some retained it permanently. *Herbertinges* in Lewes Rape (12,8) now Harpingden, had ½ hide in Pevensey Rape; *Herbertinges* in Pevensey Rape is now known as Harebeating (EPNS 436 and 325). Sedlescombe in Hastings Rape is entered as 'outside the Rape' of Hastings, an outlier of a manor in another Rape, probably of Saddlescombe in Lewes (9,122 note). DB does not distinguish Lower Beeding (TQ 22 27) from Upper Beeding, 12 miles away, because both were in Bramber Rape; but one of the outliers it surrendered to Lewes Rape was still called Beeding (*Bedinges*) in 1086, while another was not (13,1. 12,20; 47).

East Sussex differed. Outliers were smaller and more numerous, and had not yet been transferred to their geographical Rapes. In Hastings Rape, several Hundreds begin with a manor in that Hundred and follow with a long list of small places said to be 'in' or 'in the manor of' a Pevensey place, each with the comment 'it never paid tax', meaning that it had been taxed in its parent Pevensey manor, not in its own Hastings Rape.

The Count of Mortain, lord of Pevensey Rape, was also lord of East Grinstead Hundred (10,96 ff.) on the Surrey Border. Twelve of its thirteen holdings 'did not pay tax' in the Rape, and were 'outside the Rape', two of them specified as in Lewes Rape. Most were outliers of named manors, all but one of them in Lewes Rape, in the original South Saxon heartland, near to Lewes. Three holdings in adjoining Hundreds are similarly described. The reasons for the apparent anomaly were practical. These places were in Lewes Rape because they were outliers of Lewes manors. Only one, Standen (10,107), is said to have been transferred to a Pevensey manor, but it still remained 'outside Pevensey Rape'.

There were common sense reasons for placing this area under the lord of Pevensey. In the DB record, it was the only populated area on the Surrey border. It was reached from the coast by the Roman road from Lewes to London, and also by the road from Pevensey, whose course is not now known. These roads ran entirely through Pevensey Rape, and were flanked by villages in Pevensey Rape, rarely more than a few miles apart. But within Lewes Rape, it was separated from the downland manors by many miles of roadless woodland, where DB records no population. Communications and cultivation linked it with Pevensey. In all later records, it was incorporated within Pevensey Rape. The transfer was probably made soon after 1086, but it had not then taken place. The approximate 1086 boundary is here mapped; part perhaps followed the upper waters of the Medway.

The DB Survey describes a drastic reorganisation of Sussex, not yet completed. Before 1066, the county was taxed and administered through manors, many of which had outliers in other Rapes. Though the Rapes existed, there is no indication that they had any governmental function. After 1066, the county was governed and taxed through the lords of the Rapes and their Sheriffs. West of the Ouse, most manors had been stripped of outliers situated in other Rapes, but in the east such transfer had barely begun. DB itself, at pains to identify the mass of tiny holdings, gave the information upon which further reorganisation could be based. The essence of DB's Survey of Sussex is the record of a change over from administration through the manor, before 1066, to administration through the Rape; but the change was not yet completed by 1086.

LANDHOLDERS...ALDRED. Included in ch. 14 in the text.
1,1   8s 10d. . DB uses the English currency system which remained in use until 1971. The pound
       contained 20 shillings, each of 12d. The abbreviations £.s.d. preserved the DB terms *librae,
       solidi, denarii.*
1,2   HOLDING. . See 11,8 note.
2   ARCHBISHOP. Of Canterbury. DM, written about 1100, assembles documents closely
       related to DB, almost all concerning Kent. The pages, photographed in the modern edition,
       are numbered in a recent hand, and the MS distinguishes sections by huge capital letters.
       The top of page 10 (folio 10 v. in the transcript.p.99) gives 8 entries in other counties.
       1 Croydon, 2 Mortlake and Hayes, 3 Harrow are in Middlesex; 4-8 Malling, (West) Tarring,
       Pagham, Lavington, and Tangmere are in Sussex. The text reads, with a stroke (/) marking
       the ends of lines,
            (4) *Mallinges de firma c lib. Gablum / x lib & x & ix sol, et xxx / sol. archiepiscopo.
                 De costum. iiii / lib & xiiii sol. /*
            (5) *Terringes de firma x & viii / lib.   Buresto viii / lib. /*
            (6) *Pagaham de firma lxxx lib / Gablum viii lib. De costum / lx sol. /*
            (7) *Loventune de firma x & viii / lib. Gablum xxxv sol. De/ costum xxiiii sol. /*
            (8) *Tangemere de firma x lib / & i uncia auri, et xl sol/ numerantur pro
                 ii hidis os/ mellini*
       The *firma* of DM closely matches the *valet* of DB. In 1086 the value of Malling was £70;
       if the values of the Archbishop's men are additional, £18 10s plus the omitted value of
       'Alchin', which, if at the same rate as the only other virgate holding (1g), would be 30s, a
       total of £90. Godfrey had held Malling *ad firmam pro* £90. DM gives a *firma* of £100. At
       Pagham and Lavington, DM *firma* and DB *valet* are identical. At Tarring, DM has £18,
       DB's two holdings £18 10s between them. DM has £10 for Tangmere, while DB has £6
       on 6 hides, but notes that it answered for 10 hides before 1066. Most, and probably all
       the men who held from the Archbishop in Sussex, except for William of Keynes, with a
       single virgate, are listed among the Archbishop's *milites* on p. 13 of DM. DB omits the
       lesser dues claimed by DM, amounting to a little over a tenth of the *firma* at Malling and
       Pagham, but one third at Lavington. DM omits the manors held by or for the monks and
       the Malling Canons (DB 2,3; 2,4; 2,8).
2,1   MALLING (later Loxfield) Hundred and manor were coextensive; the constituent
       villages or outliers in the same Rape are not named.
       GODFREY. Called Godfrey of Malling in DM's version of DB Kent.
2,1e   WALTER. Probably of Ricarville, listed among the Archbishop's *milites;* see 10,60 note.
2,1f   ST. MICHAEL'S. Of Malling.
2,1g   KEYNES. Probably Cahagnes in Calvados, OEB 79. He or his descendants named Horsted
       Keynes, Milton Keynes in Bucks., and many other places in England.
2,2   OTHER PART. See 10,99, Burleigh.
2,5   PAGHAM. A frequented residence of the Archbishop, see, e.g. Eadmer *Historia Novorum*
       (Rolls, 1884, p.198).
       ONE PIG...FROM SEVEN. So in parts of Surrey (19,23; 30,1); elsewhere in Surrey one in
       ten (19,11); but at Bishopstone (3,1 below) and perhaps parts of Surrey and Middlesex,
       one in three (Middlesex 2,1 note; Surrey 1,2 note). The customs of Tidenham in Gloucs.
       (Robertson cix, p.206 = BCS 928 = KCD 461), probably 11th century, required 3 of the
       first 7 pigs, thereafter one in ten.

	CHURCH IN CHICHESTER. Probably All Saint's in the Pallant.

CHURCH IN CHICHESTER. Probably All Saint's in the Pallant.

OSMELIN. DM assigns him 2 hides in Tangmere, at 40s; Pagham and Tangmere adjoin.

2,7   LAVANT. East and West, EPNS 50.

2,9   TARRING. DM lists *Buresto* under Tarring, evidently as an outlier. The place should be Burstow in Surrey (TQ 31 41), *Burestou* in 1121, EPNS Surrey 286. Other Sussex manors had Surrey outliers, see 11,36 (Compton) note.

3   MS error, II for III.

3,1   ONE PIG IN THREE. See note 2,5 above.

      10 [d?]. *x sol* perhaps a MS error for *x den.* See 12,45 note below.

3,2   MAN-AT-ARMS. Evidently the *miles* named below. The gap in the MS, with possible traces of deletion, is too long for *miles;* it has room for a byname.

3,5   GUARD. *Huscarle* (Guard) is not uncommon as a personal name.

3,8   EAST WITTERING. The Bishop held the eastern portion of Selsey peninsula, including one Wittering, as Somerley Hundred; Earl Roger held the western portion, including the other Wittering, as Wittering Hundred. Earl Roger's repulsive son forfeited his lands in 1102, and in all later records the Bishop held both Witterings. Since Somerley itself is listed in Wittering Hundred, this Hundred was probably a recent and temporary creation. Since all other DB Sussex Hundreds are a geographical unit; it is probable that the Wittering in the Bishop's eastern Hundred in 1086 was East Wittering.

      SITES. *Hagae*, probably in Chichester; the figure is too large for rural hunting enclosures.

5,1   RYE. The modern name is a corruption of middle English *at ther eye*, since the place was an island in marshes until the 14th century, EPNS 536, and is probably DB's 'new Borough'. It was formed from the earlier manors of *Rameslie* and *Brede,* probably replacing the earlier Borough of *(H)Eorepeburnan,* east of Hastings, see note on Rapes, above. The account of the Borough is omitted; see index, and 9,13 note.

5,2   HAROLD. Here, and in several other 1066 references, probably King(Earl)Harold.

5,3   COUNTESS GODA. King Edward's sister; see 11,4 note.

6   BISHOP OSBERN (1072-1103). Brother of Earl William of Hereford. He was a chaplain of King Edward when he first received Bosham.

6,1   BOSHAM. See also Hants. 5,1 (43 a) 'Bishop Osbern of Exeter holds FARRINGDON (SU 71 35) from the King. Godwin the priest held it from King Edward. It belongs to the church of Bosham'.

      HUGH...RALPH. See 12,33, Saddlescombe, and 12,42, Plumpton.

      ACQUIRED IT. After 1066, since he had already relinquished the hides outside the Rape, presumably at King William's confirmation of existing holdings, probably early in 1067.

      THORNEY. West Thorney, in contrast with Thorney in East Wittering, EPNS 62.

6,4   EAST LAVINGTON. Also called Woolavington.

8   BATTLE. The site of the Abbey is not entered. It may have been Branshill ('Bramble Hill', *Brembelshulle* c. 1240, EPNS 496), preserved as a farm name on the hill above the Abbey, since under the Abbey's only Surrey holding (Limpsfield, Surrey 11,1 and note), DB records that *Brameselle* ('Bramble Hill') belonged to it before 1066. If the site of the Abbey was an outlier of a Surrey manor, that manor was necessarily granted to the Abbey.

8,1   ALNOTH. Or Aethelnoth, of Canterbury, a prominent Kentish noble.

8,3   THESE SECTIONS, to 8,16, are in smaller writing.

      HIS RAPE. Possibly meaning Hastings Rape, in which Battle lies; but possibly meaning the *leuga*, territory or 'Liberty', of the Abbey, for whose government and taxation the Abbot was responsible, as were the lords of Rapes in their Rapes.

      WULFBALD. PNDB 418.

      6 HIDES. Possibly a total of the following entries; 4-11 total 6 hides; 12-15, 2½ hides, are possibly those of 8,16.

8,4   THE ABBOT HAS. Repeated in sections 5-15.

8,5   BATHURST. EPNS 496. The 's' and 'g' of *Wasingate* do not greatly differ in shape.

8,11   CATSFIELD. Population and value are omitted, by accident or because it was waste.

8a   THE ENTRY was added at the foot of the page, written across both columns, in three lines, without number, presumably because the rest of the numbers had already been entered. The beginning of each line is here exdented.

9,1   REINBERT. Sheriff of Hastings, VCH 352.

      WARING. *Werelc* probably for *Werenc.*

9,3   WIBERT. Possibly father of William son of Wibert, *vicecomes comitatus,* evidently Sheriff of all Sussex, early in the 12th century, VCH 352.

9,11   BISHOP ALRIC, or Aethelric, of Selsey, 1057-1070.

9,13   BURGESSES. Presumably of Hastings.

9,15   HIDES. The 1086 holdings total 4½ hides, the 1066 assessment.

9,16   ...HOLDS. The holder's name is omitted, presumably accidentally.

9,22	GODA. The name could be masculine or feminine; if feminine, it might mean Countess Goda, whose name is commonly written Goda, with *comitissa* usually added above the line in correction, possibly here overlooked.

9,22   GODA. The name could be masculine or feminine; if feminine, it might mean Countess Goda, whose name is commonly written Goda, with *comitissa* usually added above the line in correction, possibly here overlooked.

9,28   EYELID. The Hundred boundary evidently cut through its lands; the value, not stated, is probably included in 9,27.

9,35   PEVENSEY RAPE. See note on Outliers, above.

9,39   WILTON ABBEY. In Wiltshire, a women's house, richly endowed and rebuilt in stone by Queen Edith, consecrated in 1065, Freeman *Norman Conquest* (ed.3) 2,520. DB shows that the Sussex grants were not confirmed by King William.

9,47   FURLONG. *Quarentina*, a fourth part, or quarter, commonly used in DB for measurements of length, as a quarter of a league. Elsewhere, for a quarter of a virgate, DB uses English ferlang, in Sussex, *ferdinc* (10,117), *ferding* (11,22), etc. The word is also used for a quarter of a Borough, see 9,107 note.

9,49   EAST DEAN. It is probable that all Countess Goda's land in *Dene* (2 hides less 1 virgate, 9,44; 49; 80) were East Dean, as expressly stated in 9,44, with the 10 hides of 10,33-34 constituting West Dean.

9,60   HOLDING. See 11,8 note.

9,61   PEVENSEY RAPE. See note on Outliers, above.

9,73   JEVINGTON. *Lovingetone* for *Iovingetone*. The DB script, and the returns which it copied, easily confused capital I and L; so also with Yeverington and Lavant, similarly spelt, and with *Luet* (Lidham), 9,106; 113.

9,83   DRIGSELL. See SAC 111 (1973) 77.

9,88   PEVENSEY RAPE. See note on Outliers, above.

9,93   BURGHAM. Perhaps Burgham in Etchingham in Henhurst Hundred; but not listed after 9,82, with Reinbert's other Henhurst manor. It might be a Pevensey outlier; or a lost place in Pevensey Rape.

9,105   ULCOMBE. In Kent.

9,106   LIDHAM. *Luet*, explicitly entered under both Baldslow and Guestling Hundreds; therefore Lidham, on the border between these Hundreds.

           HE HAS. *Habet* omitted before accusative *villanum*.

9,107   QUARTER. *Unum Ferlang*. Assessed at 6 hides, value £6. Not a quarter of a virgate; and not a place name. When spelt, as here, with a capital letter, *Ferding*, or *Ferling*, a quarter, is also used for a 'quarter' or 'ward' of a Borough. (e.g. Huntingdon B 1; B 7 and Winchcombe, Gloucs. 12,10..166 a). Here it probably refers to Hastings, on the border of Guestling Hundred, or possibly to Rye.

9,114   CLAVERHAM. In Shiplake Hundred, Pevensey Rape. Perhaps entered here perhaps because William so returned his two small holdings; but see 9,115 note.

           THEIR VALUE. The plural, *valuer(unt)*, is unusual.

9,115   NETHERFIELD HUNDRED. The two places named are nowhere near this Hundred; Chalvington, and possibly also 'Heighton', are in Pevensey Rape. Perhaps a DB mistake. But it may be that a manor in Netherfield, to which these places were outliers, has been omitted; if so, the heading may be misplaced, and should have come before 9,114. Such misplacement is not uncommon in DB.

9,118   HEIGHTON. Perhaps the lost *Hecton* or *Heghton* in Beckley, in Goldspur Hundred, Hastings Rape (EPNS 527). Possibly South Heighton in Pevensey Rape, which is however *Estone* in DB (10,47).

9,120   FOREGONE. *Retro*, literally either 'in arrears' (of tax), or 'on the other hand', in either case equivalent to 'outside the Rape', usually implying 'never paid tax'.

9,122   SEDLESCOMBE' *Salescome; Selescome* in 9,125-127. Entered under Staple Hundred in Hastings Rape, therefore Sedlescombe in that Rape and Hundred, EPNS 524. But in all these entries, DB states that it 'was outside the Rape' (of Hastings). It was therefore an outlier of a manor in another Rape, probably *Salescome* (Saddlescombe) in Lewes Rape, which had itself belonged to Bosham Church immediately before 1066, see 12,33, note on Earl Godwin. EPNS 524 suggests a different etymology for the two place-names, on the basis of an alleged 'persistent *e* ' spelling in Sedlescombe; but *e* and *a* spellings are used indifferently for both places.

9,123   ½ HIDE. *Una* underlined for deletion.

9,127   VILLAGER..HOLDS. Or 'held'; *ten(et)* normally 'holds', is sometimes also used in DB for *ten(uit)*, 'held', here perhaps intended, in view of *iacuit*, 'lay', above.

9,130   1 HIDE. There 'is' 1 hide, and it answered for 1 hide, before 1066 and in 1086; but the details total 13 virgates (3¼ hides), which correspond to the value of 66s at both dates. The arable had been much extended before 1066, but the assessment had not been raised. Since 'there was nothing but a hall' apparently when acquired, in or after 1067, it had presumably been wasted in 1066, but the damage had been made good.

10,1   MONKS OF MORTAIN. See also 10,60 note.

GILBERT THE SHERIFF. Probably of Pevensey Rape.

10,6   TOTNORE HUNDRED. The heading is misplaced; it should be at 10,11. See 12,6.

10,7   WILLIAM OF KEYNES. Probably Cahagnes in Calvados, OEB 79. He or his family names Horsted Keynes, Milton Keynes in Bucks, and several other places.

10,33   WEST DEAN. See 9,49 note, above.

10,35   WILLINGDON HUNDRED. The heading is unnecessarily repeated.

10,42   GODA. See 9,22 note.

1½ PLOUGHS. *cum car 7 dimid.* A figure may have been omitted before *car.*

10,44   FIRLE. The value, not stated, was perhaps included in 10,45.

10,51   FREEHOLD. A continental term, *alodium,* defined as *haereditas quam vendere et donare possum..mea propria;* as *praedium, id est alodium,* from the 9th century on, Du Cange *Glossarium,* with references. Landed property not held from a lord. Used in DB in the south-east, often with *sicut,* 'like a', for holdings that resembled continental *alodium.* The Sussex returns identify the DB meaning; the same holding, held by the same person, is described in the return of Pevensey Rape as *sicut alodium,* but in the Hastings return as 'he could go where he would', or 'she was a free woman' (10,56 and 9,47; 10,92 and 9,58); in other counties, *libere tenuit, se recedere potuit* and similar phrases have the same meaning. The word is not of course at all points identical with modern 'freehold'. In DB it is virtually confined to the south and south-east. In Sussex it is used frequently in the returns of Earl Roger and of the Count of Mortain, but not in those of the King, of the Churches or of the Count of Eu; in other chapters it is rare.

10,58   THE HALF. Probably half of their time or services, rather than 'metayage'.

10,59   HARTFIELD HUNDRED. Partly in Pevensey, partly in Lewes Rape; see note to 10,96, below.

10,60   WALTER. Probably of Ricarville, near Dieppe, Sheriff of Pevensey about 1095, who deprived the monks of Mortain of lands at Withyham (TQ 49 35) in Hartfield, which are not reported in DB.

5 PIGS. Unusually, *iiii* for *v.*

10,61   OUTSIDE THE RAPE. See note on Outliers, above.

10,67   WOOTTON. Uncertain identification, EPNS 412, followed by DG, without query; VCH 415 suggests 'Doddington', which it locates about 2 miles north of Wootton.

10,67   8d? Perhaps a MS error, *sol* for *den.*

10,70   WILLINGDON. In Willingdon, not Pevensey, Hundred; the manor had 36 hides, and its lands may have included ½ hide beyond the Hundred border.

10,77   HOOE. Evidently Hooe Level, with coastal salt-pans.

SALT-HOUSES. *Salina* comprehends all kinds of salt workings from coastal pans to the boilers of Worcester and Cheshire, with their associated sheds and buildings. 'Salt-house' is the most comprehensive term.

10,84   THE MARGINAL ENTRY repeats 10,82.

10,85   HIM. The meaning is clear in the Latin, not interrupted by the marginal entry.

10,95   MILLER. Probably; but possibly intending *molinarium,* in the sense of 'mill-site'.

10,96   EAST GRINSTEAD HUNDRED. All places except Brambletye were outside the Rape, necessarily in Lewes Rape, where two are expressly stated to lie. Most of them had been outliers of downland Lewes manors, and 'never paid tax' on their own, but through their manors. Rushmonden and Hartfield Hundreds were similarly divided by the Rape boundary, but were all included in the Pevensey chapter, and were later transferred to Pevensey Rape, probably not long after 1086. See not on Outliers, above.

10,99   HOLY TRINITY. Of Canterbury. Wootton (2,2) was held by the Archbishop for the monks.

10,102   EDWARD. MS error, *e(st)* for E(dwardus).

FORGE. *Ferraria,* used for a smithy or forge, as, e.g., Surrey 8,18; possibly here meaning iron-workings.

10,105   BRAMBLETYE. Probably Brambletye House, or the moated site across the river.

10,106   FULK. PNDB 251 and 257 distinguishes between Scandinavian 'Folki', for Fulchi, here, and Old German 'Fulcwig' for Fulcoius (11,14; 31-32, in 1066 and 1086) and Fulcui (14,1 and Surrey 27,3, in 1066); but does not list the 1086 landholders north of the Thames, e.g. Fulcui (Hunts. 11,1); Fulcui and Fulcheius (Cambs.); Fulcuius and Fulco (Shrops.), in both cases probably the same person. Since 'Fulcwig' is virtually unknown among the numerous Old English Folc- names, all these spellings are probably variants of the common Norman Fulco, which, like other Norman names, reached Sussex before 1066. 'Fulcoius' looks like a Latin ending added to Fulco.

LAVANT. Probably Mid Lavant (11,5) in Chichester Rape, though the other named manors in this section were in Lewes Rape. Jevington, occasionally spelt without a 'g', EPNS 421, and Yeverington are possible alternatives, see 9,73 note, but both were in Pevensey Rape.

10,107 STANDEN. Exceptionally listed as now assessed in a Pevensey manor, though formerly in a Lewes manor; but still 'outside the Rape' of Pevensey.

10,110 BALMER. MS error, *Bergeinere* for *Bergemere*.

10,116 'INWOOD'. MS *jnode*, one word, not *in Ode*. For the occasional use of a small letter for capital, see 10,102.

NEW MINSTER. Winchester (Hyde) Abbey.

10 SHILLINGS. The MS has a gap between x and ., sufficient to permit xii or xiii.

10,118 MAYFIELD. Probably *Mesewelle* for *Megevelle*, EPNS 381; capital S and G are somewhat similar in 8,5, as in other 11th century hands; DB may have misread the return it copied.

11,2 ST. NICHOLAS'. Of Arundel.

ROUGH CORN. Rye, or a mixture of corns including rye.

ROBERT SON OF THEOBALD. Sheriff of Arundel. On his death bed, in 1087, he bequeathed Toddington (11,61), to St. Martin of Sees, with his wife Emma, the witnesses including Robert, the priest of Petworth (11,18), Corbelin (11,23; 31), Hamelin (11,27-29) and Thurstan (11,20), Round, *Calendar of Documents in France*, cited VCH 378. Probably all the holdings of 'Robert' from Earl Roger were his.

11,4 COUNTESS GYTHA. Wife of Earl Godwin, mother of King Harold; in some counties she is confused with her namesake, wife of Earl Ralph, whose son was also named Harold, and is sometimes wrongly entered as Goda.

11,5 LAVANT. Probably Mid Lavant, since East and West Lavant were the Archbishop's (2,7).

11,6 10 PLOUGHS. MS *.x.c* at the end of the line; 'c' is the first letter of *car*, beginning the next line, and should have been deleted.

11,8 HOLDING. *Feudum* translates Old English *feoh*, normally meaning 'possessions', 'property', 'holding' in general, e.g. 2,1 *de feudo*. But *in feudo*, as here and in 9,60, and occasionally elsewhere, describes a special kind of English grant, before 1066, and sometimes afterwards. Here, as the whole manor was held for life only, Offa's 2 hide manor was presumably also held by a grant for a lifetime. Other instances may denote a grant for a fixed period, or otherwise revocable, not necessarily for life. *Feudum* was not used in England before 1066, and in DB neither it nor *feuum (feoff)* appear to have yet acquired their 12th century connotation.

11,17 ROBERT. Correcting Ralph (*Radulf*), with deletion mark omitted.

11,18 189 EELS. Deletion mark under *ix* perhaps omitted, intending 180.

11,22 WHEN ACQUIRED. *Post* deleted, *cum recepit* substituted.

11,31 MARDEN. 'Down on the border' (of Hampshire), originally including Compton, EPNS 51. The four DB entries presumably concern North, West, East and Up Marden; only the last, whose church was held by Engelhere's heirs (11,33), seems identifiable.

11,36 COMPTON. See Surrey 18,1 'In Wotton Hundred Earl Roger has 1 hide from the King, which lies in (the lands of) his manor of Compton in Sussex. Before 1066 the holder of Compton held this hide from the King'.

11,37 1500 PIGS. The holding was probably in the woodland in the north of the Rape.

11,44 SOMERLEY HUNDRED. See 3,8 note.

11,63 NUNMINSTER. Probably West Preston, A.H. Allcroft *Waters of Arun* (1930) 97; E.A. Fisher *Saxon Churches of Sussex* (1970) 141. The editor is indebted to Mr. G.R. Burleigh for this identification and these references.

ESMELT. MS *Esmund*, in error, PNDB 367. Old English 'Eastmund', always with a 't', is well evidenced only for the 9th century, dying out in the 13th century, after a few sporadic survivals, one of them in DB (Suffolk 1e 3...287a,*Estmunt*). Modern Esmond appears to derive from Thackeray's *Henry Esmond* (1852).

11,76 MARTIN. MS *Marun*, in error.

12,1 THE KING HAS THE...MAN. Meaning the fine from the man.

TWO PARTS WERE. *sunt* corrected to *erant*.

12,5   163 VILLAGERS. 'cxlxiii' emended by deletion mark to 'clxiii'.

12,6   STREAT HUNDRED. Swanborough is a MS error. See 10,6.

12,9   EARL. So also in Hunts. 14,1, *comes Willelmus,* evidently intending William of Warenne (Hunts. 13). He is never called *comes* in relation to Normandy. He was created Earl of Surrey in or soon after 1087. It seems probable that these entries were written after that date.

12,16   FALMER HUNDRED. The heading should have been placed before, not after, Balmer.

12,20   ALDRINGTON HALF-HUNDRED. Called a Hundred in 13,28.

12,22   BENFIELD. See SAC 111 (1973)77 and references there cited.

12,26   PAWTHORNE. EPNS 285.

12,29   SHIPLEY. Omitted in DB. In West Grinstead Hundred. This Hundred, with its neighbour, Steyning, is given 235 hides; if Shipley were a 5 hide manor, the total would be 240.

12,32   CARUCATES. Evidently for 'land for 2 ploughs'; *car* abbreviates *carrucatas,* occasionally used elsewhere in this sense, see Appendix; unless there is an MS error.

12,33   RALPH. Of Quesnay, 6,1.

SADDLESCOMBE. See 9,122 note, and 6,1 note.

EARL Godwin. In 6,1 both Saddlescombe and Plumpton (12,42) are said to have belonged to the Church of Bosham, held by (Bishop) Osbern from King Edward. In ch. 12 (William of Warenne's return) both were said to have been held from Earl Godwin by Godwin the priest. Godwin the priest, presumably of Bosham, also held East Lavington from Osbern in 1086. They had perhaps been granted to Osbern after Godwin's death.

12,35   THEN 2 HALLS...NOW 1 MANOR. Here DB defines the manor as a place with a hall, and therefore with the jurisdiction attached thereto.

12,36   ROBERT HOLDS. A gap in the MS between *Rotbertus* and *de,* where possibly a duplicate *ten(et)* has been erased.

12,45   VALUE 12s. *denar* partly erased in MS, corrected to *sol.*

12,47   BEEDING. In Bramber Rape, as stated, here included with Hugh's Lewes return.

12,49   7 HIDES...4 HIDES. Wulfeva held 7 hides in Earl Roger's Rape, Arundel (11,69), and 4 hides from the Count of Mortain (10,109), which were 'outside the Rape' of (Pevensey), in the lands of Hamsey, in Lewes Rape, evidently the 4 hides less 1 virgate here listed. DB has here inverted the figures. She also held a 2 hide manor in East Grinstead from the Count of Mortain, in Lewes Rape (10,100).

12,53   ½ PLOUGH. MS *dim vcar.* The 'v' is evidently virgate, corrected to *car,* but not marked for deletion.

13,1   BEEDING. Perhaps including Lower Beeding (TQ 22 27), in the same Rape and Hundred.

SESTER. A measure, usually of liquid, of uncertain and probably variable size.

HEARTH-TAX. *Herdigelt,* probably with this meaning, not reported elsewhere in DB by that name, but called *fumagium* 'smoke' or 'hearth' payment in Herefordshire (1,50...181 a, first entry).

13,3   BERTH. Omitted from DB.

13,27   CATTLE. *Animalia,* in Exon DB and elsewhere commonly called *animalia otiosa,* 'idle animals', beef, dairy etc. cattle, in contrast with ploughing oxen.

13,28   RALPH. Of Bucy, from whom the place was called Kingston-Bucy, corrupted to Kingston-by-Sea, EPNS 245.

13,30   ROBERT. Probably Robert Savage, whose heirs held most of these lands, VCH 447.

BROADWATER. See Hants 69,40 (50 c) 'In Clare Hundred Alwin White holds 2 hides... Alwin held...before 1066 under Wigot (of Wallingford) for protection *(tuitione);* now he holds it under Miles (Crispin). It was delivered to Wigot through Humphrey Wolf-face (a Berkshire landholder) in exchange for Broadwater, as he (Alwin) states himself. But the Hundred knows nothing of it'.

13,38   GORING...ELSEWHERE. An alternative but less likely translation is '..Roger's Rape. In Goring and elsewhere are 3½ hides...'

13,46   HOOE. The name is preserved by Hoecourt Barn, EPNS 200.

13,54 IFIELD HUNDRED. MS *Tifeld*, from Old English *aet Ifeld*.
WILLIAM. William of Ifield was one of the Archbishop's *milites*, see 2 note.
14,2 ALFRED. Brother of Odo (of Winchester).
OUALET. Or possibly Ovalet. The name is not otherwise known.
E 1 SURREY. *Lodesorde* (Surrey 36,9 and note) is probably Lollesworth in Surrey,
rather than Lodsworth in Sussex, as EPNS Sussex 26.

APPENDIX

The **HIDE** was the unit of land measurement and assessment. Its use abounds in apparent contradictions, whose discussion has sometimes prompted oversimple generalisations. Since DB states some of its meanings more clearly in the Survey of Sussex than of many other counties, it is appropriate to list here the main evidence. But its interpretation cannot be adequately attempted until all the DB information in each place in each county has been closely studied, in relation to earlier records and to the nature and extent of the lands concerned.

The evidence is clear in outline. In the 7th and 8th centuries the Hide meant 'land for one family'; in DB it normally meant a number of acres, usually, but not always, 120, and it was regularly divided into four virgates. The detail is complex, chiefly because land use changed, by the extension or abandonment of cultivation at different times in different places, and because the assessments both of land cultivated and of land taxed were often revised piecemeal, so that many were out-of-date.

The Sussex Evidence

Throughout England, DB reports either hides that are (or were) 'there', or 'held, or else hides 'taxed' or 'answerable'. Usually, one wording or the other is dominant in one county, chapter or district. When only the hides 'there' or 'held' are given, the text usually states or implies that they are the same as the taxed hides, since its main concern was with the present. But Sussex is one of the few counties whose entries often give different figures for hides 'there' and hides taxed, both before and after 1066. At Bosham (1,1) 'there were then 56½ hides; it paid tax for 38 hides; now the same'; and similar large reductions before 1066 are recorded at Westbourne and Stoughton (11,30; 11,37), both about 4 miles from Bosham. One Hampshire entry (2,15...40c) suggests a possible explanation. At Fareham 'the hides are 30 in number', but King Edward had reduced the taxable hides 'because of the Vikings, since it is on the sea'. Whatever the occasion or risk of 'Viking' damage, Bosham and its neighbourhood, 15 miles from Fareham and in the same waters, was exposed to the same attacks.

Reductions after 1066 are differently explained. Up Waltham (11,112) 'answered for 6 hides then; now for 4'; 2 hides were in Earl Roger's park. The hides of other places were reduced because they lost their outliers, as at Iford, where 77½ hides were reduced to 58, and Rodmell, 79 to 64, because the other hides were in different Rapes (12,3-4); Bosham Church was reduced from 112 hides to 65 because 47 hides were taken away (6,1). Bosham Church answered for all its remaining 65 hides, but at Iford the 58 hides answered only for 36, at Rodmell the 64 hides for 33. In 1086, DB still distinguished 'hides there' from 'hides taxed', though here it offers no explanation for the difference. Its incidental notices make the same distinction. At Stoughton there were '36 hides there, but then and now it answered for 15 hides. 16 of these hides were put in the manor of Westbourne, but they are now in Stoughton again'. The 16 hides were part of the 36, not of 15, and constituted a recognisable piece of land, that could be transferred from one manor to another. Men knew what a hide was, irrespective of tax liability.

The Seventh Century Hide

Sussex has many instances of revision. Other evidence has much to say of when, where and why revisions were undertaken.

The earliest evidence is a Mercian survey, the so-called 'Tribal Hidage' (BCS 297), of the 7th century (Wendy Davies *Fruemittelalterliche Studien* 8, 1974,226, superseding earlier studies). It groups smaller districts into multiples of three hundreds of hides, with larger round figures for the greater southern kingdoms; Sussex, and six other medium sized regions, are also allocated a round figure, 7,000 hides each; Wight, recently conquered by the Mercians, is listed at 600 hides.

About fifty years later Bede gave a number of individual figures, and explained what the word meant to him. His 9th-century English translator spoke of hides, but his own polished Latin translated the word as *possessiones*, or *terra*, land, of so many *familiae*. He still rated Sussex at 7,000, but Wight had increased to 1200. These figures do not concern 120 acre hides, for the entire surface of Wight (about 95,000 acres) has only room for about 700 such hides. But the figures fit Bede's 'family' hide. In 1086 the fertile Downs and coasts of Sussex, with their dependent pig pastures and sheep folds, supported a rural population of roughly 6,000 *villani*, with about 4,000 cultivators of lesser status. 7,000 is a not unreasonable hit and miss estimate of the 7th century population.

'Land for one family' cannot mean a fixed acreage, irrespective of the terrain; it is a measure of productivity, akin to the late Roman *iugum* (yoke), which in some provinces included more poor land than average, less good land. A similar notion persisted in Kent, where the English took over a relatively undamaged Roman economy in the 5th century. There land was normally granted not by the hide, but by the *aratra*, the classical Latin word for a plough, called in English 'sulung', from *sulh*, plough, and divided into four *ioclets*, yokes, called *iuga* in Latin.

Early laws and charter also equate hide with family, and explain the meaning of 'family'. Many of the early charters simply grant a named place, without mention of its hides. The oldest known grants that record the hides are Northumbrian, reported by Bede, a single hide before 651 (4,23) and twelve holdings, each of 10 hides, in 655 (3,24). Early Sussex charters commonly grant so many *tributarii*, the Roman technical term for tax-paying provincials, the literal equivalent of Old English *gafolgelda*, taxpayer; one such charter, of about 725 (BCS 144), which probably preserves the original Latin and English wording, granted 20 *tributarii* in Latin, but 20 *hida* in English. Elsewhere, the neutral term *manentes*, inhabitants, is more usual.

The early laws (LEEK) classified men by the value set upon their lives or the fines they paid. In 7th century Wessex, King Ine's values equate the *gafolgelda* with a man who 'has one hide', rated much above the humble cultivator, *(ge)bur* (6,3(where the Quadripartitus reading of 30s. is probably right); 23,1; see LEEK notes). He is also called *ceorl*, man, and *twyhunda*, because his life was valued at 200 shillings, in contrast with the noble *twelfhunda*, valued at 1200 shillings. A 9th century law (Alfred and Guthrum 2) distinguishes the noble from the *ceorl* who 'occupies taxland' (*the on gafollande sit*). The 7th century Kentish laws explain that the *ceorl*'s household, his *familia*, included his dependents, his 'loaf-eaters' and his maidservants (Aethelbert 16; 25). A 12th century restatement of Ine's laws (*Consuetudo West Sexe* 70,1....Liebermann 1,462, cf. 458) equates these 7th century classes with the terms used in DB, stating *twyhindi, id est villani.......twelfhindi, id est taini.*

The evidence is clear and consistent. A hide meant land sufficient to maintain one taxpayer and his dependents. That was the basis of the Mercian assessment. But assessments were not revised systematically to keep pace with change. Some charters give figures that remained unaltered between the 7th or 8th centuries and 1066, but others show differing figures. The researches of the last 20 years have recorded very many thousands of English villages that shrank, moved, or were abandoned, as well as others that grew and later declined, and others that maintained their growth. There is no reason to suppose that population change and movement was any less before the 11th century than after. It may well have been greater, for in and after the 9th century Scandinavian invasions caused extensive destruction, and also disrupted the basis of assessment.

Tenth Century Changes

The wars also greatly changed the status of the cultivator. Seventh century England had distinguished the noble from the commoner, the lord from his dependent, but prolonged warfare much extended lordship. More evidence of lands granted to laymen survives, partly because more was written and more has been preserved. But language also changed. Charters increasingly granted *cassati*, men installed in a *cot*, or cottage, by their lords, and *mansae*, parcels of land, rather than taxpayers and inhabitants. When the King granted a charter, he gave or sold to its recipient the annual tribute he had received from it, its *census, gafol* or *'gablum'*. Until 1066 there were still plenty of 'free men', but they were already a small minority; most men owed dues to a lord, in cash, in kind, or in labour, and could not quit their land. Changed relationships outstripped existing vocabulary. DB found no generalised terms for such payments, and modern attempts to supply them tend to blur understanding. Modern English distinguishes tax, paid to the central government, from rates paid to a local authority and rent paid to a private landlord; but neither Latin nor Old English had words for these distinctions. The Latin *tenere* means 'to hold', and nothing else. The modern terms 'rent' and 'tenant' are best avoided, for they imply a contract, to be ended by agreement, altogether different from the *census, gablum* and *tenet* of DB. 'Tax' is best confined to DB's *geld*, then the main royal tax, 'which no man escapes'. Most cultivators paid varying dues to lords great or small, and held a small acreage from them. The taxpaying *ceorl* with a family hide ceased to be a practicable basis for assessment.

The wars also caused both sides to construct numerous fortified Boroughs, whose population was necessarily recruited from the surrounding countryside. In the midlands, many became the centres of later Shires; but in the south, Shires or ancient smaller kingdoms already existed. There, the 'Burghal Hidage' (see note on Rapes, above) gives detail, probably at about 915. In Sussex about 4,000 hides, much less than the earlier Mercian figure, were assigned to Borough defence, at one man per hide. Most doubtless served only in emergency, but the five Sussex Boroughs may well have absorbed up to 1,000 men between them, perhaps a tenth of the rural population. The Scandinavians accelerated the break-down of earlier assessments; in many areas where they settled permanently, the 'carucate' replaced the hide; elsewhere they disturbed the structure and location of the rural population.

DB records three major innovations in assessment, whose origin or first record arises from the wars. In the late 9th century, in face of the second major Danish onslaught, King Aethelred levied a *geld*, or tax, upon each hide, which was continued after the wars, probably raised annually by 1086. DB also regularly records an assessment of plough capacity, 'land for so many ploughs', sometimes meticulously noting the shortfall, when ploughs in use were fewer; occasionally, in counties where land was reckoned by the hide, *carrucata* is used as an alternative (e.g. Hereford 1,15...181a; see also Sussex 12,32 note). Both the word, and the estimate that differs from ploughs in use, imply a count or assessment. Its occasion may have been the imposition of payments on each plough, chiefly, though not entirely, for church dues, first attested in the 920s (Edward and Guthrum 3; and references under 'Plough', indexed in LEEK and LKE). The differences in DB between plough capacity estimates and ploughs in use may mark changes in land use over a period of up to 150 years or more.

At about the same time, in the decades after the defeat of the first Danish invasions south of the Humber, the 'measured (*ametenes*) acre' (e.g. Robertson 40, p.80) and the 120 acre hide (e.g. Whitelock *Anglo-Saxon Wills* 2 (Alderman Algar), p.8, lines 26-27; Ely 2,32-33) are first recorded, in southern East Anglia. The need to specify the measurements suggests that not all acres were then measured, nor all hides of 120 acres. In the same years some smaller arable holdings in Worcestershire and Northamptonshire were measured in units of 60 and 30 acres (e.g. Robertson 55; 40 = KCD 612 (Heming 1,163); BCS 1130), the equivalents of DB's half-hide and virgate. But not all hides were confined to arable; in 10th century Warwickshire (Robertson 43 = BCS 1182 = Heming 1,206) a 3 hide holding apparently included 20 acres of meadow and a 3 acre mill-site; in 1086 DB noted (Gloucs. 6,3...165 b) that 'in this hide there are only 64 acres of land, when it is ploughed (*quando aratur*)' The wording suggests both that hides normally contained more than 64 acres, and that the acreage was greater than the arable. DB also sometimes lists hides of woodland (e.g., Beds. 32,14; 39,3; Essex 24,1-2). Measurement however took centuries to become universal. In the early 13th century the 'St.Paul's Domesday' (Camden Society 69, 1858, 69) reported that at Runwell in Essex (near Southend),an 8 hide manor, the hide contained 120 acres, although the 'Old Inquiry' stated that it customarily contained only 80, the reason being that the lands had subsequently been investigated and measured (*hida continet sexcies viginti acras, set antiqua inquisitio dicit quod non consuevit continere nisi quattuor viginti; quia postmodo exquisite sunt terre et mensurate*). The modern parish contains about 2070 acres. The measured hides account for 960 acres. DB (5,9..13 b) enters 8 hides, cultivated in 1066 by 8 *villani*, 8 *bordarii* and 2 *servi*, a population probably of the order of between 50 and 100 persons; in 1901 the population was 239.

The Surrey Evidence

Comparable evidence survives only from a few districts and places. There it indicates that the 120 acre hide was introduced piecemeal over a long period, not all at once over the whole country; and that the hide might be confined to the arable, or might include all cultivated land.

Areas cannot be measured in Sussex, for many manors included unnamed outliers of unknown size. But measurement is possible in Surrey, where

DB also records large reductions in the number of hides between 1066 and 1086, especially in the crowded areas by the Thames. There the adjacent manors of Mortlake (with Putney and Barnes) and Battersea were assessed at 153 hides in 1066, 43 hides in 1086. Their approximate area is known, for their neighbours are listed on all sides, and the bounds of some are recorded. The largest reckoning of their superficial area is not much above 12,000 acres, only 100 hides at DB reckoning. The 1066 assessment could not have been based on 120 acre hides; the 1086 assessment might have been.

The records of Chertsey afford some insight into these assessments. In a contemporary copy of a grant of 947 (BCS 820) Merstham contained '20 *mansae*, called in English 20 hides'. The bounds are given. They have been identified and mapped (A.R. Rumble in JEPN 3, 1970-1971, 6; 4, 1971-1972, 12). They are almost identical with the bounds of the modern parish, and enclose a little over 2500 acres; if these hides had been 120 acres each, then almost every acre would have been cultivated in the 10th century. Chertsey also preserved three lists of holdings which gave the numbers of hides in each place (BCS 39; 1195; KCD 812). Merstham remained at 20 hides in each, and is also entered in DB (2,5) as answerable for 20 hides in 1066; but by 1086 it answered for only 5 hides, cultivated by 21 *villani*, with 4 *bordarii*. The original assessment remained valid until revised over 100 years later. In DB, the number of villagers was almost identical with the number of old hides; in relation to the population, these were family hides.

Nearly all the places in the Chertsey lists which were still church land resembled Merstham, rated at the old hides in 1066, but greatly reduced thereafter, and similar reductions were made throughout Surrey, in church and lay lands alike. On some 50 large holdings, listed at 10 or more hides in 1066, the hides of all but two had been cut by 1086, the majority to a quarter or less of their former total. On most of these holdings, DB records one villager or less for each old hide, with varying numbers of other cultivators, and none had more than two villagers to the hide. Widespread drastic reductions are reported on this scale for Surrey alone; they cannot be explained by 'beneficial hidation' or campaign damage in 1066, for the King's indulgence was not indiscriminately spread over an entire county, and the values show no corresponding fall. There is no direct evidence for the origin of the old hides, but the DB Survey demonstrates that most were much smaller than 120 acres, and that on the larger holdings there were about the same number of villagers as hides in 1066. The implication of this evidence is that in Surrey the large measured hide was still exceptional in 1066, and in much of the county did not replace the family hide until after 1066.

The Middlesex Evidence

On the north bank, the DB record is quite different. There are no such sweeping reductions in Middlesex. But Middlesex is the only county where the individual holdings of the cultivators are systematically recorded, down to the cottager's half acre. On average, there were about 4 villagers to the hide (see Middlesex Appendix). In most manors, there is some discrepancy, usually not large, between the totals of the land cultivated and the hides held, or answerable. The exception is Westminster. On all the Abbey's manors the cultivated and assessed hides correspond at 120 acres to the hide, either exactly or within a few acres, with the exception of the last-named, Hendon, where cultivated land coincides with plough assessment, but not with hide assessment. All Westminster grants were very recent, most of them made in the last years and months of King Edward's reign. In Middlesex they were assessed on the land then cultivated, at 120 acres to the hide; in Surrey they were assessed in the old hides still prevalent in the county, which King William reduced. In both counties the 1086 hides, at 120 acres, seem to account for about one third of the acreage of comparable modern parishes; the figure is not unreasonable, for about two thirds of the acreage of modern England is cultivated, nearly half of it arable, with more building but less woodland, and there is much more arable in the south than in the country as a whole. The evidence suggests that Middlesex had been assessed in 120 acre hides before 1066, but that Surrey had not.

Sussex Regional Variation

Hide figures comparable with those of both Middlesex and Surrey are reported in DB in different parts of Sussex. In the 7th century, Sussex had been roughly estimated at somewhere about 7,000 families or hides. The 'Burghal Hidage', about 250 years later (see note on Rapes, above), assigned about 4000 hides to the county's Boroughs. It does not say that all hides were so assigned; but in East Sussex it enters about the same figures as the total hides of 1066 and 1086, with virtually no revision after 1066, as in Middlesex. But the West Sussex hides were almost halved in the 150 years before 1066, and were further reduced soon after, in round figures by about 100 in Lewes Rape, 110 in Bramber, 30 in Arundel and 130 in Chichester. These reductions, of the order of a little over 10% of the total, are much less than those of Surrey, but are parallelled in Berkshire and Hampshire. As in Surrey, they have nothing to do with value, for the manors of the three western Rapes, whose taxable hides were reduced by 270 between 1066 and 1086, increased their combined values by about £130 in the same period, while in the eastern Rapes, where reduced values 'when acquired' mark the damage done in 1066, values had about regained their 1066 level in Lewes and Hastings, though not yet in Pevensey. Yet the reduced taxed assessment is reported in the relatively undamaged west, not in the war-scarred east.

Such revision had a cause. One of the express instructions to the DB commissioners was to ascertain 'whether more could be had'. Several of their reports of Cities and Boroughs emphasise where more could not be had, recording that the present levies could not be met. In the countryside, the past changes noted are almost always reductions in tax liability. Those made after 1066 may have substituted the 120 acre hide for earlier hides of smaller or unfixed extent, but others spotlight places where it seems that more could reasonably be had. DB credits the three large manors of the Bosham area with 128½ hides between them, but they were still assessed at the 65 hides to which King Edward had reduced them, very possibly after a disaster whose damage had long since been made good; for though their values were standardised at £40 each, their payments totalled £165, well above the coastal average of around £1 a hide. At the other end of the county, at Wellhead (9,13), near the Kentish border, 'there is 1 hide... Before 1066 and now it answered for 1 hide'. But 'of this hide' five named men held between them more than 3 hides, and the value, 66s before and after 1066, fits 3 hides. In this part of Sussex, the overall assessment was still much as it had been 170 years earlier; it seems probable that more land had been brought into cultivation, without revision of the assessment. Similar reports are numerous. DB provided evidence of 'where more could be had'; but the King died, and his successors did not undertake the thorough revision of assessments which the information collected in DB made possible.

The Midland Evidence

The Mercian Shires were organised in their permanent form about 1008 (Warwicks. 1,6 note), though some of them closely corresponded with the areas assigned to

Boroughs a century earlier. The 'County Hidage' (abstracted in Maitland *Domesday Book and Beyond* 475 ff.), held to have been compiled in the middle decades of the 11th century, probably preserves their original assessment, expressed in multiples of hundreds of hides, for the English Mercian Shires assessed in hides. In most of these Shires, the numbers of hides and of Hundreds were little changed in DB. There, as elsewhere in England, many individual places were assessed in multiples of 5 hides. The neat symmetry of these figures has an outward appearance of artificiality, arbitrarily imposed by a central government for the convenience of the tax-collector. But multiples of 5 hide units are common in grants and laws from the 7th century, long before *geld* was imposed on the hide. Then, the main recorded obligation on the hide was personal service or food. That obligation severely restricts the extent of artificiality; for though a government may seek to impose excessive money taxes, it cannot levy more men or provisions than there actually are in the place. Some of these grants, particularly those which concern places ending in *-tun*, are quite near to the date when the place was named and defined, and the bounds may well have been drawn to include approximately the number of hides stated, though Hundred boundaries were doubtless rearranged at the formation of Borough districts and Shires. The probable size of these Mercian hides is not known. At 120 acres they would, with two exceptions, account for less than half the Shire acreage, often much less, and they were deemed valid in 1086, for they were not revised, like the hides of Surrey and West Sussex, Berkshire and Hampshire.

The exceptions were Northamptonshire and Cambridgeshire, where the County Hidage figures would have covered two thirds of the total area, at 120 acres to the hide. Before 1066, the hides of Cambridgeshire had been halved. More is known of Northamptonshire. A tax return survives, dated to about 1070 or soon after (Ellis, folio lix = quarto 1,184; Robertson p.230; discussed by Round, *Feudal England* p.147 (1964 reprint, p.175) and VCH Northants. 1, 258, and by C. Hart *Hidation of Northamptonshire* Leicester, 1970, with tabulated analysis and figures). The 'County Hidage' records 3200 hides. The tax return lists 32 Hundreds, a few of them regrouped as a 'double Hundred' or 'Hundred and a half', and states the number of hides in each Hundred 'as in King Edward's time', and in each holding which had not yet paid tax. In the south and east fifteen Hundreds each retained their 100 hides apiece; in the centre and north two Hundreds had been cut to 90 hides, six to 80. But in the north and east, reductions were greater, a double Hundred to 108½ hides, four Hundreds to 62, one to 60, one to 47 and one to 40. As in Sussex, there had been a regional and erratic revision.

The tax return also reported the aftermath of recent disaster; in 1065 Earl Morcar's men had ravaged Northampton, so that it 'and the neighbouring Shires were the poorer for many years', and 900 hides, more than a third of the revised total, were entered as waste. Action was soon taken. By 1086 King Edward's partial revision had been scrapped. The few identifiable holdings were cut from 10 to 4 hides, or in like proportion; and each of the 32 Hundreds was evenly reduced from 100 to approximately 40 hides; though the tabulated DB figures require some adjustment, adjustment tends to bring them nearer to the norm rather than further. The virgate was similarly reduced to 12 acres, and was known to later records as the 'small virgate', so that the standard hide was reduced to 48 acres.

There are also signs of smaller hides in the south-west. The 1084 Tax Returns in the Exeter Book occasionally record sums paid on the acre. In Wiltshire, in Dole, Damerham and probably Calne Hundreds, tax seems to have been paid at 72 acres to the hide, but in Dorset at 40 acres in Charborough Hundred, 48 in Longborough. However, these returns have not yet been critically analysed.

King Edward's partial revision may have been part of a wider reassessment, for some of the unusual figures seem to recur in Sussex. On a provisional count, Easewrithe, Holmestrow and Streat Hundreds each had 108 or 108½ hides in 1066, Binsted 90, Preston and Malling 80, with Totnore at 160 and Steyning perhaps at 240 (12,29 note); Alciston had 62, Pagham, Westbourne and Eastbourne 60, Baldslow 40. But DB hides are not easy to count, for it is often uncertain whether one figure is included in another, or is additional thereto. Interpretation of the figures for Sussex and other counties must await painstaking analysis.

Summary

The texts here cited were written by men who knew what they meant, and there are many more such texts. Much of the meaning is obscure, and will probably remain so. But a thorough sifting of the evidence for each place and county is likely to increase understanding. To aid such study, this edition will, if possible, include regional analytical volumes. In the meantime, a few conclusions seem warranted. The evidence warns against overeasy generalisations, purporting to give the hide the same meaning in all contexts all over the country, as a 'purely fiscal notion' which was 'arbitrarily imposed', its variations dismissed without scrutiny as 'beneficial hidation' or 'campaign damage', its size always 'reckoned at' 120 acres. There is strong evidence that the hide was originally the holding of a substantial family, but that by 1086 it meant both an assessment for tax and also an area, sometimes identical, sometimes not, the differences sometimes distinguished by the DB phrases, hides held, hides there, and hides taxed. There is evidence that several 11th century administrators tried to organise a neat administration, in which each Hundred contained 100 hides and each hide a hundred acres; and that a 'hundred' sometimes meant a decimal 100, sometimes 80, like the *centuria* of the Roman army, but that the English 'long' hundred, 120, was preferred; but there is also evidence that piecemeal revision in some areas, and lack of revision in others, thwarted such attempts at orderly arrangement. The evidence shows that 120 acre hides predominated in some counties and districts, but not in others; and in many counties DB gives no indication of how many acres it reckoned to the hide.

The constants are the virgate, almost always a quarter of a hide, whatever its size, and the acre. The acre varied regionally, but its meaning was real, as much land as could be ploughed in a long day. Where the variations were abnormally large, DB makes corresponding adjustments. Across the Severn, it distinguishes the smaller Welsh hide; in Cornwall, entry after entry assesses taxable hides at precisely half the hides there; in Cheshire, where an acre two and a half times the size of the standard acre lingered into modern times, the County Hidage assessment of 1200 acres had been cut to a little over 500 by 1086, after the damage done in 1069 had been put right; at 120 standard acres, these hides amount to less than a tenth of the total area. In Shropshire, the Hundreds and hides were both halved, to cover about a sixth of the acreage. Since hides were reduced when acres were unusually large, very wide variations are unlikely when no adjustment was made.

The tenor of the evidence defies generalities. The size of the hide varied from county to county, and within counties; and so did its relation to the taxable hide. There are specific reasons for these variations, but in each county and district the reasons differ. In each, decisions to estimate the extent or liability of particular lands, to revise older estimates or leave them unrevised, were taken by different men at different periods in their history. When all the evidence is studied locally in detail, it is likely to suggest the probable occasions and causes of some of these decisions. The selection of evidence listed above is intended to help such study, and in particular to provide a context in which the Sussex statistics may be investigated.

INDEX OF PERSONS

Familiar modern spellings are given when they exist. Unfamiliar names are usually given in an approximate late 11th century form, avoiding variants that were already obsolescent or pedantic. Spellings that mislead the modern eye are avoided where possible. Two, however, cannot be avoided: they are combined in the name of 'Leofgeat', pronounced 'Leffyet', or 'Levyet'. The definite article is omitted before bynames, except where there is reason to suppose that they described the individual. The chapter numbers of listed landholders are printed in italics.

Churches and Clergy. Archbishop (of Canterbury) 2. **Bishop** of Bayeux 1,2. Chichester 3. 1,1. 10,1. 11,8. Exeter, see Osbern. Selsey, see Alric. **Abbeys** Almenesches 11,63-64; 75. Battle 8. (Canterbury) Holy Trinity 10,99. Fecamp 5. Grestain 10,14; 39-41; 44-45. (Lewes) St Pancras 12,3; Mortain 10,1. St Evroul 11,3. Sees 11,2; 39; 76; 93. Shaftesbury 8a. Treport 9,13. Troarn 11,111-112. Westminster 4. Wilton 9,38-39; 56; 63; 65; 71; 75; 81; 102. 10,22. 12,8. Winchester 7. 11,8; (New Minster) 10,16. **Churches and Clergy** of (Arundel) St Nicholas 11,2; 6. Bosham 6,5. Boxgrove 11,102. (Eastbourne?) St Michael's 10,73. (Lewes) St John's 10,44; 63; St Pancras 10,22. 12,3;7. Malling, see Canons. Singleton 11,3. Tangmere 2,6. **Saints** (Abbeys) Edward...Shaftesbury. Holy Trinity...Canterbury. Martin...Battle, Sees. Peter...Westminster, Winchester. (Churches) John... Lewes? Michael...Eastbourne?, Malling. Nicholas...Arundel. Pancras...Lewes. **Canons** of Chichester 3,10. Malling, St Michael's 2,1f; 3. See also Geoffrey. **Clerics** see Alfward, Eustace, Geoffrey, Godfrey, Hugh, Osbern, Robert, Roger, William. **Priests** see Acard, Aldred, Doda, Edmer, Esmelt, Godfrey, Godwin, Ordmer, Ralph, Theobald, Venning, Wulfmer, Wulfnoth, Wulfward. **Monks** of St.Evroul 11,3. Mortain 10,1. St.Pancras (Lewes) 12,3. Treport 9,102.

Secular Titles and Occupational Names. Bowman (*arbalist*)... Hugh. **Cook** (*cocus, coquus*)... Robert. **Count** (*comes*)... of Eu, of Mortain. **Countess** (*comitissa*)...Goda, Gytha. **Earl** (*comes*)... Godwin, Gyrth, Harold, Leofwin, Roger, Tosti, William (?). **Queen** (*regina*)...Edith. **Sheriff** (*vicecomes*)...Gilbert. **Young** (*cild*)...Alnoth, Wulfmer.

INDEX OF PLACES

The name of each place is followed by (i) the initial of its Hundred and its location on the Map in this volume; (ii) its National Grid reference; (iii) chapter and section references in DB. Bracketed figures denote mention in sections dealing with a different place. Unless otherwise stated, the identifications of EPNS and the spellings of the Ordnance Survey are followed for places in England; of OEB for place abroad. Inverted commas mark lost places with known modern spelling; unidentifiable places are given in DB spelling, in italics. The National Grid reference system is explained on all Ordnance Survey maps and in the Automobile Association Handbooks; the figures reading from left to right are given before those reading from bottom to top. In the 100 km grid square lettered SZ are, in Chichester Rape, places mapped and indexed as So 1-3, Wi 3-4, A 2; and in Arundel Rape Bi 12. In square SU are places in the rest of Chichester Rape, and those in Arundel Rape which begin with figures from 94 to 99. In square TV are Pevensey Rape, W 6-10 and E 3-5. All other places are in square TQ.

The DB Hundreds, with the abbreviations used in the index, are listed below, immediately before the maps. S stands for Surrey.

The modern form of eight of the Hundred names is not known; for these a later name is used, namely for *Avronehelle* Longbridge, *(H)Ailesaltede* Netherfield, *Babinerode* Gostrow, *Edivestone* Shiplake, *Ghidentroi* Westbourne, *Hamesford* Dumpford, *Riseberg* Poling, and *Wandelmestrei* Alciston. The names and boundaries of Hundreds changed considerably in and after the 12th century; these changes are noticed in EPNS.

Border villages divided by the boundary between two Rapes or Hundreds are indexed under only one of them, but are mapped by linked dots.

	Map	Grid	Text
Barlavington	A R6	97 16	11,23
Barnham	A Bi9	96 04	11,82
'Bassingham'	H St		9,131
Bathurst	H Ne11	76 15	8,5
Battle	H Ne9	74 15	*8*
'Bechington'	P W8	54 98	10,66
Beddingham	P T2	44 07	9,35-37. 10,3; 14
Beech	H Ne8	72 16	8,4. 9,25
Beeding	B Bu3	19 10	12,(20); 47. 13,1
Bellhurst	H St3	86 25	9,124
'Benefeld'	L Wy3	25 19	12,54-55
Benfield	L A1	26 07	12,22
Bepton	C E10	85 18	11,15
Berth	L St1	33 20	13,3
Berwick	P A6	51 05	9,89; 94
Bevendean	L F5	34 06	(10,107). 12,18
'Beverington'	P E2	59 00	10,5; 7
Bexhill	H Be2	74 07	9,11
Bignor	A Bu2	98 14	11,78
Bilsham	A Bi10	97 02	11,86
Binderton	C Si3	84 10	11,4
Binsted	A Bi6	98 06	11,80
Birchgrove	L Ru1	40 29	10,110
Birdham	C Wi2	82 00	11,44
Bishopstone	P Fx3	47 00	3,1
Bodiam	H St1	78 25	9,120
Borham	A Bi		11,90
Bosham	C Bm1	80 04	1,1. 6,1;(5) (12,33)
Bowley	P P3	60 08	10,83
Boxgrove	C Bx5	90 07	11,102
Bramber	B S8	18 10	(13,9)
Brambletye	L G7	41 35	10,105
Brightling	H Ne2	68 20	9,31
Brighton	L Wh1	31 05	12,13-15
Broadwater	B Br8	15 04	(12,22). 13,30
Brockhurst	L G3	40 37	10,104
Broomham	H Ne12	72 13	9,26
Broughton	P L3	55 02	9,51
Buddington	C E1	88 23	11,13
Bullington	H Be1	76 09	8,12. 9,13
Buncton	B S3	14 13	13,56
Burgelstaltone	P		9,79
Burgham	H He1	70 28	9,93
Burleigh	L G2	35 37	10,99
Burpham	A P2	04 08	11,68
Burton	A R5	96 17	11,27
'West Burton'	P W10	54 97	10,28
Bury	A Bu3	01 13	5,3
Catsfield	H Ni1	72 13	8,11. 9,2
Chalvington	P S8	51 09	9,61; 115. 10,90-91
Chancton	B S2	13 14	13,17-18
Charleston	P T5	49 06	10,15
Charlston	P W5	52 00	10,30
Chenenolle	P P		10,69
Chichester	C St1	86 04	(1,1. 2,5-6. 3,7. 6,4. 7,2. 8a,1) 11,1;
Chichester (cont'd.)			(11,3; 5; 6; 8-12; 14-15; 18-19; 21; 25; 30-34; 36-37; 39 104-105; 107)
Chiddingly	P S3	54 14	10,95
East Chiltington	L St4	36 15	12,43-44
West Chiltington	A E4	09 18	11,57. 13,48
Chithurst	C D1	84 23	11,9
Chollington	P E5	60 97	10,6
Clapham	B S13	09 06	13,15
Claverham	P S9	53 09	9,94; 114. 10,87-88
Clayton	L Bu4	29 13	12,37
Climping	A P9	00 02	11,75-76
Cocking	C E11	87 17	11,11
Cokeham	B Br4	17 05	13,41; 45
Compton	C We1	77 14	11,36
Compton	P T1	47 08	10,23
Coombes	B S11	19 08	13,19
Cootham	A E9	07 14	11,50-51
'Cortesley'	H Ba6	77 08	9,16
Crowhurst	H Ba3	75 12	8,13. 9,18
'Cudnor'	P P8	61 05	10,72; 74
Dallington	H Ne4	65 19	9,32
Dankton	B Br1	17 07	13,42
East Dean	P W9	55 97	9,44; 49; 80
West Dean	P W7	52 99	10,33-34
Ditchling	L St2	32 15	(10,102; 108) 12,6
Donnington	C St4	85 02	7,2
'Drigsell'	H He3	75 23	9,83
Duncton	A R4	96 17	11,21
Durrington	B Br6	11 04	13,33-34
Eastbourne	P E3	61 99	10,2;(81-82) 84)
(East?) Bourne			9,88; 90
Eastergate	A Bi8	94 05	11,93
Easthall	P E4	61 98	10,4; 9
Eatons	B G2	18 16	13,53
Eckington	P S7	51 09	9,41; 55; 76; 97. 10,89-90
Elsted	C D4	81 19	6,2
Erringham	B Bu4	20 07	13,4
Etchingwood	P S1	50 22	9,54
Evebentone	H Gs		9,108
Ewhurst	H St4	79 24	9,120
Exceat	P W6	52 99	10,24; 29
Eyelid	H Ne1	76 23	9,27-29
Fairlight	L G1	41 38	10,108
Falmer	L F4	35 08	12,7; (16-17)
Felesmere	L G		10,98
Felpham	A Bi12	95 99	8a,1
Ferring	A P13	09 02	3,4
Filsham	H Ba7	78 09	8,10. 9,14
Findon	B S10	12 08	13,(7); 11
Frog Firle	P Fx4	51 01	10,44; 49. (12,10)
West Firle	P T4	47 07	9,38; 56; 71; 75; (91); 102. 10,22
Fishbourne	C St2	84 04	11,39
Fletching	P Ru4	42 23	10,112-113

	Map	*Grid*	*Text*
Folkington	P L2	55 03	10,42
Footland	H St7	77 20	9,128
Frankwell	H F1	66 14	9,8
Fulking	L Po4	24 11	12,29
Glatting	A R8	97 14	11,24
Glossams	H Gs3	84 22	9,111
Goring	A P14	11 02	11,71-73. (13,10; 16; 38)
Graffham	C E12	92 17	11,17
Greatham	A E7	04 15	11,56
Grittenham	C E5	94 21	11,20
Guestling	H Gu2	85 14	9,105
Hailsham	P P2	59 09	10,68
Halnaker	C Bx2	90 08	11,104; 114
East Hampnett	C Bx6	91 06	11,103
Westhampnett	C Bx4	88 06	11,105
Hamsey	L Ba3	41 12	(10,109). 12,49
Hangleton	L A2	27 06	12,23
Hankham	P P6	61 05	10,81-82
Hardham	A Bu1	03 17	11,79
Harebeating	P P1	59 10	12,8 note
Harpingden	L Ho3	42 04	12,8
Hartfield	P Ha2	47 35	10,60
Harting	C D3	78 20	11,6; (7)
Hastings	H Ba8	80 09	(5,1; 9,11). 9,107 note
Hawkridge	P D2	57 13	10,51
Hazelden	L G5	37 36	10,103
Hazelhurst	H Sh1	68 32	9,60
Heene	B Br9	13 03	13,31
'Heighton'	H Gs1	87 24	9,116-118
South Heighton	P Fx2	44 02	10,47
'Hendon'	P D1	59 13	10,52
Henfield	B H2	21 16	3,2
Herstmonceux	H F3	64 10	9,5
Higham	H St2	82 25	9,121
Hoe	B Br2	19 06	13,46
Hollington	H Ba5	79 11	8,15; 9,15
Hooe	H Ni3	68 09	8,9; 9,1
Hooe Level	P P5	68 06	10,77
Horns	P P4	61 06	10,75-76
Horsey	P P13	62 00	10,73
Horsted Keynes	L Ru2	38 28	10,109
Little Horsted	P Fr2	47 18	10,66
Hunston	C St5	86 02	11,43
Hurst	H St8	78 19	9,129
Hurstpierpoint	L Bu1	27 16	12,36; (13,46)
Iden	H Gs2	91 23	9,110
Ifield	B I1	25 37	13,54
Iford	L Sw4	40 07	12,3
'Inwood'	P Ru		10,116
Iping	C E2	85 22	14,2
Itchenor	C Wi1	79 01	(6,1); 11,45
Itford	P T8	43 05	10,11
Jevington	P W3	56 02	9,73; 10,26
Keymer	L Bu3	30 15	12,(18); 39
Kingston	B A4	22 05	(12,23). 13,28-29
Kitchenham	H Gt1	88 25	9,103
Lancing	B Br5	18 05	13,43-44
Langney	P P12	62 02	10,80
Laughton	P S4	49 13	9,40; 50; 52; 78. 10,(23); 93. (12,2)
Lavant	C Si4	85 08	2,7. (10, 106). 11,5
East Lavington	A R3	94 16	6,4
Lewes	L Sw1	41 10	2,(3); 4 (3,2). 7,1. 12,1; (3); 4; (5-6) 8-9; 11; 14; 19; 26-28; 31-33; 37-44; 48; 50-51)
Lidham	H Ba1	83 16	9,106; 113
Linch	C E9	84 18	11,12
Littlehampton	A P10	02 02	11,77
Lordine	H St6	80 22	9,123
Lordington	C We4	78 09	11,35
Lyminster	A P6	02 04	11,59-60. (13,15)
South Malling	P M1	42 11	2,1; (4)
Marden	C We2	79 14	11,31; 33-34; 38
Mayfield	P Ro3	58 77	10,118
Medehei	H Ni		9,3
Merston	C Bx8	89 03	11,110
Middleton	A Bi1	97 00	11,83
Morley	B Wy5	23 17	13,26
Moulstone	L F3	34 08	12,53
Mountfield	H Ne3	73 20	9,22
Mundham	C St6	87 02	11,41
Muntham	B E12	11 09	13,50
Netherfield	H Ne5	71 18	8,7. 9,23
Newtimber	L Po1	27 13	12,34
Ninfield	H Ni2	70 12	9,4
'Nunminster', see West Preston			
Nutbourne	A E3	07 18	11,53
Nyetimber	A E1	08 20	11,54
Offham	A Bi3	02 08	11,92
Offington	B S14	13 05	13,21
'Orleswick'	L Ho4	43 03	12,9
Ovingdean	L Wh2	35 03	12,11-12;(53)
Pagham	C P2	88 97	2,5
Pangdean	L Po6	29 11	12,31-32
Parham	A E8	06 14	4,1. 11,52
Parrock	L Ha1	45 35	10,63
Patcham	L Pr1	30 09	12,5
Patching	A P5	08 06	2,8
Pawthorne	L Po7	23 09	12,26
Peelings	P P9	61 04	10,71; 79
Pengest	P D		10,50
Penhurst	H Ne7	69 16	8,8
Perching	L Po3	24 11	12,27-28; 35
Petworth	A R1	97 21	11,18
Pevensey	P P10	64 04	10,1
Playden	H Gs4	91 21	9,109
Plumpton	L St7	36 13	12,42
Portslade	L A3	25 06	12,24-25
Poynings	L Po2	26 12	12,30
Preston	P T3	45 07	9,57. 10,12
Preston	C Si2	85 11	6,3

Places not in Sussex

References are to the text or Index of Persons. C refers to the Index of Churches and Clergy; CA to Abbeys, CB to Bishops and Archbishop, CM to Monks.

Elsewhere in Britain

DEVON Exeter...CB. DORSET Shaftesbury...CA. KENT Canterbury...CB; 10,99 note. Ulcombe...Robert. HAMPSHIRE Farringdon...6,1 note. Warblington...11,30. Winchester...Odo; CA; New Minster..10,116. MIDDLESEX Westminster...CA. SURREY Burstow...2,9 note. Limpsfield...8 note. Worth...E1. WILTSHIRE Wilton...CA.

Outside Britain

Almenesches...CA. Bayeux...CB. Braose (Briouze)...William. Cahagnes, see Keynes, below. Criel...Robert. Eu. Fecamp...CA. Flocques...Geoffrey. Grestain...CA. Keynes...William. Mortain; CM. Quesnay...Ralph. St Evroul...CM. Sees...CA. Sept-Meules...William. Treport...CA; CM. Troarn...CA. Warenne...William. Watteville...William.

SYSTEMS OF REFERENCE TO DOMESDAY BOOK

The manuscript is divided into numbered chapters, and the chapters into sections, usually marked by large initials and red ink. Farley however did not number the sections. References in the past have therefore been to the page or column. Several different ways of referring to the same column have been in use. The commonest are:

(i)	(ii)	(iii)	(iv)	(v)
152a	152	152a	152	152ai
152b	152	152a	152.2	152a2
152c	152b	152b	152b	152bi
152d	152b	152b	152b.2	152b2

The relation between Vinogradoff's notation (i), here followed, and the sections is

16 a	Landholders			21 a	10,19	-	10,28		26 a	12,1	-	12,4
b	1,1	-	2,1e	b	10,29	-	10,38		b	12,4	-	12,9
c	2,1f	-	2,8	c	10,39	-	10,51		c	12,9	-	12,18
d	2,8	-	3,4	d	10,52	-	10,65		d	12,18	-	12,29
17 a	3,4	-	4,1	22 a	10,65	-	10,80		27 a	12,29	-	12,37
b	5,1	-	6,1	b	10,80	-	10,93		b	12,37	-	12,44
c	6,1	-	7,2	c	10,93	-	10,105		c	12,44	-	12,53
d	8,1	-	8a,1	d	10,106	-	10,118		d	12,54	-	12,56
18 a	9,1	-	9,6	23 a	11,1	-	11,5		28 a	13,1	-	13,9
b	9,7	-	9,14	b	11,6	-	11,12		b	13,9	-	13,17
c	9,14	-	9,19	c	11,13	-	11,21		c	13,18	-	13,28
d	9,20	-	9,35	d	11,21	-	11,30		d	13,28	-	13,38
19 a	9,35	-	9,55	24 a	11,30	-	11,38		29 a	13,38	-	13,46
b	9,56	-	9,74	b	11,38	-	11,49		b	13,46	-	13,57
c	9,75	-	9,91	c	11,49	-	11,60		c	14,1	-	14,2
d	9,92	-	9,109	d	11,61	-	11,71		d	*blank column*		
20 a	9,109	-	9,123	25 a	11,71	-	11,81					
b	9,123	-	9,131	b	11,82	-	11,92					
c	10,1	-	10,4	c	11,93	-	11,105					
d	10,4	-	10,18	d	11,106	-	11,116					

MAPS

Chichester and **Arundel** Rapes
Bramber and **Lewes** Rapes
Pevensey Rape
Hastings Rape

The **Abbreviations** used for the Hundreds are

Chichester Rape

Bm	Bosham
Bx	Box
D	Dumpford
E	Easebourne
P	Pagham
Si	Singleton
So	Somerley
St	Stockbridge
We	Westbourne
Wi	Wittering

Arundel Rape

Bi	Binsted
Bu	Bury
E*	Easewrithe
P	Poling
R	Rotherbridge

Bramber Rape

A*	Aldrington
Br	Brightford
Bu	Burbeach
E*	Easewrithe
G	West Grinstead
H	Henfield
I	Ifield
S	Steyning
Wy*	Wyndham

Lewes Rape

A*	Aldrington
Ba	Barcombe
Bu	Buttinghill
F	Falmer
G*	East Grinstead
Ha*	Hartfield
Ho	Holmestrow
Po	Poynings
Pr	Preston
Ru*	Rushmonden
St	Streat
Sw	Swanborough
Wh	Whalesbourne
Wy*	Wyndham

Pevensey Rape

A	Alciston
D	Dill
E	Eastbourne
Fr	Framfield
Fx	Flexborough
G*	East Grinstead
Ha*	Hartfield
L	Longbridge
M	Malling
P	Pevensey
Ro	Rotherfield
Ru*	Rushmonden
S	Shiplake
T	Totnore
W	Willingdon

Hastings Rape

Ba	Baldslow
Be	Bexhill
F	Foxearle
Gs	Goldspur
Gt	Gostrow
Gu	Guestling
Ha	Hawksborough
He	Henhurst
Ne	Netherfield
Ni	Ninfield
Sh	Shoyswell
St	Staple

A star (*) marks Hundreds divided by a Rape boundary.

On the maps, places divided by a Rape or Hundred boundary are shown by linked dots. Places held by the Count of Mortain in East Grinstead and adjacent Hundreds are shown both on Map 2 and Map 3.

In the map keys, places not numbered are not mapped, since their location is not known.

The National Grid is shown in the map border, at 10 km. intervals.

Each 1km (four figure) grid square contains about 247 acres, approximately two hides at 120 acres to the hide.

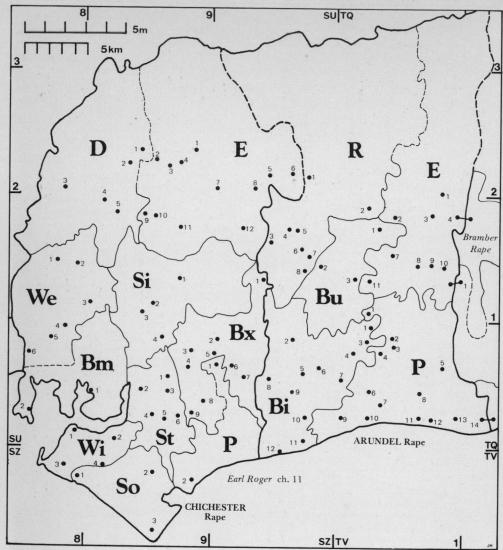

CHICHESTER   **Bm** 1 Bosham. 2 Thorney. **Bx** 1 Up Waltham. 2 Halnaker. 3 Strettington.
4 Westhampnett. 5 Boxgrove. 6 E.Hampnett. 7 Aldingbourne. 8 Merston. 9 Runcton.
D 1 Chithurst. 2 Trotton. 3 Harting. 4 Elsted. 5 Treyford. **E** 1 Buddington. 2 Iping. 3 Stedham.
4 Woolbeding. 5 Grittenham. 6 Tillington. 7 Todham. 8 Selham. 9 Linch. 10 Bepton. 11 Cocking.
12 Graffham. **P** 1 Tangmere. 2 Pagham. **Si** 1 Singleton. 2 Preston. 3 Binderton. 4 Lavant.
So 1 E.Wittering. 2 Sidlesham. 3 Selsey. **St** 1 Chichester. 2 Fishbourne. 3 Rumboldswyke.
4 Donnington. 5 Hunston. 6 Mundham. **We** 1 Compton. 2 Marden. 3 Stoughton. 4 Lordington.
5 Racton. 6 Westbourne. **Wi** 1 Itchenor. 2 Birdham. 3 W.Wittering. 4 Somerley.

ARUNDEL   **Bi** 1 S.Stoke. 2 Slindon. 3 Offham. 4 Arundel. 5 Walberton. 6 Binsted. 7 Tortington.
8 Eastergate. 9 Barnham. 10 Bilsham. 11 Middleton. 12 Felpham. *Borham.* **Bu** 1 Hardham.
2 Bignor. 3 Bury. **E*** 1 Nyetimber. 2 Pulborough. 3 Nutbourne. 4 W.Chiltington. 7 Greatham.
8 Parham. 9 Cootham. 10 Storrington. 11 Amberley. **P** 1 N. Stoke. 2 Burpham. 3 Wepham.
4. Warningcamp. 5 Patching. 6 Lyminster. 7 Toddington. 8 Angmering. 9 Climping.
10 Littlehampton. 11 W.Preston. 12 E.Preston. 13 Ferring. 14 Goring. **R** 1 Petworth. 2 Stopham.
3 E.Lavington. 4 Duncton. 5 Burton. 6 Barlavington. 7 Sutton. 8 Glatting.

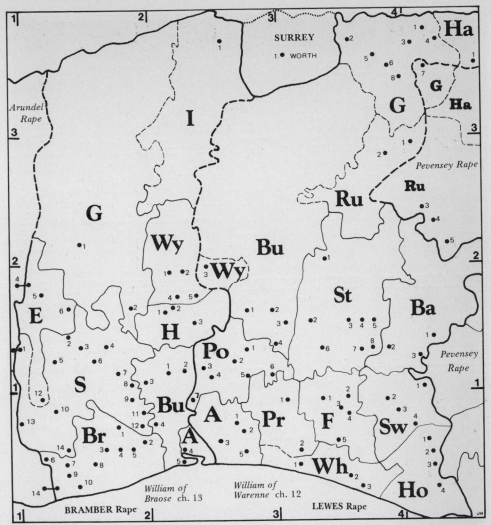

BRAMBER A* 4 Kingston. Br 1 Dankton. 2 Hoe. 3 Sompting. 4 Cokeham. 5 Lancing.
6 Durrington. 7 W.Tarring. 8 Broadwater. 9 Heene. 10 Worthing. Bu 1 Tottington. 2 Truleigh.
3 Beeding. 4 Erringham. 5 Shoreham. E* 5 Thakeham. 6 Ashington. 12 Muntham. G 1 Shipley.
2 Eatons. H 1 Wantley. 2 Henfield. 3 Woodmancote. I 1 Ifield. S 1 Sullington. 2 Chancton.
3 Buncton. 4 Wappingthorne. 5 Washington. 6 Wiston. 7 Steyning. 8 Bramber. 9 Annington.
10 Findon. 11 Coombes. 12 Applesham. 13 Clapham. 14 Offington. Wy* 1 Shermanbury.
2 Sakeham. 4 Woolfly. 5 Morley.

LEWES A* 1 Benfield. 2 Hangleton. 3 Portslade. 5 Aldrington. Ba 1 Barcombe. 2 Allington.
3 Hamsey. Bu 1 Hurstpierpoint. 2 Wickham. 3 Keymer. 4 Clayton. F 1 Stanmer. 2 Balmer.
3 Moulstone. 4 Falmer. 5 Bevendean. G* 1 Fairlight. 2 Burleigh. 3 Brockhurst. 4 Shovelstrode.
5 Hazelden. 6 Standen. 8 Whalesbeech. *Felesmere. Sperchedene. 'Warley'. ?Wildetone.*
Ha* 1 Parrock. Ho 1 Rodmell. 2 Southease. 3 Harpingden. 4 'Orleswick'. Po 1 Newtimber.
2 Poynings. 3 Perching. 4 Fulking. 5 Saddlescombe. 6 Pangdean. 7 Pawthorne. Pr 1 Patcham.
2 Preston. Ru* 1 Birchgrove. 2 Horsted Keynes. St 1 Berth. 2 Ditchling. 3 Streat. 4 East
Chiltington. 5 Wootton. 6 Westmeston. 7 Plumpton. 8 Warningore. Sw 1 Lewes. 2 Ashcombe.
3 Winterbourne. 4 Iford. Wh 1 Brighton. 2 Ovingdean. 3 Rottingdean. Wy* 3 'Benefeld'.

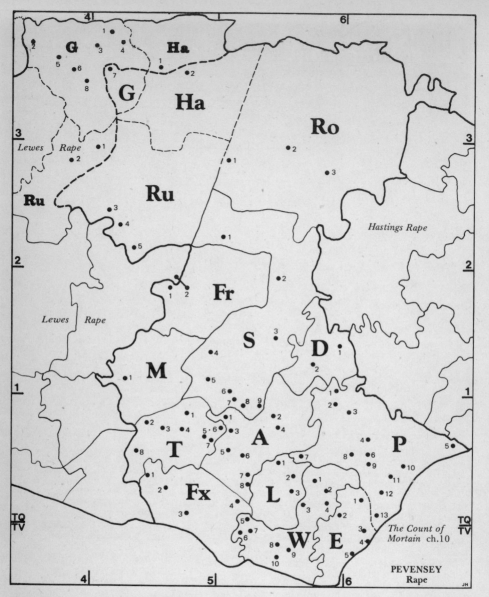

PEVENSEY **A** 1 'Sidnor.' 2 Sessingham. 3 Selmeston. 4 Arlington. 5 Alciston. 6 Berwick. 7 Winton.
8 Alfriston. **D** 1 'Hendon'. 2 Hawkridge. *Pengest.* **E** 1 Yeverington. 2 'Beverington'. 3 Eastbourne.
4 Easthall. 5 Chollington. **Fr*** 1 Worth. 2 Little Horsted. **Fx** 1 Tarring Neville. 2 S.Heighton.
3 Bishopstone. 4 Frog Firle. **G*** 7 Brambletye. **Ha*** 2 Hartfield. *Wildene.* **L** 1 Wilmington.
2 Folkington. 3 Broughton. **M** 1 S.Malling. **P** 1 Harebeating. 2 Hailsham. 3 Bowley. 4 Horns.
5 Hooe Level. 6 Hankham. 7 Wootton. 8 'Cudnor'. 9 Peelings. 10 Pevensey. 11 'Renching'.
12 Langney. 13 Horsey. *Chenenolle.* **Ro** 1 'Alchin'. 2 Rotherfield. 3 Mayfield. **Ru*** 3 Sheffield.
4 Fletching. 5 Barkham. 'Inwood'. **S** 1 Etchingwood. 2 Waldron. 3 Chiddingley. 4 Laughton.
5 'Stockingham'. 6 Ripe. 7 Eckington. 8 Chalvington. 9 Claverham. *Burgelstaltone. Segnescombe.*
T 1 Compton. 2 Beddingham. 3 Preston. 4 W.Firle. 5 Charleston. 6 Sherrington. 7 Tilton.
8 Itford. **W** 1 Wannock. 2 Willingdon. 3 Jevington. 4 Ratton. 5 Charlston. 6 Exceat. 7 W.Dean.
8 'Bechington'. 9 E.Dean. 10 W. Burton.

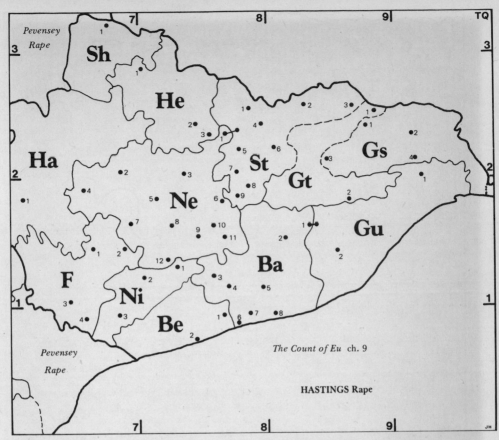

HASTINGS   **Ba** 1 Lidham. 2 Westfield. 3 Crowhurst. 4 Wilting. 5 Hillington.
6 'Cortesley'. 7 Filsham. 8 Hastings. **Be** 1 Bullington. 2 Bexhill. **F** 1 Frankwell.
2 Ashburnham. 3 Herstmonceux. 4 Wartling. **Gs** 1 'Heighton'. 2 Iden. 3 Glossams
4 Playden. *Evebentone.* **Gt** 1 Kitchenham. 2 Udimore. **Gu** 1 Rye. 2 Guestling.
Ha 1 Warbleton. **He** 1 Burgham. 2 Salehurst. 3 'Drigsell'. **Ne** 1 Eyelid.
2 Brightling. 3 Mountfield. 4 Dallington. 5 Netherfield. 6 Whatlington.
7 Penhurst. 8 Beech. 9 Battle. 10 Uckham. 11 Bathurst. 12 Broomham.
Ni 1 Catsfield. 2 Ninfield. 3 Hooe. *Medehei.* **Sh** 1 Hazelhurst. **St** 1 Bodiam.
2 Higham. 3 Bellhurst. 4 Ewhurst. 5 Wellhead. 6 Lordine. 7 Footland. 8 Hurst.
9 Sedlescombe. 'Bassingham'.

TECHNICAL TERMS

Many words meaning measurements have to be transliterated. But translation may not dodge other problems by the use of obsolete or made-up words which do not exist in modern English. The translations here used are given in italics. They cannot be exact; they aim at the nearest modern equivalent.

ALODIUM. See 10,51 note.   *freehold*

BEREWIC. An outlying place, attached to a manor.   *outlier*

BORDARIUS. Cultivator of inferior status, usually with a little land.   *smallholder*

COTARIUS. Inhabitant of a *cote*, cottage, often without land.   *cottager*

DOMINIUM. The mastery or dominion of a lord *(dominus)*; including ploughs, land, men, villages, etc., reserved for the lord's use; often concentrated in a *home farm* or *demesne*, a 'Manor Farm' or 'Lordship Farm'.   *lordship*

FEUDUM. See 11,8 note.   *Holding*

FIRMA. Old English *feorm*, provisions due to the King or lord; a fixed sum paid in place of these and of other miscellaneous dues.   *revenue*

GABLUM. Old English *gafol*, tribute or tax to the King or a lord, see Appendix.   *tribute*

GELDUM. The principal royal tax, originally levied during the Danish wars, normally at an equal number of pence on each *hide* of land.   *tax*

HIDA. A unit of land measurement or assessment, see Appendix.   *hide*

HUNDRED. A district within a shire, whose assembly of notables and village representatives usually met about once a month.   *Hundred*

TAINUS, TEGNUS. Person holding land from the King by special grant; formerly used of the King's ministers and military companions.   *thane*

T.R.E. *tempore regis Edwardi*, in King Edward's time.   *before 1066*

VILLA. Translating Old English *tun*, town. The later distinction between a small *village* and a large *town* was not yet in use in 1086.   *village* or *town*

VILLANUS. Member of a *villa*, usually with more land than a *bordarius*.   *villager*

VIRGATA. A quarter of a hide.   *virgate*